Debbie Morris

CW01590124

WHS

Teacher's resource

150 Numeracy Hour Lessons

YEAR R

Contents | Page

First published 2001
exclusively for WHSmith by

Hodder & Stoughton Educational,
a division of Hodder Headline Ltd
338 Euston Road
London NW1 3BH

A CIP record for this book is available from the British Library.

Author: Jan Thomas
Series editor: Paul Broadbent

ISBN 0340 79002 4

Typeset by Servis Filmsetting Ltd
Printed and bound in Spain by Graphycems

Reception
Summary of objectives

	Theme	Topics	Objectives – children will be taught to:
Autumn Term			
1	**Counting to 5**	Counting	Say and use the number names to 5 in order in familiar contexts. Recite the number names in order to and back from 5. Count reliably up to 5 everyday objects, giving just one number name to each object.
2	**Counting to 10**	Counting	Say and use the number names to 10 in order in familiar contexts. Recite the number names in order to and back from 10. Count reliably up to 5 everyday objects, giving just one number name to each object.
3	**Flat shapes**	Shape and space	Use language such as round, circle, bigger and smaller to describe the shape and size of flat shapes. Begin to name flat shapes such as circle, triangle, square, rectangle. Use a variety of shapes to make pictures and describe them.
4	**Length**	Counting Measures	Count reliably up to 5 objects. Use language such as more or less, longer or shorter to make direct comparisons of two lengths.
5	**One more**	Counting Adding (one more)	Say and use the number names to 10 in order in familiar contexts. Begin to recognise 'none' and 'zero' in stories, rhymes and when counting. Find one more than a number from 1 to 5.
6	**Comparing and ordering**	Counting Comparing and ordering numbers	Say and use the number names to 10 in order in familiar contexts. Recite the number names to ten in order, continuing the count forwards or backwards from a given number. Use language such as more and less, greater or smaller to compare two numbers up to 10 and say a number which lies between two given numbers.
7	**One more, one less**	Counting Adding and subtracting (one more, one less)	Recite the number names in order from 1 to 20. Count reliably up to 10 everyday objects, giving just one number name to each object. Find one more or one less than a number from 1 to 10.
8	**Solid shapes**	Shape and space Reasoning	Use language such as round, flat, bigger and smaller to describe the shape and size of solid shapes. Begin to name solid shapes such as cube, cone, sphere … Use a variety of shapes to make models and describe them.
9	**Measures**	Counting Measures, including time	Recite the number names in order from 1 to 20. Count reliably up to 10 objects Use language such as more or less, heavier or lighter to make direct comparisons of two masses. Begin to understand and use the vocabulary of time. Sequence familiar events.
10	**Problems**	Counting Money and 'real life' problems	Count reliably up to 10 – both everyday objects and in other contexts, such as clapping sounds or hopping movements. Solve practical problems involving counting and comparing in a real or role play context. Begin to understand and use the vocabulary related to money. Sort coins, including £1 and £2 coins, and begin to understand the similarities and differences. Use up to five 1p coins in shopping role play situations.

Summary of objectives

	Theme	Topics	Objectives – children will be taught to:
Spring Term			
1	**Ordering numbers**	Counting Comparing and ordering numbers	Say and use the number names beyond 10 in order in familiar contexts such as number rhymes, songs, stories, counting games and activities. Count reliably up to 10 in a variety of contexts. Use appropriate language to compare two numbers. Order a given set of selected numbers to 10 *(e.g. 1 to 6 in random order)*.
2	**Adding**	Counting Adding and subtracting	Recite the number names forwards to 20 and backwards from 20. Count reliably up to 10 in a variety of contexts. Begin to use the vocabulary involved in adding. Begin to relate addition to combining two groups of objects, counting all the objects.
3	**Patterns**	Shape and space Reasoning	Begin to name flat and solid shapes. Use a variety of shapes to make patterns and describe them. Use everyday words to describe position.
4	**Capacity**	Counting Measures	Recite the number names to 20 in order, continuing the count forwards from a given sequence of numbers. Recognise small numbers without counting. Use language such as full, empty, holds more/less to make direct comparisons of two capacities. Compare the capacity of two containers by filling and emptying.
5	**Taking away**	Counting Adding and subtracting Money and 'real life' problems	Count reliably up to 15 – both everyday objects and in other contexts – clapping sounds or hopping. Begin to use the vocabulary involved in subtracting. Begin to relate subtraction to 'taking away' and counting how many are left. Compare coins, including £1 and £2 coins, and recognise the similarities and differences. Use up to ten 1p coins in shopping role play situations.
6	**Counting and reading numbers**	Counting and reading numbers Comparing and ordering numbers	Say and use the number names to 20 in order in familiar contexts such as number rhymes, songs, stories, counting games and activities. Recognise numerals 1 to 5. Use appropriate language to compare two numbers. Order a given set of selected numbers to 10 *(e.g. 2,5,1,8,4)*.
7	**Combining and counting on**	Counting and reading numbers Adding and subtracting	Count reliably up to 15 in a variety of contexts. Recognise numerals 1 to 5. Begin to relate addition to combining two or three groups of objects, counting all the objects. Begin to relate addition to counting on.
8	**Shapes and sorting**	Shape and space Reasoning	Begin to name flat and solid shapes, using appropriate language to describe their shape and size. Talk about and recognise symmetrical patterns in the environment. Put sets of objects in order of size. Sort and match objects, shapes, pictures or children themselves, justifying the decisions made.
9	**Measures**	Counting and reading numbers Measures, including time	Recite the number names to 20 in order, continuing the count forwards or backwards from a given sequence of numbers. Recognise numerals 1 to 9. Use language such as more or less, longer or shorter, heavier or lighter … to compare two quantities. Use the vocabulary of time to make comparisons. Begin to know the days of the week in order.
10	**Using number**	Counting and reading numbers Adding and subtracting Money and 'real life' problems	Recite the number names to twenty in order, continuing the count forwards or backwards from a given number. Recognise numerals 0 to 9. Begin to relate addition to counting on and subtraction to 'taking away' and counting how many are left. Sort and match objects, pictures or the children themselves, justifying the decisions made.

	Theme	Topics	Objectives – children will be taught to:
Summer Term			
1	**Counting and ordering**	Counting, reading and writing numbers Comparing and ordering numbers	Say and use the number names beyond 20 in familiar contexts. Count reliably to 20 everyday objects. Recognise numerals 0 to 10. Order a given set of selected numbers to 10 *(e.g. 2,5,1,8,4)*. Begin to understand and use ordinal numbers.
2	**More addition**	Counting, reading and writing numbers Adding and subtracting	Count reliably up to 20 in a variety of contexts. Recognise numerals 0 to 10. Begin to relate the addition of doubles to counting on. Find a total by counting on when one group of objects is hidden.
3	**Shape movements**	Shape and space Reasoning	Use everyday words to describe position, direction and movement: for example, follow and give instructions about directions and movements in PE and other activities. Use a variety of shapes to make models, pictures and patterns and describe them. Make simple estimates and predictions.
4	**Comparing quantities**	Counting, reading and writing numbers Measures	Begin to record numbers to 5, initially by making marks, progressing to simple tallying and writing numerals. Record numbers beyond 5 by tallying. Compare more than two quantities by making direct comparisons of lengths or masses, and by filling and emptying containers.
5	**Counting back and problems**	Counting, reading and writing numbers Adding and subtracting Money and 'real life' problems	Count in tens to 100 and backwards from 100. Recognise numerals beyond 10. Remove a smaller number from a larger and find how many are left by counting back from the larger number. Solve simple addition and subtraction problems in a practical context including using 1p, 5p and 10p coins.
6	**Estimating and comparing**	Counting, reading and writing numbers Comparing and ordering numbers	Estimate a number in the range that can be counted reliably, then check by counting. Write numerals to 10. Begin to understand and use ordinal numbers in different contexts. Use language such as more and less, greater or smaller to compare two numbers up to 20 and say a number which lies between two given numbers.
7	**Patterns and problems**	Counting, reading and writing numbers Adding and subtracting	Count in twos to 20 and backwards from 20. Write numerals to 10 and beyond. Select two groups of objects to make a given total. Separate (partition) a given number of objects into 2 groups.
8	**Shape and space**	Shape and space Reasoning	Talk about, recognise and recreate patterns, for example simple repeating or symmetrical patterns in the environment, or patterns from different cultures. Solve simple problems or puzzles in a practical context, and respond to 'What could we try next?'
9	**Time**	Counting, reading and writing numbers Measures, including time	Count to 20 and beyond, forwards and backwards. Count reliably up to 20 everyday objects. Begin to understand and use the vocabulary of time. Begin to read o'clock time.
10	**Using number**	Counting, reading and writing numbers Adding and subtracting Money and 'real life' problems	Count in tens and twos, forwards and backwards. Begin to write numerals to 20. Begin to find out how many have been removed from a larger group of objects by counting up from a number. Work out by counting how many more are needed to make a larger number. Use developing mathematical ideas and methods to solve practical problems involving counting or comparing.

Reception

Mental maths starters

1. Number rhymes

Every reception teacher needs a variety of number rhymes to use with the children (see Homework Copymasters 1 and 2 and lesson copymaster). Record some on a tape so that the children can listen to them at different times throughout the day.

2. Counting books

There are a large number of counting books on the market. Many of these are suitable for counting together in mental/oral sessions. A few examples are:

Count with Maisy, by Lucy Cousins (Walker Books)
Ten in a Bed, by Penny Dale (Walker Books)
Lucy and Tom's 1, 2, 3, by Shirley Hughes (Picture Puffin)
Numbers, by David Bennett (Picture Mammoth)
The Very Hungry Caterpillar, by Eric Carle (Picture Puffin)
Ten Tall Girraffes, by Brian Moses (Picture Ladybird)
One Bear all Alone, by Caroline Bucknall (Macmillan)
One Green Island, by Charlotte Hard (Walker Books)

3. Remember a number

Give each of the children a number from 1 to 10 to remember. Then hold up any number of fingers from 1 to 10 and ask those children remembering that particular number to stand up. Repeat, showing different numbers of fingers.
You could also show some fingers and ask children remembering a number which is bigger or smaller than that number to stand up.

4. Counting and miscounting

Recite the numbers together to and back from 5, 10 or 20.
Say the numbers forwards or backwards, leaving out one or more. *Can the children spot which numbers have been left out?*
Use a counting stick to illustrate the above.

5. What comes next?

Say the numbers in order, forwards or backwards to/from 5, 10 or 20, but stop part way. *Can the children continue the count?*
Give three (then two, then one) numbers in forwards or backwards order to the children and ask, *What comes next? (e.g. 6, 7, ?)*
Give two selected numbers to the children and ask them to say the number(s) that come between them. *(e.g. 4, ?, 6 or 16, ?, 14)*

6. Which number?

Show the children a large number track or line with numbers 1 to 10, or 1 to 20 on. Point to a number and ask questions like:
What number is this?
What is the number before/after this one?
What is one more/less than this one?
Tell me any number bigger/smaller than this one.

7. Number tracks and grids

The following numbers can be found on a number track or grid showing numbers up to 5, 10 or 20. If all of the children have a small copy of the number track or grid, they can respond to the instructions by placing a counter on the correct answers.
Put your counter on … number 3 … or number 15 … or number 6
Put your counter on … a number bigger/smaller than 3 … 9 … 12
Put your counter on … the number in between 4 and 6 … 7 and 5
Put your counter on … the number that comes before/after 4 … 3 … 7
Put your counter on … an odd/even number
Put your counter on … a number with a straight top … or with only curved lines

8. Number statements

Use a puppet or soft toy to make a statement about numbers. The children can decide whether it is right or wrong. *If it is wrong, can they correct the statement?*

e.g. *5 is more than 6*
7 comes after 6
8 is smaller than 5
3 comes between 4 and 2

9. Counting in twos and tens

Count in twos to 20 or backwards from 20, clapping on every even number. Repeat the counting, performing a different action on the even numbers – blink, jump, wave, make a sound with a percussion instrument, nod.
Count in tens to 100 and backwards from 100, showing ten fingers for each multiple of ten. Count to ten around the class, sometimes starting the count in a different place.
Count from a given multiple of 2 or 10 and stop at another *(e.g. count in twos from 6 to 14).*

10. Using interlocking cubes

Make a row of 10 or 20 interlocking cubes, changing the colours every 2, 5 or 10 cubes. Use the row as a counting stick to count forwards or backwards.
Break the row in different places and count the cubes in each piece. Encourage the children to move beyond counting in ones, by using the blocks of colour – counting in twos, fives or tens, then the ones at the end *(e.g. 6 could be seen as 5 and one more, if the cubes are in groups of 5 of each colour).*

11. Digit cards

Provide each child with a set of 0 to 9 digit cards and ask them to hold up ...

... any specific number
... a number which is bigger/smaller, more/less, than a given number
... a number which comes before/after/in between

12. Using fingers

Ask the children to use their fingers to, for example ...

... count forwards to and backwards from 10
... hold up two groups and say how many altogether
... hold up some and take some away, by folding them down
... hold up some and say how many more/less are needed to reach a given number

13. Large number cards

Ask a child to come to the front, then give them a large number card from 0 to 10 (*e.g. 5*) to hold. Give a second child a number card and ask – *Would this number come before or after 5?*
Continue to give out all the number cards from 0 to 10, asking children to come and stand in the right place to order the numbers, re-adjusting their positions as necessary.

14. Number jumps

Show a large number from 1 to 10 as a starting place. Show a second number and ask the children to say something about the 'jump' from the first number, to the next (*e.g. 5 to 7, it's bigger/more*). Continue to select another number, asking how it has changed from the last.
You could give each of the children a card with an arrow on it, so they could respond by pointing the arrow up, if the next number is higher, or down if it is lower.
Point to a large number line or track to check.

15. Empty number lines

Ask the children to draw an empty number line with 0 at the beginning and 10 at the end. Hold up, in random order, cards with the missing numbers and ask the children to write them in the correct place on their number line. Try the same activity with 10 at the beginning of the line and 0 at the end.

16. Bonds to 10 (or other numbers)

Children will need to be sitting at a table with 10 counters or small counting objects each. Ask them to split the counters into 5 and 5, or 4 and 6, or 9 and 1 ... etc. Try asking them to split the counters into three groups.

17. Measures

Hold up a pencil (or similar thin object) either vertically or horizontally and ask the children to think of things which are longer, shorter, or about the same length.
Similar activities can be done for weighing *(What would be heavier or lighter?)*, or capacity *(What might hold more or less?)*.

18. 2D shapes

Hold up some paper shapes (square, circle, rectangle, triangle, star) and ask the children what they can tell you about them.
Alternatively give them one of each shape and ask them to hold up, for example ...

... a shape with 3 sides or corners
... a shape with curved/straight edges
... any named shape
... a shape like a particular object (the window?)

19. Feely bags

Put a plastic numeral, or a shape, or a number of counters in an opaque bag and pass it around the class. Ask the children to put in their hand and feel what is inside. What can they tell you about what is in the bag? Can they guess what it is? Duplicate bags are useful for increasing pace.

20. Solid and flat shapes

Hold up a real object, which is like a common 3D or 2D shape (*e.g. a die or toothpaste carton*). Ask questions about the properties of the shape. *Can the children name it?* Point to a larger object around the room, like the clock or table top, and ask similar questions.

21. More shapes

Hold up some large paper shapes and ask the children to watch as you fold them in half. *Is half of the shape the same shape as the whole shape? Does it still have the same number of edges? Are they straight or curved? What happens if I fold the shape in a different place, or fold it in half again?*

22. Coins

Use real coins for this activity – two of each if possible. Hold up a coin and ask children to describe it. *What colour is it? ... what shape? Does it have a smooth or grooved edge? Is it thick or thin? Do they know how much it is worth? Can they see another one the same?*

23. Real life problems

Take in a packet of four cakes. Show them to the children and ask them real life questions about them. *How many have I got? If 3 people came to tea, would I have enough? ... and if 6 people came? If I ate one, how many would I have left? How many would there be in two packets?*
Ask similar questions with different numbers of items and quantities.

24. Smiley faces

Give each child a card with a smiley face on one side and a sad face on the other. Then make some statements about numbers or shapes. Ask the children to show the smiley face if you are right and the sad face if you are wrong.

e.g. *3 is bigger than 7*
1 more than 4 is 5
double 2 is 6
8 comes between 6 and 10

Theme 1 Counting to 5

Objectives

- Say and use the number names to 5 in order in familiar contexts
- Recite the number names in order to and back from 5
- Count reliably up to 5 everyday objects, giving just one number name to each object

Vocabulary

count, number, numbers 1 to 5, how many? next, show me, same number, find, separate, split, together, check

Resources

Copymasters 1 and 2, fingers, small counting objects in different colours, interlocking cubes, a small bag, a tray of sand, the story of Noah's Ark, plastic animals

Homework Copymaster 1

Mental maths starters 1, 2

Assessment

At the end of this theme is the pupil able to:

- Recite the number names to 5;
- Recite the number names backwards from 5;
- Listen to a story involving numbers;
- Join in a number rhyme;
- Count to 5 by pointing to, or moving each object in the group;
- Use their fingers to help them count?

Lesson 1

Introduction **10 mins**

Hold your hand up in a fist and demonstrate how to count up to 5 by straightening the fingers one at a time. Demonstrate to the children with both hands, asking the children to do the same action, while you count slowly. Then show how you can count backwards from 5, by folding the fingers down one at a time.

Ask the children to try this as you count, or count together.

Activities **25 mins**

Me then you (whole class/group)

Ask the children to listen carefully as you count up to 5. Then count up to 4 and ask them to say the 5 together at the end. Once they can do this, count to 3 and the children can add the 4, 5. Carry on in this way until they are able to try counting with you from 1 to 5.

Do a similar thing, counting from 5 back to 1.

Play and count (supported group/individuals)

Let the children play with some of the objects they will be using later in the week – plastic animals, counting objects, interlocking cubes. Provide them with no more than 3 of anything which are the same. The items could differ in type, shape or colour. Use every opportunity for simple counting. An adult needs to spend some time with the children, asking them questions like:

Which are the cows? pigs? horses?

Can you find just one red object?

Differentiation

Low Attainers – Keep any questioning short, or just listen to the vocabulary the children use as they investigate.

High Attainers – Ask more direct counting questions using number names and 'how many?' Use up to 5 objects.

Plenary **5 mins**

Ask the children questions about what they have been counting, ensuring that they know the names for the objects and realise there were different numbers of each.

Lesson 2

Introduction **10 mins**

Try a variety of actions counting to 2 as you do them. Encourage the children to use all of their bodies, standing up for some activities. They could do this as a 'copy the teacher (or another child) activity'.

Jump, jump, clap, clap, nod, nod, blow, blow … etc., counting 1,2 with each action.

Activities **25 mins**

Noah's Ark (whole class)

Tell the children a simple version of the story of Noah's Ark, emphasising that two of each animal went into the Ark. Enlarge Copymaster 1 to illustrate the story, encouraging the children to count the animals.

Two by two (pairs/individuals)

Provide the children with a number of plastic animals, some of which are the same. Ask them to find some pairs of animals to go into the Ark. *Can they line the pairs up ready to go in?*

Differentiation

Low Attainers – Include only 2 of each type of animal in the ones you present to the children, so they only have to find the two which are the same.

High Attainers – Ask the children to play a trick on Noah, by including one type of animal which is not in a pair. Can their friends tell which animals in the line are not in pairs? They could also try to line up the animals with the tallest first.

Plenary **5 mins**

Show the children one of the lines of animals and check that they are in pairs. Then use a line where the animals are not all in pairs and ask them what is not quite right. *If there is only 1 animal, is that enough? If there are 4 animals, is that too many?*

Lesson 3

Introduction **10 mins**

Ask the children how many they have of different parts of their bodies. Tell them to point as you count the parts.
How many noses do you have?
How many ears? … or eyes? … or thumbs? … or fingers on each hand? … or arms? … or heads?

Activities **25 mins**

Me and you (whole class)
Say the number rhyme on Homework Copymaster 1 several times asking the children to join in when they are able. Then ask them to help you think up suitable actions for the rhyme.

Draw a face (whole class)
Draw a large face shape on the board. Ask the children what you need to put on it and how many of each thing *(e.g. 2 eyes)*. Demonstrate drawing all the missing parts of the face, counting aloud as you do so.

Funny faces (individual)
Provide each child with Copymaster 2 and ask them to fill in the missing eyes, ears, noses and hats.
How many of each do there need to be?

Differentiation

Low Attainers – Add some of the above onto the copymaster before it is used, so that the children only need to add the 2 eyes and the nose.
High Attainers – Can draw their own faces or their whole bodies with the correct number of body parts.

Plenary **5 mins**

Look at some of the children's funny faces and count together to see if they have added the correct number of missing things. Say 'Me and you' together once more and the children can then take the rhyme home to learn with their parents.

Lesson 4

Introduction **10 mins**

Each pupil needs five small counting objects. Call out a number from 1 to 5. Ask the children to show you the same number of fingers and then hold up that number of objects. They can check with a friend to see if they have the same number. Continue with other numbers from 1 to 5, asking some of the children to choose the number.

Activities **25 mins**

What's in the bag? (whole class/group)
Put some counting objects in a bag with different colours for each number up to 5 *(e.g. 1 red, 2 green, 3 blue …)*
Ask the children to watch as you take them out one at a time, putting ones of the same colour together *(e.g. I've got 1 green, the next one is red, that's 1 of each, then a blue one, and another green, that's 2 green now … etc.)*.
When the bag is empty count how many of each colour as a class. *Which colour do I have 3 of? … or 4 of?*

What's in the sand? (group/individual)
Bury some small counting objects in the sand tray for the children to find. Ask them to put ones which are the same together before they count them. Start with three each of four different objects, then try different numbers.
Can the children choose a different number up to 5, and each bury that number of objects which are the same? Then the hunt can start all over again as they try to find them all.

Differentiation

Low Attainers – Use numbers from 1 to 3 only or make the number sets the same colour and shape.
High Attainers – Use larger sets of shapes, including sets of objects which vary in size.

Plenary **5 mins**

Look at some of the sets of objects the children have found in the sand and count them together. Demonstrate how it is easier to count the objects if they are put in a line or moved when they have been counted.

Lesson 5

Introduction **10 mins**

Show the children 3 cubes the same colour, count them individually, then fit them together counting as you go. Demonstrate how to check the counting of the tower, by pointing to one cube at a time. Ask the children to count with you. Take the tower to pieces again, counting backwards from 3 as you do so. Do the same thing with different numbers up to 5, sometimes using cubes the same colour and sometimes varying the colours.

Activities **25 mins**

Build a tower (whole class/group)
Each child needs 5 interlocking cubes. Call out a number from 1 to 5 and ask the children to make a tower with that number of bricks.
They can ask a friend to check whether they have the right number, or hold them up to compare with one the teacher has made. Repeat with other numbers.

Tower sort (group/individuals)
Present the children with a large pile of ready made towers with up to 5 cubes in them. Ask them to count the cubes in the towers and find some which have the same number. Once they have done this, they can make some towers of their own including some which have the same number of cubes in them.

Differentiation

Low Attainers – Use towers with up to 3 cubes of the same colour.
High Attainers – Use towers with different coloured cubes, or fit some of the threes, fours and fives together in different shapes.

Plenary **5 mins**

Use some towers which have the same number and count them all together. Reinforce counting by moving fingers to point to each cube in turn.
Does it matter whether you start counting at the top or bottom of the tower?

Theme 2 Counting to 10

Objectives

- Say and use the number names to 10 in order in familiar contexts
- Recite the number names in order to and back from 10
- Count reliably up to 5 everyday objects, giving just one number name to each object

Vocabulary

count, number, numbers 1 to 10, how many? next, show me, same number, find, together, check, each, every

Resources

Copymasters 3 and 4, home corner with 3 plates, teddies and chairs of different sizes, play bedding, interlocking cubes, opaque bags or boxes, counting objects, paper plates, plastic beakers, sorting trays

Homework Copymaster 2

Mental maths starters 1, 2, 3

Assessment

At the end of this theme is the pupil able to:

- Recite the number names to 10;
- Recite the number names backwards from 10;
- Count to 5 by pointing to, or moving each object in the group;
- Give one number name in one to one correspondence with each object;
- Begin to realise that if two different counts of a collection of objects give different answers, then something is wrong?

Lesson 1

Introduction **10 mins**

Hold your hand up in a fist and demonstrate how you can count up to 10 by straightening the fingers one at a time. Ask the children to do the same action, while you count slowly.
Then show how you can count backwards from 10, by folding the fingers down one at a time. Ask the children to try this as you count, or count together.

Activities **25 mins**

Count up to 10 (whole class/group)

Ask the children to listen carefully as you count up to 10. Then count up to 9 and ask them to say the 10 together at the end. Once they can do this, count to 8 and the children can add the 9,10. Carry on in this way until they are able to try counting with you from 1 to 10. Allow the children to hear you repeating the counting, with them adding one or more of the last numbers in the count.

Put into groups of three (individuals)

Ask the children to colour the turtles on Copymaster 3 in groups of three. There are four groups of three on the page, so they will need four different colours.

Differentiation

Low Attainers – Give the children 3 counters to match on a group of 3 turtles before they colour them.
High Attainers – Encourage them to colour some groups which are close together and some which are far apart. *Does it matter which 3 are coloured? Can they draw an additional group of 3 on the page?*

Plenary **5 mins**

Discuss the different ways the children have coloured the turtles. *Do the turtles the same colour need to be close for them to be in a group of 3? How many groups of 3 did you find? What differences were there in the ways the children coloured the sheet?* Check some of the groups by counting together up to 3, or backwards from 3.

Lesson 2

Introduction **10 mins**

Ask some how many questions relating to the work covered in week 1 and show fingers to demonstrate.
How many of each animal went into Noah's Ark?
How many eyes, ears, noses, legs, arms, do you have?
How many brothers or sisters?

Activities **25 mins**

Count back from 10 (whole class/group)

Ask the children to listen carefully as you count back from 10 to 1. Then count back to 2 and ask them to say the 1 together at the end. Once they can do this, count to 3 and the children can add the 2, 1. Carry on in this way until they are able to try counting back with you from 10 to 1. Allow the children to hear you repeating the counting, with them adding one or more of the last numbers in the count.

Find and count (pairs/individuals)

Tell the children a number from 1 to 5 and give them a sorting tray with different compartments. Ask them to look around the classroom, or use a selection of counting objects to put the same number of items in each part of the tray. They can check one another's counting, before putting things back in the right places.

Differentiation

Low Attainers – May benefit from working with a more able child, or using lower numbers.
High Attainers – Give them two numbers *(e.g. alternately put 2 objects, then 4 objects in the compartments).*

Plenary **5 mins**

Ask the children to count up to 10 with you again, this time shouting out numbers 5 and 10. Ask them to use their fingers, holding hands up clearly as they call 5 and 10. Talk for a few minutes about the things they could use at home to practise counting – stairs, windows, paving slabs. *What else?*

Lesson 3

Introduction **10 mins**

Count 5 paper plates or plastic beakers as you place them in a row. *How many? Show me on your fingers.* Show a different number up to 5. *How many now?* Count together to check, moving each object as you count. *Show me the same number on your fingers.*
Continue showing different numbers to 5. Let the children take a turn at moving the objects.

Activities **25 mins**

Goldilocks and the Three Bears (whole class/group)
Tell the children a simple version of the story of Goldilocks and the Three Bears, emphasising the number 3 whenever it comes into the story. Use different sized bowls and chairs to illustrate the story if possible.
The House in the Wood (small groups)
Ask the children to work in a group of 3 to make the home corner into the House in the Wood for the 3 bears. *Can they lay the table for 3, put 3 chairs ready and make 3 beds? What else might the bears need?*

Differentiation

Low Attainers – Will benefit from working with more confident children.
High Attainers – Challenge them to match the bears and their things to the right sizes of plates and chairs. *Are the beds the right size for each bear? What would happen if grandfather bear came to visit?*

Plenary **5 mins**

Return to the story of Goldilocks and the Three Bears. *What was different about the bears? How was their porridge different? … or chairs? … or beds? Do they know any other stories involving the number three?* (Try to read The Three Little Pigs or The Three Billy Goats Gruff stories to the children soon.)

Lesson 4

Introduction **10 mins**

Sit the children in 2 large groups facing one another. Name 4 children in one group and ask them to stand up. *Can the other group say how many are standing?* Name 3 children in the other group and ask them to put their hands on their heads. *How many have hands on their heads?* Continue asking up to five children in one group to perform a clear action, asking the facing group to count how many each time?

Activities **25 mins**

Busy people (whole class)
Say the number rhyme on Homework Copymaster 2 several times asking the children to join in when they can.
They may soon be able to say the number and 'busy people', then you can finish each line. Then ask them to help you think up suitable actions for the rhyme.
How many flowers? (individuals)
Give the children Copymaster 4. Ask them to count how many flowers in a group, then count out the same number of counters. They can check if they are right by placing the counters on the flowers in that group.

Differentiation

Low Attainers – May need adult support or they may find it easier to draw their own groups with up to 5 flowers.
High Attainers – Can draw some larger groups of flowers on the back of the page. *Which group has the most/least flowers? Which group has 1 more or less than this group?*

Plenary **5 mins**

Draw a group of 4 or 5 flowers on the board, spaced randomly. *If we counted these, where could we start? Which way could we go as we count? Would we get the same number if we started in a different place?*
Say Busy people together once more and the children can then take the rhyme home to learn with their parents.

Lesson 5

Introduction **10 mins**

Count to 5 with the children, using fingers. Then count to 5 making mistakes so the count is 6 or 4 *(e.g. count faster or slower than fingers go up). What's wrong?* Demonstrate how important it is to put up one finger for each number in the count. Show miscounting with different numbers to 5, asking the children to spot what's wrong.

Activities **25 mins**

What's in the bag? (whole class/group)
Put some counting objects in a bag with different colours for each of 3 numbers up to 10 *(e.g. 3 red, 6 orange, 4 blue)*. Ask the children to watch as you take them out one at a time, putting ones the same colour together. When they are all out of the bag, count how many of each colour as a class, as you move the objects and place them in a line. *Which colour do I have 3 of?* Explain why it is easier to count if you move the objects.
What's in your bag? (pairs/individuals)
Give the children a bag with numbers of objects from 1 to 5 *(e.g. 1 pig, 2 cows, 3 sheep …)*. Ask them to sort the objects in their bag, placing items which are the same in rows, so they can count more easily. *How many of each item?* They can then check the counting of another pair or individual.

Differentiation

Low Attainers – Will benefit from the support of an adult, or could work in a pair with a more able child.
High Attainers – Ask the children to sort their objects with the rows in order according to the number of objects.

Plenary **5 mins**

Show the children 5 objects. Demonstrate counting them more than once, but miscount *(e.g. count some twice, miss some out). Why do I keep getting different answers?* Explain that if you move the objects as you count, you are less likely to make a mistake. Also arranging things in a row helps you to count correctly.

Theme 3 Flat shapes

Objectives

- Use language such as round, circle, bigger and smaller to describe the shape and size of flat shapes
- Begin to name flat shapes such as circle, triangle, square, rectangle
- Use a variety of shapes to make pictures and describe them

Vocabulary

circle, triangle, square, rectangle, star, shape, flat, curved, straight, round, corner, side, end, make, draw

Resources

Copymasters 5 and 6, plastic or cardboard shapes, straws, paper and paper strips, objects which are different shapes, plasticine, rolling pin, cloth bag, paint and crayons

Homework Copymaster 3

Mental maths starters 1, 18, 20

Assessment

At the end of this theme is the pupil able to:

- Understand and use in practical contexts, language to describe the shape and size of flat shapes;
- Make pictures using flat shapes that vary in size and texture;
- Recognise, name and talk about 2D shapes such as square, circle, triangle, rectangle, star;
- Identify flat shapes that can be seen around the school and in the classroom?

Lesson 1

Introduction **10 mins**

Hold up some objects which are circular and some which are not and ask questions like:
Is this a circle shape? How many sides does it have? Does it have straight sides? Why is it (or is it not) a circle?
With the children, sort the objects into two groups, circles and not circles.

Activities **25 mins**

Circle patterns (whole class/group)

Use some circle shapes of different sizes and colours to build up a group of circles by fixing them to the board with blu-tak, so that the edges just touch. Change the group, so that some of the circles overlap, or are on top of one another, explaining what you are doing to the children. Ask questions like:
Which circles are touching the edge of the green circle? Which circle has a part of it covered up?

Circle drawings (pairs/individuals)

Provide the children with some shapes and objects, including some which are not circular. Ask them to select only the ones that they can draw around or inside, to draw circles. Encourage the children to help one another by holding a shape or object still.

Differentiation

Low Attainers – Provide them with shapes and objects which can all be used to draw circles.
High Attainers – Challenge them to fit smaller circles in the spaces between the ones they have drawn.

Plenary **5 mins**

Discuss some of the shapes and objects the children used to draw circles. *Why were some of the shapes not suitable? Which part of the objects did they draw around? Who do they think fitted the most on the page?* Reinforce that a circle has one continuous, curved edge. Ask them to look out for circles around the school or at home.

Lesson 2

Introduction **10 mins**

Hold up some objects which are square and some which are not and ask questions like:
Is this a square shape?
How many sides/corners does it have?
Does it have straight sides?
Why is it (or is it not) a square?
With the children, sort the objects into two groups, squares and not squares.

Activities **25 mins**

Square turns (whole class/group)

Draw around a large square shape on the board. Count the sides and corners with the children to establish the shape as a square. Turn the square a little and draw around it again. *Is it still a square?* Do this several times, demonstrating that a square can be drawn in different positions, but that it is still a square.

Shape press (pairs/individual)

Provide the children with some plasticine, a board, a small rolling pin and some circle and square shapes to press into the plasticine. Ask the children to roll the plasticine flat and press the shapes into it, with the circles on one side and the squares on the other. *Can they trace the edges of the shapes with their fingers?*

Differentiation

Low Attainers – Press the shapes anywhere into the plasticine. Ask them to show you a square and a circle.
High Attainers – Challenge them to press the squares in different orientations. *Does it matter which way up it is? Is it still a square?*

Plenary **5 mins**

Choose some of the plasticine prints to discuss. Ask one of the children to close their eyes and feel the print. *Can they tell what the shape is? How did they know?* Emphasise the differences in the edges of circles and squares.

Lesson 3

Introduction **10 mins**

Hold up some objects which are triangular and some which are not and ask questions like:
Is this a triangle shape?
How many sides/corners does it have?
Does it have straight sides?
Why is it (or is it not) a triangle?
With the children, sort the objects into two groups, triangles and not triangles.

Activities **25 mins**

Shape skeletons (whole class/group)
Use four straws of the same length. Fix them together as the sides of a square and ask the children if they can name the shape you have made. *How many sides/corners does it have?* Change the length of one of the straws. *Is it still a square? Why not? Does a square have four sides the same length?*

Do a similar thing with three straws starting with ones the same length, then changing one side. *Is it still a triangle? Can triangles have sides of different lengths?*

Making shapes (pairs/individuals)
Provide the children with some strips of coloured paper which are mostly the same length, a large sheet of paper and some glue. Ask them to make some triangles and squares to stick on their paper.

Differentiation

Low Attainers – Provide strips which are all the same length.
High Attainers – Encourage them to cut the strips to different sizes and make some squares with sides of different lengths.

Plenary **5 mins**

Discuss some of the shapes the children have made. Emphasise the number of sides and corners in triangles and squares, and that the edges are straight. Stress that the sides of a square are the same length, but triangles can have sides of different lengths.

Lesson 4

Introduction **10 mins**

Show the children five different shapes – circle, square, triangle, rectangle, star. Hide the shapes, choose one and show a part of it sticking out behind a book.
Which shape could it be? … why?
Repeat with the other shapes.

Activities **25 mins**

Shapes feely bag (Whole class/group)
You need two of each of the above shapes. Spread one of each out, so the children can see them. Put one of the remaining shapes into an opaque bag and pass it around for the children to feel, without taking it out. *Can they guess which shape it is and point to one the same?* Try the same with the other shapes, sometimes allowing a child to choose which shape goes into the bag.

Shape matching (individuals)
Use Copymaster 5 for the children to find matching pairs of shapes and objects.

Shape printing (pairs/individuals)
Provide the children with paper, paint and a selection of shapes and objects with which they can make shape prints. Alternatively they could make prints in damp sand.

Differentiation

Low Attainers – No simplification should be necessary.
High Attainers – Challenge the children to sort their prints by printing, the circles and squares in groups.

Plenary **5 mins**

Draw a square on the board. Ask the children its name and properties. Draw a different four-sided shape on the board. *Is this a square? Why not?* Try with a rectangle and a square drawn at a different angle. Emphasise the properties of squares and rectangles, which do not change when the position of the shape changes.

Lesson 5

Introduction **10 mins**

Place a square, circle, triangle, rectangle and star where the children can see them.
Tell the children you are thinking of a shape. *Can they guess which one?*
Provide them with a clue like 'it has three corners'.
Try the same with the other shapes, using words to describe their properties in the clues.

Activities **25 mins**

Draw a robot (whole class/group)
Use the board to demonstrate how you could draw a robot, using the shapes the children have worked with during the week. Model the use of shape vocabulary as you draw – *It's going to have a square body, so I need to draw four sides the same length. It has two round buttons on its body …*

Make pictures with shapes (pairs/individual)
Ask the children to draw their own pictures, using the shapes they have been working with. They could use crayons or paint to do this. Houses, boats and other vehicles are good things to try, but the children will have their own ideas!

Differentiation

Low Attainers – Provide sticky shapes or plastic shapes for the children to make pictures.
High Attainers – Include some additional geometric shapes like a hexagon.

Plenary **5 mins**

Discuss some of the pictures the children have made. *Which shapes have you used?* Check that the children can recognise and name a circle, square, triangle, rectangle and star.

Theme 4 Length

Objectives
- Count reliably up to 5 objects
- Use language such as more or less, longer of shorter to make direct comparisons of two lengths

Vocabulary
numbers 1 to 5, count, how many? count up to, length, width, height, depth, long(er/est), short(er/est), tall(er/est), high(er/est), more, less

Resources
Copymasters 7 and 8, a variety of long and short objects, strips of paper, washing line, clothes pegs, string, large building bricks, classroom toys, piece of elastic, interlocking cubes.

Homework Copymaster 4

Mental maths starters 1, 2, 3, 17

Assessment
At the end of this theme is the pupil able to:
- Count a number of objects up to 5, giving just one number name to each object;
- Begin to realise when counting that the number of objects is not affected by their size or position, or whether or not they are of the same type;
- Begin to realise that no matter in which order a collection of objects is counted, the number remains the same;
- Compare the lengths of two objects and say which is longer/shorter/taller;
- Begin to use appropriate language to compare lengths;
- Find, pick or make objects that are the same, shorter, wider, longer … than a given one?

Lesson 1

Introduction 10 mins
Say the Humpty Dumpty nursery rhyme for and with the children, adding two additional lines:
'How many horses and how many men?
Use your fingers and count to ten.'
Count to ten using fingers.

Activities 25 mins
Building bricks (whole class/group)
Give each child 5 interlocking cubes (all one colour), which will fit together in 2 dimensions. Ask them to fit 3 cubes together to make a brick for Humpty's wall. Compare and discuss any different shapes they have made. Do the same with different numbers up to 5.
Humpty's wall (pairs/individuals)
Provide the children with Copymaster 7 and some interlocking cubes. Ask them to work out how many cubes were used for each brick and colour the wall using the right colours. They may need to match the bricks to the spaces on the wall.

Differentiation
Low Attainers – Underline the words in the colouring key with the corresponding colour and allow them to work with a more able child.
High Attainers – Once they have coloured the wall, ask them to make it using cubes the same colour. Or, they could make some bricks of different sizes and make their own wall.

Plenary 5 mins
Draw some of the brick shapes from Humpty's wall on the board and ask the children to explain how they managed to count how many cubes were in each one. Draw lines to show the individual cubes to help the children visualise how each brick is made up.

Lesson 2

Introduction 10 mins
Choose two children of different heights to stand up.
Who is the taller/shorter of the two?
Is there anyone in the class who is taller/shorter than both?
Can we find someone who is in between the two heights?
Do we know any adults taller/shorter than the teacher?
Who has a brother or sister taller/shorter than themselves?

Activities 25 mins
Tall and short pairs (whole class/group)
Ask the children to find a partner who is a different height. Then give the pairs instructions to follow using taller and shorter. *Stand up the taller child. The shorter child clap 3 times.* Allow the children to swap partners, so that they are not always the taller or shorter, and continue the instructions … or put the children into groups of 3 and use middle sized as well.
Tall and short towers (pairs/individuals)
Ask the children to use large building bricks to build a tower which is the same height, shorter or taller than themselves (or a classroom toy). *What is the tallest tower they can build? How many bricks can they pile up before the tower falls over?*

Differentiation
Low Attainers – Working with a more able child may help them to develop associated vocabulary.
High Attainers – Provide additional challenges. *Can they build a wall they can step over? … or one too tall for this?*

Plenary 5 mins
Discuss the things the children have discovered in their building. *Who made a tower the same height as themselves? Can you show us?* Compare the height of their towers with things around the classroom.

Lesson 3

Introduction **10 mins**

Ask the children to hold up their hands and look at the lengths of their fingers and thumbs.
Show me the shortest/longest finger.
Show me two the same length.
Show me a finger which is shorter/longer than this crayon.
Compare the length of your little finger with that of a friend.

Activities **25 mins**

Longer or shorter (whole class/group)
Hold up two strips of paper, which are different lengths. *How can we find out which is the longer or shorter of the two?* Put the ends together to demonstrate, then do a similar thing with different strips including some, which are the same length.

Washing line pairs (small group/pairs/individuals)
Peg a selection of strips of paper of different lengths to a washing line. Use two of each length in a random order. Ask the children to sort out the strips, so that the ones which are the same length are next to each other.

Differentiation

Low Attainers – Use a small number of strips for them to pair.
High Attainers – Ask them to arrange the strips in order of length, with the shortest or longest first. Or ask them to cut a third strip of each length to go with the pairs.

Plenary **5 mins**

Discuss the pairs of strips the children have made and ask them to think of things in the classroom or at home, which are about the same length as each pair.

Lesson 4

Introduction **10 mins**

Use a piece of elastic which stretches easily. Stretch it to different lengths and each time ask the children if they can think of things which are about the same length as the elastic.
What is the same length as the elastic when it is fully stretched?
… or not stretched at all?

Activities **25 mins**

As tall as teddy (whole class/group)
Ask one of the children to hold one of the classroom toys (a teddy?), while you cut a piece of string which is the same height. Demonstrate clearly how it needs to match both ends of the toy. *What would you do if you cut it too long? … or too short?* Continue with other toys of different heights.

Cut it the same (pairs/individuals)
Provide the children with a selection of objects of different lengths (pipe cleaner, brick, pencil … etc.) and ask them to cut some pieces of string or strips of paper which are the same length as each object.

Differentiation

Low Attainers – Provide them with thin objects, so the length is easy to determine.
High Attainers – Ask them to cut string or paper strips which are the same length, longer and shorter than each object.

Plenary **5 mins**

Show the children three of the objects, hold up one of the pieces of corresponding string and ask if they can tell which object it is the same length as. Or, pick an object and see if they can choose the piece of string which is the same length.

Lesson 5

Introduction **10 mins**

Give the children 5 interlocking cubes each to use. Make a tower with any number of bricks up to 5 and ask the children to build one which is taller, shorter or the same height. They can hold up their towers and count the bricks to check. Repeat with towers of different heights.

Activities **25 mins**

Matching heights (whole class/group)
Use a small classroom toy (a plastic farm animal?) and demonstrate how you would make a tower of interlocking cubes which is about the same height. Put the toy and the tower together for comparison. *How will you decide what the closest tower height is if a whole number of cubes does not match the toy?* Demonstrate building some more towers to match toys of different heights.

Measuring with cubes (pairs/ individual)
Use common classroom objects or Copymaster 8, and ask the children to fit some interlocking cubes together to make rows the same length as the objects or pictures.

Differentiation

Low Attainers – The pictures on the copymaster are all related to 2 cm, so should match a whole number of cubes and be easy to use.
High Attainers – Ask them to draw some pictures of objects which are the same length as a given number of cubes up to 5, or 10 if appropriate.

Plenary **5 mins**

Ask the children if they can tell which is the longest and which the shortest object of their collection, or pictures on the sheet, by just comparing the rows of cubes. Hold up some cube rows of different lengths and ask the children to think of other things, which are about the same length.

Theme 5 One more

Objectives
- Say and use the number names to 10 in order in familiar contexts
- Begin to recognise 'none' and 'zero' in stories, rhymes and when counting
- Find one more than a number from 1 to 5

Vocabulary
count, numbers 1 to 10, how many? next, same number, find, together, check, each, every, none, zero, more/less than, one more, next, after

Resources
Copymasters 4, 9 and 10, number tracks from 0 to 5 with the numbers shown as spots, counters, counting toys, deep tray with dry sand, six pots with from 0 to 5 flowers in them, dot dice marked 1, 1, 2, 2, 3, 3, counters, pictures of animals, birds, mini-beasts, large soft toys

Homework Copymaster 5

Mental maths starters 1, 3, 4, 5

Assessment
At the end of this theme is the pupil able to:
- Recite the number names to 10;
- Recite the number names backwards from 10;
- Begin to recognise 'none' and 'zero' in stories and when counting back;
- Say the number that comes after a number up to 5;
- Add one more to a collection of objects and recount?

Lesson 1

Introduction 10 mins
You need some pictures of different animals, birds, mini-beasts. Hold the pictures up one at a time and ask how many questions. *How many legs? … wings? … ears? … spots? … stripes?* Use the phrase 'more than ten' where counting would exceed ten. Continue with more than/less than questions. *Are there more legs than tails? … less spots than legs?*

Activities 25 mins
Make an alien (whole class/group)
Draw two matching body shapes on the board. Draw some features (1 eye, 2 ears, 3 fingers on each hand, 4 legs) on the first body, then ask children to the board to draw as many and one more of these features on the second body (2 eyes, 3 ears, 4 fingers on each hand, 5 legs). Count the features to check there are one more on the second alien.

Along came another one (individuals)
Ask the children to draw all the people in their family and then draw one more person. *Who could that person be? Why have they joined the family? How long will they stay? How many in the family? … and how many is one more?*

Differentiation
Low Attainers – May need adult support to help them include all of their family members.
High Attainers – Can they draw their family with the oldest or youngest first? Are they able to include details like ears, fingers, feet? How many of these are there?

Plenary 5 mins
Tell the children a made up story about five of the soft toys from the classroom. One can go for a walk with the others joining in, one at a time, along the way. Every time another toy joins the 'walkers', recount and decide how many one more is. Invent things for the toys to count along the way *(e.g. 3 rosy apples on a tree)*.

Lesson 2

Introduction 10 mins
Altogether recite the numbers up to 10 several times, slowly to start with, then gradually faster and then as fast as you can. Repeat backwards from 10 to 1. Then introduce zero and show the children how to 'blast off' by putting their hands together in a point over their heads and standing up quickly. Recite the numbers from 10 to 0 several times, including the 'blast off' at the end.

Activities 25 mins
Spiders at play (whole class)
Read the Spiders at play rhyme from Copymaster 9 to the children. Then read it again asking the children to keep track of the spiders on their fingers. Read it a third time, asking the children to join in with verses 1, 3, 5 and 7 if they are able. *How do we show 'none' on our fingers?*
How many spiders? (pairs/individuals)
Ask the children to draw a series of pictures to illustrate the rhyme. They will need to draw 10 spiders to start with, then 7, then 3, then 2 and 0 in the last picture.

Differentiation
Low Attainers – May need groups of counters (10, 7, 3, 2) to help them and adult support to check and repeat the rhyme.
High Attainers – Challenge them with questions like, *How many spiders would have to be blown away for there to be none after each verse?* (Do they realise that $10 - 10 = 0$, or $7 - 7 = 0$?)

Plenary 5 mins
Recite the rhyme again, asking the children after each verse to point to the appropriate picture they have drawn. Stop for them to count their spiders and check that they have the right number. *Where is a good place in their picture to start counting? Does it matter where they start? If they started in a different place, would they still get the same number?*

Lesson 3

Introduction **10 mins**

Show the children a large spotty number track with the numbers from 0 to 5 (draw the spots as they appear on a dice). Point to the box with no spots. *How many would I have if there was one more spot than in this box?* Point to the box with one spot and repeat the question. Say, *one and one more makes two.* Move your finger along the track to 2. Continue right along the track in the same way, then jump about in random order.

Activities **25 mins**

One more (whole class/group)

Give each child a spotty number track with numbers from 0 to 5 (see Copymaster 22) and a counter. Call out some *one more* questions and the children can all put their counters on the correct number on their number track. *What is one more than 3? … or 1? … or 4? One more is 2, what is the number? What is one bigger than 4?*

One more sets (pairs/individuals)

Bury lots of different coloured counting toys in the sand tray with more in a box on the table. Ask the children to look in the sand to find numbers of objects from 1 to 5 in different colours *(e.g. 1 red, 2 blue, 3 green … etc.)*. They can use the objects in the box on the table to make sets which have one more than the ones found in the sand. *How many red objects did you find? How many in the set with one more?*

Differentiation

Low Attainers – Ask them to find numbers of objects up to 3 only in the sand.

High Attainers – Could try 6 and 7 as well, or could try to draw sets with one more than those in the sand.

Plenary **5 mins**

Compare some of the objects found in the sand, with the ones the children made with one more. Relate the sets found and made to the spotty number lines. Emphasise that one more relates to moving one space along the track.

Lesson 4

Introduction **10 mins**

Ask the children to show you 2 fingers. Now put up one more. *How many do you have now?* So, 3 is one more than 2. Point to 3 and then 2 on the spotty number track used in Lesson 3 as you say this. Continue, but use different numbers from 0 to 4. Try calling out a number and asking the children to show you one more finger straight away.

Activities **25 mins**

Stand up one more (whole class/group)

Tell each child a number from 1 to 5 and ask them to remember it. If necessary, give then from 1 to 5 counters to hold. Ask all the ones, then two, then threes … etc. to stand up to check that they know their numbers. Then call out a number between 1 and 4 and ask the *one mores* to stand up *(e.g. if you call out 2, then the number 3s stand up)*. Repeat with different numbers.

Draw one more (individuals)

Use Copymaster 10. Ask the children to count the objects, draw one more, then recount. Encourage them to say how many they started with and how many one more is. *Can they record in the box how many they now have?* This could be done with the same number of spots or tally marks.

Differentiation

Low Attainers – Many benefit from working with a more able child.

High Attainers – May be able to record one more as a numeral, or draw one more than 5 on the back of the page.

Plenary **5 mins**

Ask a variety of one more questions to consolidate the language of more, less and one more. *Is 5 one more than 4? Is 3 one more than 4? What is 2 one more than? Think of 4 and 5, which is more? Think of 2 and 0, which is less? Is 3 more than 2? Is it one more? Is 5 more than 1? Is it one more?* Refer to the spotty number track as appropriate.

Lesson 5

Introduction **10 mins**

Ask a variety of 'how many?' questions relating to numbers up to 10 around the classroom.

How many doors/windows/display boards/taps?

Ask some questions where the answer is none or zero and some where the number is too big to count and there are 'more than 10'.

Activities **25 mins**

One more flower (whole class/group)

You need six pots with from 0 to 5 flowers in them and a spare flower. Arrange them in order to start with, but the same questions can be repeated with the pots in random order later. Count the flowers in any pot together. *If I put one more flower in the pot (the spare one), how many flowers will there be now? Which other pot has the same number?* Repeat with each of the other pots.

The one more flower game (pairs/trios)

Each pair/trio needs a die marked 1, 1, 2, 2, 3, 3 as dots, counters and Copymaster 4 for each player. Before playing the game, ask the children to draw one more of each type of flower on their sheet and recount the groups. They then take turns to throw the die and put counters – one more than the number shown – on to the flowers. The winner is the first to cover all their flowers.

Differentiation

Low Attainers – Change the die so that it only has one or two dots.

High Attainers – Could have larger numbers of dots on the die, but they will need to draw some extra flowers.

Plenary **5 mins**

Look at some of the children's flower sheets. *How many flowers were there in this group before you started? … and How many after you had drawn one more?* Repeat with other flower groups.

Theme 6 Comparing & ordering

Objectives

- Say and use the number names to 10 in order in familiar contexts
- Recite the number names to ten in order, continuing the count forwards or backwards from a given number
- Use language such as more and less, greater or smaller to compare two numbers up to 10 and say a number which lies between two given numbers

Vocabulary

numbers to 10, how many? count (up) to, count on (from, to), more/most, less/least, larger(est), bigger(est), greater(est), fewer(est), smaller(est), compare, size, next, between, what comes next?

Resources

Copymasters 11 and 12, counting objects, flowers and flower pots (you could draw these), 3 large hoops, large number line, dry sand, some large books, paper and crayons, interlocking cubes, a puppet, soft toys

Homework Copymaster 6

Mental maths starters 1, 2, 3, 5, 8

Assessment

At the end of this theme is the pupil able to:

- Continue counting forwards from a number up to 10;
- Continue counting backwards from a number up to 10;
- Recognise counting errors when someone else is counting to and back from 10;
- Recognise which is more or less than two numbers to 10;
- Give a number that lies between two numbers up to 10?

Lesson 1

Introduction **10 mins**

Use a row of 10 interlocking cubes with the first 5 in one colour and the second 5 in another (red, blue).
Count the red 5 altogether, then the blue 5. Then count all 10.
Break the row and hold up one end. *How many do I have? Can you show me the same number of fingers?*
Continue breaking the row in different places, keeping the colours, which match fingers on each hand.

Activities **25 mins**

Continue the count (whole class, group)

Count part way to 10, and ask the children to continue the count up to 10. Do this several times, stopping at different numbers. Then try saying any 3 numbers in order – *can the children continue the count when you stop?* Then give 2 number clues and finally just 1 – *can the children continue the count as the clues are reduced?*

Looking for sevens (pairs/individuals)

Give the children a large selected pile of counting objects, of which there are 7 of some things, but different numbers of other objects. Ask them to sort and count the different objects, looking for sevens. If there are fewer than 7 of any one object, put the set to one side, if more place on the other side. Lay out any sevens in a row.

Differentiation

Low Attainers – Give the children fewer of each object and ask them to look for a smaller number.
High Attainers – Ask them to find sets of 7 and 8 from their objects, or they could sort all of the objects out into groups which have the same number.

Plenary **5 mins**

Check some of the sets of 7 which were found, demonstrating putting them in a row to help counting. *If there were fewer than 7 objects, how many could there have been? What about the sets with more in?*

Lesson 2

Introduction **10 mins**

Introduce the children to a puppet, who is learning to count. Let the puppet recite the numbers to 10, but miscounting *(e.g. saying a number in the wrong place, missing a number out, saying a number twice, mispronouncing a number). Can the children put him right?* Once the puppet can count to 10 correctly, teach him to count backwards from 10 in the same way.

Activities **25 mins**

Flowers and more flowers (whole class/group)

Use 2 flower pots and some real flowers, or draw large pictures on the board. Put 2 flowers in one pot and 5 in the other. *How many flowers in each pot? Which pot has more? Which has less? Is 5 more or less than 2?* Add some more flowers to one pot to compare different numbers.

Draw some flowers (individuals)

Ask the children to draw a given number of flowers in a flower pot. Make sure that at least one child draws every number up to 10. Encourage them to compare their numbers as they draw. *Who has the bigger/smaller number? Who has drawn the most/least flowers?*

Differentiation

Low Attainers – Give them smaller numbers to draw, or ask them to put given numbers of real flowers in a pot.
High Attainers – Sow the roots of addition, by asking them to colour their flowers in 2 colours *(e.g. draw 6 as 3 of each colour)*. Or they could draw a row of 3 pots with the number of flowers increasing *(e.g. 7, 8, 9)*.

Plenary **5 mins**

Choose one of the children's drawings and count the flowers. Choose another and count the flowers. *Are there more or less flowers than the first picture?* Continue selecting more pictures until you have built a row of 10 pots showing the numbers 1 to 10 in the increasing number of flowers in them.

Lesson 3

Introduction **10 mins**

Count part way back from 10, and ask the children to continue the count to 0. Do this several times, stopping at different numbers. Then try saying any 3 numbers in reverse order – *can the children continue the count backwards when you stop?* Then give 2 number clues and finally just 1 – *can the children continue the count backwards as the clues are reduced?*

Activities **25 mins**

Hoop count (whole class/group)

Lay 3 large hoops in a row. Put 1 soft toy in the first hoop and 3 in the third. *Which number comes in between 1 and 3? How many toys go in the middle hoop?* Ask one of the children to put the correct number in. Continue in a similar way with different numbers of toys in the end hoops. Arrange the numbers in ascending or descending order, with the middle hoop empty for the children to fill.

Teddies in the sand (pairs/individuals)

Bury some small plastic teddies (or similar counting objects) in the sand tray *(e.g. 7 red and 4 blue)*. Ask the children to find the teddies and work out which colour they have more or less of. A second pair/individual could be looking for different colours or objects in the same sand. Vary the numbers up to 10. *Can they draw the sets they find and explain which has the most and least?*

Differentiation

Low Attainers – Bury smaller numbers of objects.
High Attainers – Bury 3 different sets of teddies for comparison.

Plenary **5 mins**

Using the hoops from the introductory activity, ask the children to sort the things they found in the sand and place each set in a hoop. *How many are there in each hoop? Which hoop has the most/least? Which number is more/less? … or bigger/smaller?*

Lesson 4

Introduction **10 mins**

Place 2 large books in a pile, then 3 books in a second pile. *How many books would be in the next pile?* Ask one of the children to build it (with 4 books) and check the counting. Continue with different numbers of books up to 10, arranging some piles so that there is a missing number in the middle *(e.g. 6 books, what comes in between? 8 books)*.

Activities **25 mins**

Counting spots (whole class/group)

Enlarge Copymaster 11, and cut out the separate number cards. Hold up some of the cards and ask the children to count the number of spots, always starting from an end with two spots together (except 1). Hold up any 2 cards. *Which has more/less spots? Which number is bigger/greater/smaller? Which has the most/least?* Continue with different pairs.

Spotty sort (pairs individuals)

Give the children Copymaster 11 and ask them to cut out the spotty cards and count the numbers. They can then stick some onto paper and draw a box next to them with more spots in, or one before with fewer spots in.

Differentiation

Low Attainers – Give them the lower spotty numbers only to work with.
High Attainers – Ask them to draw their own spotty numbers from 1 to 10, leaving one number out. *Can their friends, or parents, work out which number they have left out?*

Plenary **5 mins**

Again using the spotty cards from Copymaster 11, fix two on the board with a missing number in between *(e.g. 8 ? 10, or 4 ? 6 or 7 ? 5)*. Ask the children to say the number that comes between the two shown. *Can they find the correct spotty card to fit in the space?* Repeat with other numbers up to 10.

Lesson 5

Introduction **10 min**

Ask one of the children to the front, then both you and the child show any number of fingers up to 10 at the same time.
How many fingers are we holding up? Which is the bigger/smaller number? Who is holding up the most/least?
Try again, showing a different number of fingers asking different children to help.

Activities **25 mins**

Is the puppet right now? (whole class/group)

Use the puppet once again, but this time it needs to make statements and the children can decide whether it is right or wrong. Use statements involving comparing numbers … 4 is bigger than 7 … 2 is smaller than 5 … 7 comes after 6 … 5 is in between 2 and 4. *Is the puppet right? Can the children correct any wrong statements?*

What comes in between? (individuals)

Ask the children to complete Copymaster 12 by drawing the correct number of objects, so that the pictures show numbers in ascending order.

Differentiation

Low Attainers – Blank out some of the dots before photocopying, so that the copymaster shows smaller numbers.
High Attainers – Ask the children to draw some more groups of three numbers. They can draw 3 boxes, draw objects in the first and last and ask their friends if they can fill in the middle box.

Plenary **5 mins**

Use the puppet to say a number from 3 to 8 and you can say a second number that is 2 more, or 2 less. Ask the children which number comes between the two you have said *(e.g. puppet says 7, you say 5 or 9). If you say a number, and the puppet says the number which is 1 more or less, can the children continue the count to, or back from 10?*

Theme 7 One more, one less

Objectives
- Recite the number names in order from 1 to 20
- Count reliably up to 10 everyday objects, giving just one number name to each object
- Find one more or one less than a number from 1 to 10

Vocabulary
count, number, numbers 1 to 20, how many? next, show me, same number, find, together, check, each, every, one more, one less

Resources
Copymasters 13 and 14, multilink cubes, 2 cm squared paper, counters, counting apparatus, a large 0 to 10 number track, a puppet or large soft toy

Homework Copymaster 7

Mental maths starters 4, 10, 12

Assessment
At the end of this theme is the pupil able to:
- Recite the number names to 20;
- Count to 10 by pointing to, or moving each object in the group;
- Say a number that comes before or after a number up to 10;
- Say a number that is one more or one less than a number up to 10;
- Respond to simple oral questions involving one more or one less?

Lesson 1

Introduction **10 mins**
Ask a child to the front to help. The child can count to ten putting up one finger at a time, then you demonstrate continuing the count to twenty using your fingers. Count several times, encouraging all the children to join in the count. Ask them to work in pairs, trying to count to 20 together using all four hands. Ask a successful pair to demonstrate.

Activities **25 mins**
Counting to 20 (whole class/group)
Make a row of 20 interlocking cubes, mostly the same colour, but with every fifth cube in a second colour. Point to the cubes as the children count to 20. *Which numbers are a different colour?* Repeat the counting in different ways asking the children to shout or whisper or clap on each multiple of five.
Give the children some 2 cm squared paper and ask them to make their own coloured number track with 20 squares. They can colour numbers 5, 10, 15 and 20 in a different colour from the rest. *Can they use their number track for counting? Can they take it home and practise counting to 20 with their parents?*

Differentiation
Low Attainers – Make a number track up to 10 or 15 only, colouring multiples of 5 in the same way. Alternatively, they could have a ready-made interlocking cube track to copy when colouring the squares.
High Attainers – Could try to write any of the numbers they know on their number track.

Plenary **5 mins**
Use some of the children's number tracks for counting, emphasising the numbers 5, 10, 15 and 20. Count up to 20 using fingers, again emphasising the multiples of 5 for each complete hand.

Lesson 2

Introduction **10 mins**
Ask 20 children to stand in a curved row, so they can see each other. *Can they count up to 20 along the row?* Once they have done this several times, *ask some of the children which number they are. Can the children work out which number different children are? (Which number is Tom?)* Mix the children up, or swap some and repeat.

Activities **25 mins**
One more, one less (whole class/group)
Show a number of fingers up to 10 and ask the children to show you one more, or one less of their own fingers. *Can they express the relationship between the numbers in words?* (3 is one more than 2, or 2 is one less than 3.) Continue with different numbers of fingers.
More or less objects (individuals working in a supported group)
Use counters or similar counting apparatus. Give each child 3 counters the same colour and ask them to make two similar groups with one more and one less counters in them. *How many should be in the one more group? … and in the one less group?* Repeat, using different numbers from 1 to 9. Ask the children to record their groups.

Differentiation
Low Attainers – Use smaller starting numbers, check the counting and repeat the activity using different counting objects. Encourage the children to move the counters or objects as they count.
High Attainers – Use larger numbers to start with. Encourage them to say how many will be one more and one less before they make their sets.

Plenary **5 mins**
Draw a row of 5 shapes on the board. Ask a child to come to the front and below it draw a row with one more shape. Another child can draw a row above with one less shape. *How many in the first row I drew? What was one more? … and one less?* Repeat with different numbers, sometimes drawing the shapes in a vertical column.

Lesson 3

Introduction **10 mins**
Begin the count forwards to 20, but stop part way. *What will the next number be?* Repeat, but stop in different places. Encourage some of the children to count part way, so the others can say the next number.

Activities **25 mins**
What does one more or less mean? (whole class/group)
Draw 6 shapes on the board in a row. Count the shapes together, pointing as you count. *If I wanted one more, what would I need to do?* Draw one more and recount, 7 is one more than 6. *If I wanted one less what would I do?* Rub one out and recount, 5 is one less than 6. Demonstrate with different numbers of shapes from 1 to 9.
Draw one more and one less (individuals)
Ask the children to complete Copymaster 13, drawing one more and one less of the shapes shown in the boxes. *Can they then say the three numbers in order?*

Differentiation
Low Attainers – Use practical apparatus instead of the copymaster and ask them to make sets which have one more and one less than a given set.
High Attainers – Could draw some additional boxes of their own, choosing larger numbers to go in the middle box. *What if they draw 5 boxes in a row, with shapes in the middle box? Can they draw one more/less and one more/less again?*

Plenary **5 mins**
Ask the children questions like, *7 is one more than what? 5 is one less than what?* Point to numbers on a large number track to demonstrate their relative positions. Give the children some statements about one more and one less and ask if they are true or false … *5 is one less than 6 … 3 is one more than 1.*

Lesson 4

Introduction **10 mins**
Use a puppet or large soft toy who is learning to count up to 20, but can't quite do it yet. The children can help whenever the puppet gets stuck. Ask some children to demonstrate counting to 20, while the puppet listens and tries to remember.

Activities **25 mins**
More or less towers (whole class/group)
Give each child 10 interlocking cubes of the same colour. Hold up a tower of 4 cubes. Ask all of the children to make and show a tower with one more cube than yours. Repeat with different numbers of cubes, up to 10. Ask the children to make and show a tower with one more or one less each time.
Build your own towers (pairs/individuals)
Give the children a set of towers made from different numbers of yellow interlocking cubes. Their task is to make two more towers to go with each yellow one – a red one showing one more, and a green one showing one less. *Can they stand their towers in order of size and describe how many in each using more and less?* (Colours are only examples.)

Differentiation
Low Attainers – Could use towers with 5 or less cubes to start with, or they could add one more of a different colour to each yellow tower and recount.
High Attainers – Could use numbers beyond 10 or make towers which are 2 more or 2 less.

Plenary **5 mins**
Discuss and compare some of the towers the children have made, reinforcing the use of one more and one less. Encourage the children to use the same language to compare the number of cubes in their towers.

Lesson 5

Introduction **10 mins**
Draw a group of 4 linked squares on the board. Count the squares together. Draw 4 squares joined along the sides in a different shape. *How many squares in this shape?* Draw more shapes made from joining the sides of squares and ask the children how many squares. Use any number of squares up to 10.

Activities **25 mins**
More or less than 6 (whole class/group)
Make a variety of multilink shapes made from 5, 6 or 7 cubes. Use cubes of the same colour for each shape and join them in 2 dimensions only. Show the children a shape and count the cubes together. *Does the shape have 6 cubes, one more than 6 or one less than 6 cubes?* Repeat with the other shapes. Try the same thing with shapes made from other numbers like 8, 9 and 10.
Lucky sevens (pairs/individuals)
Use Copymaster 14 and ask the children to colour the groups of 7 squares red. If there is one more than 7, colour the group yellow. If there is one less than 7, use green. Groups with none of these numbers should not be coloured.

Differentiation
Low Attainers – Instead of using the copymaster, ask the children to make some multilink shapes with 4 cubes, 1 less than 4 cubes or 1 more than 4 cubes.
High Attainers – Ask them to make as many different shapes as they can using 7 multilink cubes. *Can they make some the same as the groups on the copymaster?*

Plenary **5 mins**
Show the children two of the multilink shapes used in the class activity. Use shapes with a difference of one cube. Count the number of cubes in each. *Which shape has more cubes? How many more? Which has less? How many less?* Hold up different pairs and ask similar questions.

Theme 8 Solid shapes

Objectives

- Use language such as round, flat, bigger and smaller to describe the shape and size of solid shapes
- Begin to name solid shapes such as cube, cone, sphere …
- Use a variety of shapes to make models and describe them

Vocabulary

shape, cube, pyramid, sphere, cone, circle, triangle, square, flat, curved, straight, round, size, big(ger), small(er), large(er), side, top, bottom, roll, corner, middle, hollow, solid, face, edge, end

Resources

Copymasters 15 and 16, a selection of solid shapes, small cardboard boxes and tubes, lots of junk cuboid boxes, real objects which are 3D shapes, paint, glue, opaque bags

Homework Copymaster 8

Mental maths starters 19, 20

Assessment

At the end of this theme is the pupil able to:

- Understand, and use in practical contexts, language to describe the shape and size of solid shapes;
- Make models using solid shapes that vary in size and texture;
- Recognise, name and talk about 3D shapes such as cube, sphere, cone and pyramid;
- Identify solid shapes that can be seen around the school and in the classroom?

Lesson 1

Introduction **10 mins**

Hold up some different sized cubes and cube shaped objects and ask the children questions about them.
How many faces does it have?
Are the faces flat or curved?
What shape are the faces?
How many corners?

Activities **25 mins**

What's this called? (whole class/group)
Sit the children in a circle with a collection of solid shapes in the centre. Include a cube, sphere, cylinder, cone, pyramid and cuboid. Ask a child to pick one, you say its name clearly and then ask all the children to say it together after you. After a while, ask some of the children to say some of the names first.
Rolling shapes (pairs/individuals)
Give the children a selection of solid shapes to explore, encouraging then to look for flat and curved surfaces. *Which shapes roll, and which don't? Will the shape roll in a straight line? Which shapes balance easily on top of other shapes?*

Differentiation

Low Attainers – Adult support will be needed to help develop the related vocabulary.
High Attainers – Ask them to look for the biggest face to stand the shape on. *What shape is that face? Are there any faces the same shape on the 3D shape?*

Plenary **5 mins**

Use one of each shape and ask the children if it will roll. *Why/why not?* Demonstrate to check. *Do they know the names of any of the faces? Can they remember the names of any of the shapes?*

Lesson 2

Introduction **10 mins**

Hold up some different sized cubes and cuboids. Ask questions like:
How many faces does it have?
Are the faces flat or curved?
What shape are the faces?
How many corners?
Draw attention to the similarities and differences.

Activities **25 mins**

Face shapes (whole class/group)
Use some large cube and cuboid shapes and draw around them on the board. *Do you always get the same shape if you draw around the different faces?* Emphasise the differences – you always get a square when you draw around a cube, but drawing round a cuboid sometimes gives you a rectangle. *Are these rectangles always the same shape and size?*

Printing with cubes and cuboids (pairs/individuals)
Give the children different cube and cuboid shapes (or junk boxes) and ask them to make a print with each of the six sides of the 3D shape. Look for pairs of rectangles with the cuboids.

Differentiation

Low Attainers – May need to mark each face of the cube or cuboid, so they know which they have already used to make a print.
High Attainers – Could try using different coloured paint for printing opposite sides of the shapes.

Plenary **5 mins**

Look at some of the prints and ask the children if they can decide which shape was used to make the set of 6 prints. *Was it a cube or a cuboid? How could they tell? What shape are the prints? Are there any the same?* Ask them to look around the room. *Can they see any cuboid shapes?*

Lesson 3

Introduction **10 mins**
Show the children a selection of junk packages and ask them what comes in packages like these. Include things like soap boxes, toothpaste boxes, sweet tubes etc. *What else can they think of that comes in packages of a similar shape?*

Activities **25 mins**
Unwrap a box (whole class/group)
Carefully unwrap a cuboid shaped box in front of the children and open it out flat. Ask of they can see any rectangles the same shape and size. As they recognise matching pairs, fold the box back up to show them where those sides were in relation to one another (opposite). Try to identify all 3 pairs. Continue by unwrapping several different shaped cuboids.
More unwrapping! (pairs/individuals)
Provide the children with some small cuboid packages to unwrap. Ask them to identify any matching pairs of rectangles and colour them the same colour on the inside surface of the box. (They may only find two matching pairs on some boxes, where the flaps make up the ends of the box.)

Differentiation
Low Attainers – It may help if some of the flaps are cut off the boxes first.
High Attainers – Could try to cover some of the boxes, cutting matching pieces of paper the same colour to stick on opposite sides.

Plenary **5 mins**
Emphasise the properties of cubes and cuboids. Show some different shapes which are neither and ask the children why they are not cuboids. *Do they have too many/few faces or corners? Are the faces the wrong shape? Are the surfaces flat?*

Lesson 4

Introduction **10 mins**
Use a selection of solid shapes including a sphere, cube, cuboid, cylinder, cone, pyramid. Hold up a shape and ask the children to tell you something about it *(e.g. cone – one curved surface, a circle at one end, it rolls, it won't roll in a straight line, it will rest steady on the circle end, you can buy ice-cream in cones)*. Repeat with the other shapes.

Activities **25 mins**
Shape feely bag (whole class/group)
Hide a solid shape in an opaque bag and pass it around to the children, asking them to feel the shape without looking and tell you something about it. *Can they guess what it is?* Try with different familiar shapes. Duplicate bags with the same shape inside will speed things up.
Model making (pairs/individuals)
Provide the children with a wide selection of 3D packages, glue and scissors and allow them to make junk models. Houses with chimneys and garages, boats and cars are fun to try, but any model is allowed.
Packages turned inside out and re-stuck are easier to paint afterwards.

Differentiation
Low Attainers – Ask them questions about the shapes they are using as they work, to develop vocabulary.
High Attainers – Encourage them to alter some of the packages to get the shapes they need, or add some folded or curved bits of card.

Plenary **5 mins**
Look at some of the models the children have made, discussing the shapes they have used and matching them to similar solid shapes. Alternatively, enlarge Copymaster 15 and discuss the shapes used in the models shown there. Reinforce both the names of solid shapes and their properties.

Lesson 5

Introduction **10 mins**
Use a selection of solid shapes including a sphere, cube, cuboid, cylinder, cone, pyramid. Ask the children to pick a shape which does **not** have 6 faces … flat faces … any corners … a circle at the end … any square faces etc. Can they tell you what the shape has instead? *(e.g. no flat faces – choose a sphere, which has only a curved surface.)*

Activities **25 mins**
Guess the shape (whole class/group)
Hold a solid shape behind your back and encourage the children to ask you three questions about it before they try to guess what it is. The questions must have only yes or no answers. *Does it have two faces? Will it roll? Are any of the faces circles?* Try with different familiar shapes. It will help the children to focus their questions if they can see the selection of shapes you are using.
Spot the pairs (individuals)
Give the children a set of solid shapes and ask them to find pairs which are the same shape. Or use Copymaster 16, and ask them to colour the same shapes the same colour. They could even try to draw some 3D shapes in their own way.

Differentiation
Low Attainers – Use solid shapes with matching pairs which are the same size.
High Attainers – Include some less familiar 3D shapes and ones which are different sizes. The children could try to match some junk packages to solid shapes.

Plenary **5 mins**
Use Copymaster 16 – one for each pair of children. Hold up one of the solid shapes shown on the sheet and ask the children to point to one the same shape on their sheet. *If you describe one of the shapes on their sheet, can they point to the one you are thinking about?*

Theme 9 Measures

Objectives
- Recite the number names in order from 1 to 20
- Count reliably up to 10 objects
- Use language such as more or less, heavier or lighter to make direct comparisons of two masses
- Begin to understand and use the vocabulary of time
- Sequence familiar events

Vocabulary
numbers to 20, heavy/light, heavier/lighter, balance, scales, time, day, morning, afternoon, evening, night, bedtime, dinner time, playtime, today, before, after, early, late, takes longer/less time

Resources
Copymasters 17 and 18, balance scales, real objects of differing weights, sizes and materials, everyday classroom objects, counting objects, plasticine, pictures of day and night scenes (or a day/night story) if available, paper, paint

Homework Copymaster 9

Mental maths starters 1, 2, 4, 10, 17

Assessment
At the end of this theme is the pupil able to:
- Recite the number names in order from 1 to 20;
- Count reliably up to 10 objects giving just one number name to each object;
- Begin to use appropriate language to compare weight;
- Compare the weights of two objects and say which is heavier or lighter;
- Find, pick out or make objects that are the same, heavier, lighter than a given one;
- Begin to understand and use the vocabulary of time;
- Sequence familiar events, or events in a story?

Lesson 1

Introduction **10 mins**
Sit in a circle with the children. Count up to 20 altogether, loudly then softly, whispering, then in a croaky voice. Then call 1 and point to children who have to call the next number to continue the count to 20. Repeat, pointing to different children, until all have been included. Now tell a child to start with 1 and ask them to point to the person they want to continue … and so on to 20.

Activities **25 mins**
The significance of 5 (whole class)
Ask 20 children to stand in a curved row, so they can see each other. Tell them to count to 20 along the row, but children calling out 5, 10, 15 or 20 must sit down as they call the number. Discuss the pattern made. Move the children around and repeat the counting asking the children who say the multiples of 5 to turn to face the other way as they say the number. Repeat with different children, emphasising the multiples of 5 in some way.
Number find (pairs)
Ask the children in pairs to make sets of objects of every number from 1 to 10, using things they find around the classroom *(e.g. 1 book, 2 pencils, 3 farm animals, 4 counters …)*. When they have finished, ask them to check the counting of another pair, before putting all the objects back in the right places.

Differentiation
Low Attainers – Ask them to make sets of objects from 1–5.
High Attainers – Could continue beyond 10.

Plenary **5 mins**
Use the sets of objects that one pair have made. Ask all the children to check the counting together. Then ask questions involving more/less, bigger/smaller/greater. *Are there more counters or more teddies? Is the number of cubes smaller than the number of crayons?*

Lesson 2

Introduction **10 mins**
Use a collection of real objects of different sizes and materials to sort with the children (or use an enlarged version of the pictures on Copymaster 17). View them one at a time asking questions like:
Is this heavy or light?
Does this look heavier/lighter than … ?
Are large objects always heavy?

Activities **25 mins**
Introducing the scales (whole class/group)
Demonstrate what happens to the balancing scales when an object is put into one of the pans. Ask the children to predict how much the pan will go down when different objects are put into it.
Put one object into each pan.
Which pan has the heaviest/lightest object?
How do you know?

Practical weighing (pairs/individuals)
Give the children an object and some pan scales to share and ask them to find some things that are heavier.

Differentiation
Low Attainers – Provide 2 objects with the scales and ask which is heavier.
High Attainers – Ask the children to find objects that are heavier and lighter than their own.

Plenary **5 mins**
Discuss some of the comparisons the children have made, emphasising the fact that the pan goes down when things are put in and up when things are taken out. *What happens if you weigh two objects which are about the same weight?*

Lesson 3

Introduction **10 mins**

Demonstrate to the children how you would make a ball of plasticine to balance a 50 g weight. Stop at times as you check the weight.
Do I have enough/too much?
What do I do if the ball is not heavy enough?
... or too heavy?

Activities **25 mins**

Plasticine shapes (whole class/group)
Show children two 50 g balls of plasticine, checking they are the same by weighing on the scales. Break one into two pieces or make a sausage of it. *Will it still balance the other ball?* Change the same ball in different ways and weigh against the unchanged ball each time.
Plasticine models (individuals)
Give a 50 g ball of plasticine to each child and ask them to use all of it to make a model or a different shape. Encourage them to make something different from everyone else.

Differentiation

Low Attainers – No simplification necessary, but emphasise that they must use all of their plasticine.
High Attainers – Can make their own 50 g ball, by comparing with a ready made one, before they start.

Plenary **5 mins**

Compare the children's models by weighing some on the pan scales. Emphasise the fact that different shapes can weigh the same, and that their models should all weigh the same if they used all of their plasticine.

Lesson 4

Introduction **10 mins**

Discuss the differences between the children as they are now, what they were like in the past, and what they will be like in the future.
What couldn't you do when you were a baby?
What are you learning to do now?
How might you change in the future?

Activities **25 mins**

A school day (whole class/individual)
Discuss the sequence of events in a school day from when the children wake up to when they go to sleep at the end of the day.
What do you do when you wake up? ... before you come to school? ... when you arrive in school? ... at playtime? ... in the afternoon? ... when you get home? ... before you go to bed?
My day (individual)
Provide the children with a wide strip of paper and ask them to draw a sequence of pictures to show their day, including something they do before, at and after school.

Differentiation

Low Attainers – Use Copymaster 18, ask the children to cut out the pictures and stick them in a suitable order for their day.
High Attainers – Encourage them to include more events in their sequence, or add some things that could happen after they have gone to bed.

Plenary **5 mins**

View some of the children's drawings and discuss them to develop the use of language associated with time. *Would the pictures be different at the weekend? ... or if you were ill and had to stay at home? What else might make you draw different things?*

Lesson 5

Introduction **10 mins**

Use the vocabulary early/late and yesterday/today/tomorrow in questions to the children.
Are you usually early for school?
What might make you late?
What did you do yesterday?
What might happen today? ... or tomorrow?

Activities **25 mins**

Day and night (whole class/group)
Introduce day and night to the children, using appropriate illustrations or a story book if available. Ask questions like: *Why does it go dark at night? Which animals come out at night? What do you do at night? Who might go to work at night? How many hours do most people sleep?*
Day and night pictures (pairs/individuals)
Draw or paint a picture of the daytime or night-time. Show what people and animals are doing. Put the Sun or the Moon in your picture.
Day and night collage (whole class/groups)
Ask the children to draw, paint, cut and stick things to go on a large class collage of day and/or night.
They could make 2 large collage pictures, one for day and one for night (*e.g. child asleep in bed/child playing, owl in a tree/blackbird in the tree*).

Differentiation

Low Attainers – Will be supported if they work with a more able child.
High Attainers – Could be the ones who sort the pictures and decide where they go on the collage.

Plenary **5 mins**

Discuss some of the pictures and clarify the differences between day and night. Explain simply how the Sun and the movement of the Earth is involved. Talk about the fact that the daytime is longer in Summer and shorter in Winter.

Theme 10 Problems

Objectives

- Count reliably up to 10 – both everyday objects and in other contexts, such as clapping sounds or hopping movements
- Solve practical problems involving counting and comparing in a real or role play context
- Begin to understand and use the vocabulary related to money
- Sort coins, including £1 and £2 coins, and begin to understand the similarities and differences
- Use up to five 1p coins in shopping role play situations

Vocabulary

numbers to 10, repeat, count, copy, money, compare, coin, penny, pence, pound, bigger/smaller, round, thick/thin, buy, sell, spend, copper, silver

Resources

Copymasters 19 and 20, real coins, large coin pictures, plastic coins, dice marked with 1p and blank faces, a class shop with items from 1p to 5p, teddy bears, tea-set, play food, drum, recorder

Homework Copymaster 10

Mental maths starters 3, 4, 5, 8, 22, 23

Assessment

At the end of this theme is the pupil able to:

- Count reliably up to 10 sounds or movements;
- Solve a problem in a practical play context;
- Talk about how the problem was solved;
- Recognise similarities and differences between real coins;
- Pay for things up to 5p, with the correct number of pennies?

Lesson 1

Introduction **10 mins**

Count altogether up to 5, then count again as you clap 5 times, then blink 5 times, than tap your knees 5 times. Build up a rhythm in the movements. Choose a different number up to 10 and repeat the activity. *What else could you do as you count?*

Activities **25 mins**

Listen and count (whole class/individuals)

Make a number of beats on a drum and ask the children to listen, count and show the same number of fingers. Start with small numbers, then larger ones up to 10. Try the same with a recorder, sometimes playing different notes so the children can see your fingers move, at other times repeating the same note, so there are no movement clues. Then try making the same sounds, asking the children to reply with an equal number of actions, like jumps, hops or claps.

Follow me (pairs, working as part of a class)

With the children in pairs, ask one child to repeat an action any number of times up to 10. *Can their partner count the actions and copy the actions the same number of times?* Swap places and try with a different number and/or action. Then ask one child to call out a number, so their partner can perform the same number of actions.

Differentiation

Low Attainers – Could do the same activities in a small group with an adult helper.

High Attainers – Try using two actions, so that 5 might be – jump, clap, jump, clap, jump. *Do you always end with the same thing?* This could be the beginning of odd and even numbers.

Plenary **5 mins**

Clap 6 times and ask the children to respond by clapping one more (7) or one less (5) times. Repeat with different numbers to 10 and different actions, always asking the children to respond with one more, or one less.

Lesson 2

Introduction **10 mins**

Choose 2 children and ask the class who they think is taller. Check by standing back to back. Continue with different pairs, choosing children that are closer in height. *Who do they know that is taller/shorter than themselves? … or about the same height?*

Activities **25 mins**

Who is the tallest? (whole class/group)

Choose 3 or 4 children and ask them if they can stand in height order. *Who is the tallest/shortest?* Divide the children into groups of 3 and ask them to do the same. *Hands up tallest/shortest in each group.* Continue varying the groups of 3, so that different children may be the tallest/shortest in a different group. Increase group size if appropriate.

Who is the tallest of all? (pairs/individuals working for a class comparison)

How could we find out who is the tallest of all in the class and show this to other classes? Discuss ideas like drawing around each child, cutting string or a paper strip the same as each child and labelling it, making a named mark on the wall at each child's height. Allow the children to follow up some or all of the ideas and use the results for comparisons.

Differentiation

Low Attainers – Will need adult help with some of the above.

High Attainers – Ask them to begin to make the comparisons, putting the lengths of string or body shapes together to compare their heights. Can they make predictions as to who will be the tallest and shortest?

Plenary **5 mins**

Once all the bodies have been drawn around, or bits of string cut, or marks made, make comparisons using the language associated with length. *How could you use what you have made to find out the tallest/shortest in the class.*

Lesson 3

Introduction **10 mins**
Sit 5 different sized teddy bears at the front. Ask the children questions like:
Which is the biggest/smallest/fattest/thinnest?
Which has the longest/shortest arms/legs?
Which do you think would eat the most?
How old do you think they are?

Activities **25 mins**
Teddy bear problems (whole class/group)
Using the 5 teddy bears, ask the children simple word problems like:
If each teddy needed a plate to eat from, how many would that be? If two teddies already had plates, how many more would be needed? If each teddy ate two biscuits, how many is that?
... and if one teddy didn't like biscuits?
Use fingers to help with the counting.

Teddy bear's picnic (small group/pairs)
Ask the children to set the scene for a teddy bear's picnic in the home corner. They will need to decide how many plates, cups etc. *What will each one eat and how many? Do different sized teddies eat different amounts of food? Do they have enough for all the teddies?*

Differentiation
Low Attainers – Will need some support from an adult helper to develop number vocabulary.
High Attainers – As they are playing, give them additional information to take into consideration *(e.g. one teddy feels sick and goes to bed). Do they need to make any changes?*

Plenary **5 mins**
Ask the children to talk through their teddy bear's picnic. Question them about the numbers they have used and ask the class to check their counting. Ask questions involving one more and one less *(e.g. if one more teddy came to tea, how many plates would be needed?).*

Lesson 4

Introduction **10 mins**
Ask the children questions about their shopping experiences.
Where would you go to buy bread? ... clothes? ... petrol?
How often do you buy these things?
How might you pay for these things?
Where would you get the money from?

Activities **25 mins**
All about the coins we use (whole class/group)
Hold up a real coin (or a large picture of a real coin) and ask the children what they can tell you about its colour, shape and size. *Is it round? Is it thick? Does it have a smooth edge?* Pass the coins around so the children can look at them closely.
Coin sort (pairs/individuals)
Ask the children to sort through a pile of real (or plastic) coins and find one of each type, or matching pairs. *Can they describe the coins? Can they draw around them and colour them the right colour?*
Purse full of pennies (pairs/individuals)
Use Copymaster 19, asking the children to colour the odd purse in each line.

Differentiation
Low Attainers – Work with an adult, who describes one of the coins for the children to find *(e.g. find a small, round, silver coloured coin).*
High Attainers – Ask them to sort the coins in different ways *(e.g. silver/not silver, round/not round).*

Plenary **5 mins**
Hold up some of the coin shapes the children have drawn, or draw some coin shapes on the board keeping the relative sizes correct. Ask the children to find a similar coin, or guess which coin it is by just looking at the shape.

Lesson 5

Introduction **10 mins**
Ask the children questions about the relative cost of different things.
Which costs more, a car or a bicycle?
Which costs less, a house or a garden shed?
What sort of things do you buy with your pocket money?
What would be too expensive?

Activities **25 mins**
What's different? (whole class/group)
Hold up two real coins. Ask the children what is different about them. *Is it the colour? ... the shape? ... the size?* Hold up in turn the 1p, 2p, 5p and 10p coins and ask the children to hold up fingers to match the value in pence.
Go shopping (supported pairs/individuals)
Set up a class shop with items priced from 1p to 5p and allow the children to use it for role play, paying for items with the correct number of 1p coins.

Buy a snowman (pairs)
Pairs need Copymaster 20, using a snowman each. They take turns to throw a die with 1p on three faces and blank on the other three. If they throw a 1p, they collect a 1p coin and save these until they have enough to 'buy' a part of the snowman. Placing coins on the picture. The winner is the first to buy all of their snowman.

Differentiation
Low Attainers – Can be given support from an adult helper or more able child when shopping.
High Attainers – Write 2p on one of the faces of the die in the snowman game and the children can collect the amounts they need using both 1p and 2p coins.

Plenary **5 mins**
Take coins up to a value of 20p, and ask how many 1p coins they would be worth. Display each coin with its corresponding number of 1p coins. The children can count the 1p coins together. Which is worth the most?

Theme 1 Ordering numbers

Objectives

- Say and use the number names beyond 10 in order in familiar contexts such as number rhymes, songs, stories, counting games and activities
- Count reliably up to 10 in a variety of contexts
- Use appropriate language to compare two numbers
- Order a given set of selected numbers to 10 *(e.g. 1 to 6 in random order)*

Vocabulary

number names to 10 and beyond, the same, as many as, bigger(est), greater(est), fewer(est), smaller(est), compare, size, next, between, what comes next? order, first, altogether

Resources

Copymasters 11, 21 and 22, a large set of dominoes, small sets of dominoes, interlocking cubes, a large number line or number track, small 0 to 10 number cards, cards and number tracks made from the copymasters

Homework Copymaster 11

Mental maths starters 6, 7, 8, 13, 24

Assessment

At the end of this theme is the pupil able to:

- Count a collection of 10 objects in different arrangements, using a strategy for keeping track of where the count begins and ends;
- Find out by counting which of two collections has more/fewer objects;
- Know that a number following another number in the counting sequence is bigger;
- Know that a number preceding another number in the counting sequence is smaller;
- Say what comes before/after, or between two numbers to 10;
- Order a complete set of numbers selected from 1 to 10?

Lesson 1

Introduction **10 mins**

Show the children some large dominoes and explain how the spots are grouped at each end. Hold some of them up and count the number of spots together. Include some of the more unusual ones, like those with blanks and doubles. Hold up any domino and ask the children, *How many spots?* They can hold up a corresponding number of fingers.

Activities **25 mins**

Who's got the number ...? (whole class/group)

Give each child in the class a domino and ask them to count the total number of spots and remember the number in their head. Call out any number from 0 to 12 and ask the children to hold up their domino if it has the same number of spots (or more spots, or fewer spots). Continue the questions, selecting different numbers and asking the children to swap dominoes from time to time.

Domino sort (pairs/trios)

Give the children a complete set of dominoes and ask them to count the spots and put them on top of one another, if they have the same number of spots. They should end up with piles of dominoes representing numbers from 0 to 12.

Differentiation

Low Attainers – Give them fewer dominoes with matching pairs with from 2 to 10 spots. They can count the spots and find the pairs that match.

High Attainers – Ask them to put their piles in order according to the number of spots. *Which number of spots is there most of? ... least of?*

Plenary **5 mins**

Ask the children to describe any two dominoes they found with the same number of spots. *Which numbers were at each end? Does it matter which end you start counting from? Could the spots be counted in a different order? Will you get the same number of spots altogether?*

Lesson 2

Introduction **10 mins**

Recite the numbers to 12 together, then around the class. Give each child a domino to hold it up if:

... it has a particular number of spots.

... it has more/less than a given number of spots.

... it has one more/one less spot than a given number.

... it has the number before/after given numbers.

Activities **25 mins**

More or less than 6? (pairs)

Ask the children to spread a complete set of dominoes face down on the table and take turns to pick one. The first child turns over a domino and counts the spots, keeping it if there are more than 6 spots. The second child turns over a domino and keeps it if it has less than 6 spots. Dominoes with exactly 6 spots are placed on one side. They continue until all the dominoes have been used. *How many have more, or less than 6 spots?*

Domino count (individuals within a group)

The group needs a set of dominoes and Copymaster 21 for each child. The children need to find dominoes with the same total number of spots as those on the sheets and draw them in the space provided.

Differentiation

Low Attainers – Ask them to draw any domino and count the number of spots. When they have drawn several, *can they match their dominoes to the correct drawing?*

High Attainers – Ask them to draw any domino, then draw one with one more spot next to it.

Plenary **5 mins**

Sit the children in a circle around the large dominoes spread face up. *Which domino has the least number of spots? How many spots does it have?* Place to start a row. *Can you see one with one more spot?* Place this next. Continue to build up the dominoes in order according to the number of spots, placing ones with the same number of spots on top of each other.

Lesson 3

Introduction **10 mins**
Ask the children to show an appropriate number of fingers to respond to the instruction. *Show me: any number from 0 to 10, more/less than a given number, bigger/smaller/larger/greater/fewer than a given number, one more than/one less than a given number, a number in between 2 others, the number before/after.*

Activities **25 mins**
Jump to it (individuals working as a whole class/group)
Give the children a counter and a spotty 0 to 10 number track from Copymaster 22. Ask questions similar to those in the introduction, but this time the children must respond by placing their counter on an appropriate number. Where a question has more than one answer, ask some children which number they chose and why.

Sort the spots (pairs/individuals)
The children need the spotty number track with numbers in random order from Copymaster 22. Ask them to cut up the track and stick the numbers in the right order.

Differentiation
Low Attainers – The number track has been arranged so that it can be cut part way along to give children only the numbers from 0 to 5.
High Attainers – Use the track with numerals instead of spots (Copymaster 42).

Plenary **5 mins**
On the board, go through the process of ordering the spotty numbers from 0 to 10, reinforcing all the relevant vocabulary. *Which is the smallest number? What comes next? Is this the right one? Why/why not?* Refer to the numerals on a large number line or track to see what comes next. Model how you would keep counting the numbers ordered so far to check.

Lesson 4

Introduction **10 mins**
Display in random order, any three consecutive spotty numbers from Copymaster 11. *Which shows the biggest number? Which shows the smallest?* Move the smallest to start a new row. *Of the two left, which is the smaller?* Move this, positioning it after the smallest. Then move the one with the most spots, so they are in increasing order. Repeat with different sets of 3 or more consecutive numbers.

Activities **25 mins**
What's missing? (individuals)
Use the spotty 0 to 10 number track from Copymaster 22, but blank out the spots in three or more of the squares before photocopying. One example has been done for you, but you may wish to produce alternatives with different, or more numbers missing. Ask the children to fill in the spots for the numbers which are missing.

Growing numbers (individuals)
Give the children a pile of spotty numbers cut from Copymaster 22. They need more than one of each. Ask them to find any 3 (or more) numbers that come next to each other and stick them in ascending order.

Differentiation
Low Attainers – Provide them with a copy of the spotty number line (ascending order) for support. In 'Growing numbers' they could find 2 consecutive numbers.
High Attainers – For 'Growing numbers' give them a mixture of spotty numbers and numerals to select from and order (see Copymaster 44).

Plenary **5 mins**
Use the spotty numbers cards from Copymaster 11. Hold up one and ask the children where it would go on a 1 to 10 number track. Place it on the board. Pick another card. *Is this number more or less? Where would it go?* Place this one. Continue until the numbers are in order from 1 to 10.

Lesson 5

Introduction **10 mins**
Display in random order, any three consecutive spotty numbers from Copymaster 11. *Which shows the smallest number? Which shows the biggest?* Move the biggest to start a new row. *Of the two left, which is the bigger?* Move this, positioning it after the biggest. Then move the one with the least spots, so they are in decending order. Repeat with different sets of 3 consecutive numbers.

Activities **25 mins**
What's missing now? (individuals)
Use the spotty 0 to 10 number track with numbers in descending order from Copymaster 22, but blank out the spots in three or more squares before photocopying. You may wish to produce alternatives with different or more numbers missing. Ask the children to fill in the spots for the numbers which are missing. Again they could try several different ones, some with more to fill in.

Shrinking numbers (individuals)
Give the children a pile of spotty numbers cut from Copymaster 22. They need more than one of each. Ask them to find 3 (or more) numbers that come next to each other, and stick them in descending order.

Differentiation
Low Attainers – Could start with any 2 numbers that come next to each other, sticking the largest first.
High Attainers – Give them a mixture of spotty numbers and numerals to select from and arrange in descending order (see Copymaster 44).

Plenary **5 mins**
Use the spotty numbers cards from Copymaster 11. Hold up one and ask the children where it would go on a 10 to 1 number track (note descending order). Place it in a suitable position on the board. Pick another card. *Is this number more or less? About where would it go?* Continue until the numbers are in descending order from 10 to 1.

Theme 2 Adding

Objectives

- Recite the number names forwards to 20 and backwards from 20
- Count reliably up to 10 in a variety of contexts
- Begin to use the vocabulary involved in adding
- Begin to relate addition to combining two groups of objects, counting all the objects

Vocabulary

number names to 20, forwards, backwards, count on/back, what comes next? add, more, and, make, sum, total, altogether, one more

Resources

Copymasters 23 and 24, 6-sided dice, counters in 2 colours, multilink cubes, finger paints, paper circles, pack of playing cards, counting objects in 2 colours, 2 cm squared paper, reading books, crayons, cards made from enlarged copymasters

Homework Copymaster 12

Mental maths starters 4, 5, 16

Assessment

At the end of this theme is the pupil able to:

- Recite the number names to 20 in ascending and descending order;
- Count a collection of 10 objects in different arrangements, using a strategy for keeping track of where the count begins and ends;
- Begin to use words like more, add, total, altogether … in practical contexts;
- Say how many there are altogether by counting all the objects in two groups?

Lesson 1

Introduction **10 mins**

Count together up to 20 and back. Use a row of 20 interlocking cubes, arranged in groups of 5 the same colour. Count along the row and back together. Split the row in the middle and place one half below the other. Count to 20 and back along both rows. Split the rows again and arrange as 4 rows of 5 cubes – recount forwards and backwards again.

Activities **25 mins**

Where to start? (whole class/group)

Draw an array of squares on the board *(e.g. 8 squares arranged in 2 rows of 4). How many squares? Where could you start counting? Which way could you count? If you started in a different place, would you get the same number?*

Repeat with different familiar shapes and different arrays, with up to 10 shapes.

Finger print counting (pairs/individuals)

Ask the children to make up to 10 finger prints of the same colour in a group on a large sheet of paper. *Can they count them starting in different places? Can their friend check their counting?* Print and count some more groups, using a different colour for each group.

Differentiation

Low Attainers – Use numbers to 5 only. They may need to mark their prints in some way, as they count them.

High Attainers – Make groups of up to 15 prints.

Plenary **5 mins**

Count some of the children's groups of finger prints emphasising finding a starting point and deciding which way to count to avoid mistakes. Discuss counting errors like counting a print twice, missing some out, not saying a number name for each print. Miscount some prints and ask the children to spot your mistakes.

Lesson 2

Introduction **10 mins**

Arrange up to 20 multilink cubes of the same colour into any irregular 2D shape. *How could we count these? Where could we start?* Count forwards starting from different places, check by counting backwards. Repeat with different numbers of cubes up to 20, arranged into different shapes. Try mixing different colours in the shapes. *Does this make it easier or harder to keep track of the count?*

Activities **25 mins**

Where to start? (pairs)

Ask each of the children to make 2D interlocking shapes with up to 10 cubes. They can tell their partner how many cubes they have used and ask them to check their counting. They may be able to record some of their shapes on 2 cm squared paper. Encourage them to make some irregular shapes. They could even try 3D shapes!

It's raining (pairs)

Children play a game on Copymaster 23, taking turns to throw a 6-sided die and placing the correct number of counters on the raindrops. They will each need to use counters of a different colour, checking to see who has the most counters on the sheet when it is full to see who the winner is.

Differentiation

Low Attainers – Use a die with 1 to 3 spots, repeated twice.

High Attainers – Use an 'It's raining' sheet each and a die with numerals on and/or bigger numbers.

Plenary **5 mins**

Fix up to 20 paper circles (about 10 cm diameter) on the board in a random arrangement with uneven spacing. Ask the children to watch as you point and count, but miscount them in some way. *Am I right? Can anyone check? Could someone else check by counting in a different order? Where did I go wrong?* Repeat with different numbers of circles, spaced in different ways.

Lesson 3

Introduction **10 mins**

Ask the children to look through their reading book and look for words of different lengths. *Can they find one with four letters? What is it?* Write some of the words on the board and count the letters together. Repeat with other numbers of letters. *What is the longest word they can find?*

Activities **25 mins**

Stand up, sit down (whole class/group)

Give each child a card with up to 10 spots on and ask them to count the spots (enlarge Copymaster 11, 2 or, 27). Tell them to stand up and show their card, when you call out their number. Sometimes call 2 numbers together, or ask for numbers that are bigger/smaller, one more or one less. Repeat, with the children all standing to start with, sitting down as their numbers are called.

Cross country (pairs)

Ask pairs to play the cross country game on Copymaster 24. They take turns to throw a 6-sided die and move forward the number of spaces thrown. The winner is the first to reach the winning post.

Differentiation

Low Attainers – Ensure they have familiar numbers in 'Stand up, sit down' – or the number they are trying to learn to count. In 'Cross country', use a die with lower numbers.

High Attainers – Give them 2 numbers to respond to in 'Stand up, sit down'. In 'Cross country' use a die with numerals on and/or bigger numbers.

Plenary **5 mins**

Choose some short story books. Look at the way the pages are numbered and count them together. *Does the count always start on the very first page? Are the pages numbered?* Discuss why it is useful to number the pages in books.

Lesson 4

Introduction **10 mins**

Show the children 2 small counting objects in one hand and 1 in the other. *How can I find out how many I have altogether?* Demonstrate putting the objects together in one hand and counting, or counting those in one hand carrying on the count to those in the other hand. Repeat with different numbers in each hand, sometimes allowing the children to choose the objects.

Activities **25 mins**

How many altogether? (pairs)

Ask the children to work alongside one another as a pair. They throw a 6-sided die and both colour in the same number of joined-up squares on 2 cm squared paper. They throw the die again and colour more squares in a second colour, joined to those first coloured. *How many of each colour? How many altogether? Did you have the same total as your partner? Did you colour them in the same shape?*

Towers of 5 (pairs/individuals)

Give the children multilink cubes in 2 colours only and ask them to make a tower of 5 bricks. *How many of each colour cube in the tower? How many different towers of 5 can you make using only two colours? Can you draw your towers?*

Differentiation

Low Attainers – Could build towers of 3 or 4 as there will be fewer possibilities, but this may restrict their counting.

High Attainers – Ask the children to work with a different shape of 5 cubes (T-shape or cross). They could record the cubes in the towers as number sentences (3 + 2 = 5).

Plenary **5 mins**

Look at some of the towers the children have made and discuss the different number bonds they represent (5 + 0, 4 + 1, 3 + 2). Sort the towers according to the number bonds they show. Discuss some similar ones (*e.g. Does it matter which positions the 3 red bricks in the tower are? Does it still show 3 + 2?*). Emphasise number bonds of 5.

Lesson 5

Introduction **10 mins**

Use objects around the classroom to ask questions involving less than/more than and 1 less/1 more. *If there was one more door in the classroom, how many would there be? If there were fewer windows, how many might there be? If we gave a bookcase to another class, how many would we have left? Can the children think of any questions to ask?*

Activities **25 mins**

Boys and girls (whole class/group)

Ask 2 boys and 2 girls to the front. *How many girls? How many boys? How many altogether?* Replace a boy with a girl and repeat the questions. *How many different ways could we make a row of 4 children using boys and/or girls?* Illustrate all possible combinations and model writing as a number sentence on the board. Repeat, using different totals.

Make 6 (pairs)

The first child in the pair needs to draw less than 6 spots or tally marks on paper. Their partner then draws more marks in a second colour to make the number up to 6. *How many marks in each colour? How many altogether? Try starting with a different number?* Swap, so that a different child goes first. *How many ways can you make 6?*

Differentiation

Low Attainers – Work with totals they can count to and/or real objects.

High Attainers – Could try writing the number sentences, exploring different totals or playing in a group of 3.

Plenary **5 mins**

Ask the children to feed back some of the numbers they drew to make 6. Draw these and write as number sentences on the board. Emphasise the similarities between 5 + 1 and 1 + 5, 4 + 2 and 2 + 4. *Did anyone start with 0? How many more would you need to make 6?* Ask the children to show all the pairs of numbers that make 6 using fingers or both hands.

Theme 4 Capacity

Objectives

- Recite the number names to 20 in order, continuing the count forwards from a given sequence of numbers
- Recognise small numbers without counting
- Use language such as full, empty, holds more/less to make direct comparisons of two capacities
- Compare the capacity of two containers by filling and emptying

Vocabulary

numbers to 20, forwards, backwards, count on/back, what comes next? guess, check, count, full, half-full, empty, holds, container, more/less

Resources

Copymasters 27 and 28, yogurt pots, a wide variety of plastic containers (mostly transparent), water or dry sand, playing cards, dominoes, cards made from copymasters, paint to colour the water

Homework Copymaster 14

Mental maths starters 4, 5, 17

Assessment

At the end of this theme is the pupil able to:

- Recognise numbers to 5 without counting;
- Continue the count from any number up to 20;
- Compare the capacity of two containers, by filling and emptying and say which holds more or less;
- Begin to use appropriate language to compare capacities;
- Find, by filling or emptying, containers that hold more or less than a given one?

Lesson 1

Introduction — 10 mins

Begin to count up to 20, but stop part way. Ask 3 different children to say the next 3 numbers. Repeat, stopping in different places, sometimes asking the children to start off the count and decide where to stop and who continues. Try the same thing, but counting backwards from 20.

Activities — 25 mins

Quick as a flash! (whole class/group)

Show any number of fingers on one hand very briefly to the children. *How many fingers? Can you show me the same number?* Repeat with different numbers, using different fingers. As the children improve, show numbers up to 5 (and beyond) using fingers from both hands. Invite some of the children to show some of their fingers briefly, for everyone to guess how many.

Quick sort (pairs/individuals)

Give the children either dominoes with a total number of spots less than 5, or playing cards with numbers from 1 to 5. Challenge them to sort the dominoes or cards into different number piles as quickly as they can. *Can they do it any faster? Do they need to count all the spots/shapes? Can they race against their friends?*

Differentiation

Low Attainers – Just use numbers up to 3 or 4 initially.
High Attainers – Use dominoes and playing cards with numbers beyond 5.

Plenary — 5 mins

Use the dominoes and cards the children have been working with. Compare and discuss the different numbers from 1 to 5 as they are represented on a domino or card. Hold one up briefly and ask how many. Repeat with different dominoes and cards, holding your fingers over the numerals on the playing cards so the children only see the shapes.

Lesson 2

Introduction — 10 mins

Draw 4 large spots in a row on the board. Count them together. Then draw different arrangements of 4 spots – in a square, an L-shape, a T-shape, a random arrangement. Discuss which are the easiest to recognise without counting all four spots. *Where might you have seen 4 arranged in different ways?* (window panes, on a dice, legs on a horse, wheels on a car …)

Activities — 25 mins

Sharp shooting (whole class/group)

Enlarge Copymaster 27 and cut into individual cards. Hold one up briefly and ask how many. *Show me the same number of fingers.* Show again and count to check. Repeat with different cards. *Was there more or less than the card before?*

Spot your number (supported group of 5)

Use the cards showing numbers 1 to 5 from Copymaster 27. Each child in the group is told a number from 1 to 5 to spot. An adult then shows the cards briefly, one at a time and the children try to spot their number. They can, if correct, have the card. Once all the cards have been spotted, the children all swap numbers and play the game again.

Differentiation

Low Attainers – Only use the cards with lower numbers and show them for a longer time.
High Attainers – Before photo-enlarging Copymaster 27, amend the sheet so that the cards have more shapes on them including some with a mixture of shapes *(e.g. 2 triangles and 3 circles).*

Plenary — 5 mins

Discuss and draw on the board different ways of representing the number 5 visually. Include 5 in a horizontal or vertical row and 5 as represented on a die. *How do the children visualise 5 of something? What about 6?*

Lesson 3

Introduction **10 mins**
Show the children 6 different transparent containers of which 2 are full, 2 empty and 2 half-full. Ask questions like:
Which are full/empty?
What does full/empty mean?
What can we call the ones which are neither full nor empty?
What could we do to make them all full? … or empty? … or half-full?

Activities **25 mins**
Which holds the most? (Whole class/group)
Show the children two containers with different capacities and ask them how you could find out which one holds the most. Demonstrate by filling the smaller container with the contents of the larger one, and then the larger container with the contents of the smaller one. *What happens each time?*
Filling and emptying (pairs/individuals)
Give the children two containers and ask them to find out which holds the most by filling one and emptying it into the other, taking care not to spill any water or sand.

Differentiation
Low Attainers – Give them containers which have clearly different capacities.
High Attainers – Provide containers which are less obviously different and ask them to demonstrate which holds the most in two different ways. Or provide three containers.

Plenary **5 mins**
Choose pairs or individuals to show their containers, explain which one holds the most and how they found out. Reinforce the two different ways of doing this, shown in the class activity.

Lesson 4

Introduction **10 mins**
Use 6 different transparent containers, filled to varying amounts with coloured water. Discuss each one in turn and whether or not it is half-full. Adjust them one at a time to make them half-full.
Is it more/less than half-full?
Do I need to add/tip out water to make it half-full?
What does half-full mean?

Activities **25 mins**
Half-full containers (whole class/ group)
Draw some container shapes on the board and ask the children where the half-full line would go. Start with uniform cylindrical shapes, then some different ones, like a container with a balloon bottom. *Where would the half-full line be in this container?*
Make it half-full (pairs/individuals)
Give the children a selection of containers and ask them to half-fill them with water or dry sand. Alternatively ask them to colour the half-full containers on Copymaster 28.

Differentiation
Low Attainers – Can still try, but don't expect them to be too accurate!
High Attainers – Ask them to half-fill some beakers for the teddies, or water the plants with a half-full yogurt pot of water.

Plenary **5 mins**
Look at some of the half-full containers the children have made and discuss their accuracy. Emphasise the equal nature of two halves and question the position of the half-way line in any irregular containers.

Lesson 5

Introduction **10 mins**
Discuss the different containers used in everyday life with the children.
What do we keep milk/lemonade/petrol … in?
What are different containers made from?
Why are they different shapes? (e.g. spout on a tea-pot)

Activities **25 mins**
A pot full of water (whole class/group)
Use a yogurt pot, some different transparent containers and coloured water. Show the children what a yogurt pot full of water looks like in each of the other containers. *Does it always come up as high in the container? Why not?*
The same water (pairs/individuals)
Provide the children with a small container and several differently shaped larger ones, with possibly one smaller. Ask them to use their small container to put the same amount of water or dry sand in each of the other containers. They can mark the level in each container with a pen.

Differentiation
Low Attainers – Give them a yogurt pot to work with as in the demonstration.
High Attainers – Ask them to make several marks on the larger containers, where one potful would come to, two potfuls … etc.

Plenary **5 mins**
Discuss some of the differences in the way the same amount of water or sand looks in different containers. *If the container is thin, is the water level higher or lower? What if the container is wide?*

Theme 5 Taking away

Objectives
- Count reliably up to 15 – both everyday objects and in other contexts
- Begin to use the vocabulary involved in subtracting
- Begin to relate subtraction to 'taking away' and counting how many are left
- Compare coins, including £1 and £2 coins, and recognise the similarities and differences
- Use up to ten 1p coins in shopping role play situations

Vocabulary
number names to 15, take (away), leave, how many are left? one less, money, compare, coin, penny, pence, pound, bigger/smaller, buy, sell, spend, how much, pay, price

Resources
Copymasters 29 and 30, real and plastic coins, large coin pictures, plasticine or playdough, rolling pins, class shop selling items up to 10p, coin stamps, shopping items and a shopping bag, interlocking cubes, small counting items, small bunches of grapes, large number line or track, one large die, small dice marked 1, 1, 2, 2, 3, 3

Homework Copymaster 15

Mental maths starters 4, 5, 12, 22

Assessment
At the end of this theme is the pupil able to:
- Count forwards up to 15 in a variety of contexts;
- Begin to use words like take away, leave, less … in practical contexts;
- Count how many are left when some of a collection are taken away;
- Recognise and explain the similarities and differences between real coins;
- Use coins to pay for things in the class 'shop';
- begin to recognise that some coins have a greater value than others?

Lesson 1

Introduction **10 mins**
Recite the numbers to 15, clearly sounding the numbers after 10. Ask the children to count with you, showing fingers as they count and emphasising the multiples of 5 once the fingers on a hand are all up. Count to 15 several times, performing 15 actions as you do so – 15 hand shakes, 15 claps, 15 blinks, 15 jumps, 15 nods of the head.

Activities **25 mins**
A bag full of shopping (whole class/group)
Use a bag with up to 15 items of shopping, some the same and some different. *How many things do you think are in here?* Ask the children to count as you take the items out one at a time. *If I used one of the things (e.g. ate the apple), how many would I have now?* Check by counting the items back into the bag. Repeat with different numbers of items, using the numbers from 10 to 15 in particular.

Rows and rows (pairs/individuals)
Ask the children to make some rows of 15 interlocking cubes, with a different pattern of colours in each. They could use all one colour, or alternate two colours, or repeat three colours along the row. *What else could they try? Can they record some of their rows of 15?*

Differentiation
Low Attainers – Try making rows of 11 cubes.
High Attainers – Challenge them to arrange the colours in different ways – in groups of 3 or 5 colours, with ten of one colour and five in another. *Can they count backwards from 15 to check they have the right number?*

Plenary **5 mins**
Ask the children to listen carefully as you recite the numbers to 15, leaving one out. *Which number was missing?* Repeat, missing out different numbers. Ask some of the children to say the numbers to 15 missing one out. Ask similar questions.

Lesson 2

Introduction **10 mins**
Hold up 8 fingers. *If I folded 3 down, how many would I have left? … and how many would I need to fold back up to get the 8 I started with?* So, 8 take away 3 is 5. Repeat with other numbers up to 10, encouraging the children to fold down their fingers and count how many are left. *If we start with 5 fingers, what is the biggest number we can take away?*

Activities **25 mins**
Bunches of grapes (whole class/group)
You need some small bunches of washed grapes, with up to 15 in each bunch. Count how many in a bunch together. *If I took 2 away (give to 2 children to eat), how could I find out how many were left?* Count remaining grapes together to check. *If I take another 3 away, how many are left?* Continue until all the grapes are gone. Repeat with a second bunch, taking away different numbers.

Count the grapes (pairs/individuals)
Give the children Copymaster 29 and ask them to count the grapes in each bunch. They need to find bunches of grapes with the same number of grapes, colouring them the same colour.

Differentiation
Low Attainers – May need to mark each grape to keep track of the count.
High Attainers – Can they work out how many would be left if 2 grapes were eaten from each bunch.

Plenary **5 mins**
Discuss the grape eating problem again, using another bunch of grapes, or an enlarged version of Copymaster 29. *If 2 grapes are eaten, how many would be left? Does it matter which 2 grapes are eaten?* Count together to check. Emphasise that whichever 2 grapes are eaten, there would be the same number left. Model how to write as a number sentence using – and =.

Lesson 3

Introduction **10 mins**

Ask some one less questions. What is one less than 4? or 7? Point to the numbers on a number line or track to illustrate. *Which numbers are less than 3? or 8? How many would I need to take away from 4 if I wanted 1 left?* Repeat similar questions, putting some into a real life context.

Activities **25 mins**

Where have the children gone? (whole class/group)

Sit the girls in a large circle, with the boys in a group in the middle. *How many boys?* Throw a large 6 spot die and ask that number of boys to stand up. *Where could they be going?* They then join the circle. *How many boys are left?* Count to check, before throwing the die again. Continue until there are no boys left, then start again with the girls in the centre group.

Take away pairs (pairs)

Each child needs 15 small counting objects, with a die marked 1, 1, 2, 2, 3, 3 for each pair. They take turns to throw the die, take 1, 2 or 3 items from their set and count what they have left. The winner is the first to take away all of their objects. *How many did you take away? How many were left? Who is winning so far?*

Differentiation

Low Attainers – Give them fewer items and a die marked 1, 1, 1, 2, 2, 2.

High Attainers – Could start with 20 items, or play a variation where they take items from their partner and aim to collect all 30 objects.

Plenary **5 mins**

Emphasise that taking away leaves you with a smaller number than you started with. Ask them to take away 1 from some familiar numbers. Explain that taking away 1 leaves you with the number that comes before in the count. *How could you take away 2? (e.g. by subtracting 1 twice) Can they take away 2 from 5? … or 8?*

Lesson 4

Introduction **10 mins**

Give each child one of each plastic coin.

Can you show me a round coin?

… the largest coin? … the smallest coin?

… a silver coin? … a 1p coin?

… a coin bigger than a 10p coin? Continue with similar questions.

Activities **25 mins**

Guess which coins (whole class/group)

Put a real coin in an opaque bag and pass it round, so the children can try to guess what it is without looking. Additional duplicate bags will speed things up. *What can they tell you about the shape and size of the coin before they guess what it is?* Try with different coins. *Who needs to be able to recognise different coins by touch?*

Plasticine coin press (pairs/individuals)

Provide the children with some plasticine or playdough and ask them to roll it flat and press coins into it, leaving a coin print. Real coins are better, but plastic ones will show the relative size and shape. A friend can then try to match the coins with the prints that have been made.

Differentiation

Low Attainers – Will need adult support to develop the appropriate language.

High Attainers – May like to try to make their coin prints in order of value, or size.

Plenary **5 mins**

Hold up some of the plasticine or playdough prints the children have made with the coins and ask them if they can guess which coin made the print. *How did they know?* Match a coin with the print to see if they are right.

Lesson 5

Introduction **10 mins**

Draw one of the class shop items up to 10p on the board, with its price. Ask one of the children to fix (blu-tak) the correct number of 1p coins next to the item. All children can count to check whether they are right. Continue with other items up to 10p.

Activities **25 mins**

A trip to the shop (small group/pairs/individuals)

Set up a class shop for shipping role play with items priced from 1p to 10p. Give them 10 × 1p coins to spend. They can pay for items with the correct number of 1p coins and count how much they have left.

Class shop price list (pairs/individuals)

Ask the children to draw pictures of the items in the class shop, copy the prices and stamp the correct number of 1p coins next to them, using a 1p coin stamp. This can become a price list for the shop.

Buy a scarecrow (pairs)

Pairs need Copymaster 30, using a scarecrow each. Children take turns to throw a die marked with 1p on three faces and blank on the other three. When they throw a 1p, they collect a 1p coin and save these until they have enough to 'buy' a part of the scarecrow. Coins can be placed on the picture. The winner is the first to buy all of their scarecrow.

Differentiation

Low Attainers – Can be given support from an adult helper, or more able child when shopping.

High Attainers – The children can use both 1p and 2p coins for shopping and the Snowman game (add 2p to die).

Plenary **5 mins**

Explain to the children that a 2p coin is worth the same as two 1p coins. Then hold up a 1p and a 2p coin and ask how much that would be altogether. Try with two 2p coins and other combinations of 1p and 2p coins to 5p.

Theme 6 Counting & reading numbers

Objectives
- Say and use the number names to 20 in order in familiar contexts such as number rhymes, songs, stories, counting games and activities
- Recognise numerals 1 to 5
- Use appropriate language to compare two numbers
- Order a given set of selected numbers to 10 *(e.g. 2, 5, 1, 8, 4)*

Vocabulary
number names to 20, straight, curved, before, after, bigger/smaller than, more/most, less/least, larger(est), bigger(est), greater(est), fewer(est), smaller(est), compare, size, next, between, what comes next? order, first

Resources
Copymasters 11, 22, 31 and 32, number tracks from 1 to 5, small counting objects, small plastic numerals from 1 to 5, plasticine or playdough, small rolling pins, large numbers from 1 to 5, enlarged spotty numbers from Copymasters 11 and 22, spotty number lines, large straws and elastic bands, safety scissors

Homework Copymaster 16

Mental maths starters 1, 2, 6, 13

Assessment
At the end of this theme is the pupil able to:
- Say and use the number names to 20 in different contexts;
- Recognise numerals from 0 to 5;
- Know that numbers following in the counting sequence are bigger;
- Know that preceding numbers in the counting sequence are smaller;
- Say what comes before/after, or between two numbers to 10;
- Order any set of numbers from 1 to 10?

Lesson 1

Introduction **10 mins**
You need 20 straws and several elastic bands. *How many straws?* Ask the children to count up to 20 and back from 20 to check. Count out 5 straws and put a band around them. *Show me 5 fingers.* Make 3 more groups of 5 straws. Ask the children to count to 20 again, shouting on the multiples of 5 as they show you their whole hand and you hold up a bundle of 5 straws.

Activities **25 mins**
Pass on the number (whole class/group)
Sit the children in a large circle, whisper a number up to 20 in the ear of one child and ask them to pass the whisper around the circle. *Can the number get all around the circle without changing?* Try a variation, where children listen to a number and whisper the following number to the next child. If they reach 20, they can start to count backwards or start again from 0. *Can anyone work out what the last number will be once the whisper has gone all around the circle?* Everyone can count aloud to check.
Straw snips (pairs/individuals)
Give the children two long straws and ask them to cut the straws so they have 15 small straws. They need to count carefully so they don't cut too many! *Can they sort the straw snips into sets to show the numbers 1 to 5? Can they match the correct plastic numeral to each set?*

Differentiation
Low Attainers – Could initially work with uncut straws.
High Attainers – Can make sets of straw snips up to 10. *Can they add 2 to each whispered number around the circle?*

Plenary **5 mins**
Ask the children to count up to 20 and back again several times, following a loud or soft action from your hands – wide apart means loud, close together means quietly. If you put your hands together, they need to keep counting in their heads until you separate them again.

Lesson 2

Introduction **10 mins**
Write the numerals 1 to 5 on the board and point to them as the children count up and back in order. Then point to numerals at random and ask what number it is. *Where would you start to write the number? Can the children draw the number in the air?* Rub out, then re-write the numerals, but randomly spaced on the board. Repeat the questions.

Activities **25 mins**
Which number? (whole class/group)
Give each child from 1 to 5 small counting objects to hold in their hand. Ensure an even spread of the different numbers. Point to a numeral from 1 to 5 on the board and ask the children to put up their hand if they are holding that number of objects. Ask some to check by counting aloud. Repeat with other numbers, then swap the objects around so that each child has a different number and continue pointing to numerals.
Number hunt (pairs/individuals)
Bury a large number of small counting objects in a sand tray along with some small plastic numerals from 1 to 5. Ask the children to find one each of the numerals from 1 to 5, put them in order and continue hunting until they find the correct number of objects to put with each numeral.

Differentiation
Low Attainers – Just bury the numerals from 1 to 3.
High Attainers – Bury numerals beyond 5 as well, and more objects to go with them.

Plenary **5 mins**
Ask a child to the front, to stand with their back to the other children. Using your finger, draw a large numeral from 1 to 5 on their back. *Can they guess which numeral you are drawing? Can the other children show you a corresponding number of fingers?* Repeat with different children and numerals. Ask the children to repeat the activity working in pairs and drawing on one another's backs.

Lesson 3

Introduction **10 mins**
Hold up a large number card from 1 to 5. *What can you tell me about this number? Is it made of straight lines or curved lines? Can you show me the same number of fingers? Which number comes before/after?* Repeat with other number cards in random order.

Activities **25 mins**
Number track to 5 (whole class/group)
Give each child a number track from 1 to 5 and a counter. Ask them to place their counter on … *the number 3, … the number 5, … the number before/after 2, … one more/less than 4, … a number made from curved lines.* Continue asking similar questions, asking the children to read back the numbers they have chosen. Encourage the children to take part in giving the instructions.
Number press (pairs/individuals)
Ask the children to roll some plasticine or playdough flat and press a plastic numeral from 1 to 5 into it. *Can they then make the corresponding number of prints next to it, by pressing in a finger, small object or shape?* Encourage them to work alongside a friend who can check their counting.

Differentiation
Low Attainers – Just use the numerals 1 to 3 to start with.
High Attainers – Use numerals beyond 5 as well and ask the children to make a set of prints with the numbers in order.

Plenary **5 mins**
Give five children the numerals from 1 to 5 and ask them to the front. *Can they arrange themselves in order from 1 to 5? What about reverse order from 5 to 1? Are they right?* Repeat with different groups of children, sometimes asking the observers to give instructions to the children holding the numbers, telling them how to move to get into the right order.

Lesson 4

Introduction **10 mins**
Display in random order, any three spotty numbers from Copymaster 11. *Which shows the biggest number? Which shows the smallest?* Move the smallest to start a new row. *Of the two left, which is the smaller?* Move this, positioning it after the smallest. Then move the one with the most spots, so they are in increasing order. Repeat with different sets of 3 or more numbers. *Which numbers in between are missing?*

Activities **25 mins**
Growing numbers (individuals)
Give the children a pile of the individual spotty numbers cut from Copymaster 22. They need more than one of each number. Ask them to find any 3 (or more) numbers and stick them in their book in order *(e.g. a sequence of 3, 7, 9 spots)*. If they can do this easily, increase the number used.
Wobbly worms (individuals)
Ask the children to fill in the missing spots on the Wobbly worms sheet, Copymaster 31. They can add any number that could come in between the ones shown either side of the spaces. If they finish, they can draw some worms of their own showing numbers in ascending order.

Differentiation
Low Attainers – Provide them with a copy of the spotty number line (Copymaster 22 – ascending order) for support.
High Attainers – Give them a mixture of spotty numbers and numerals to select from and arrange in ascending order (see Copymaster 42).

Plenary **5 mins**
Give 5 children a spotty number from Copymaster 11 and ask them to arrange themselves in order with smallest number first. *Are they right?* Repeat with more numbers, building up until all ten numbers are put in order.

Lesson 5

Introduction **10 mins**
Display in random order any three spotty numbers from Copymaster 11. *Which shows the smallest number? Which shows the biggest?* Move the biggest to start a new row. *Of the two left, which is the bigger?* Move this, positioning it after the biggest. Then move the one with the least spots so they are in descending order. Repeat with different sets of 3 or more numbers. *Which numbers in between are missing?*

Activities **25 mins**
Shrinking numbers (individuals)
Give the children a pile of the individual spotty numbers cut from Copymaster 22. They need more than one of each number. Ask them to find any 3 (or more) numbers and stick them in their book in decending order, with the largest first *(e.g. a sequence of 8, 4, 1 spots)*. If they can do this easily, increase the number in the sequence.
Smart snakes (individuals)
Ask the children to fill in the missing shapes on the Smart snakes sheet, Copymaster 32. They can add any number that could come in between the ones shown either side of the space. If they finish, they can draw some snakes of their own showing numbers in descending order.

Differentiation
Low Attainers – Provide them with a copy of the spotty number line (Copymaster 22 – descending order) for support.
High Attainers – Give them a mixture of spotty numbers and numerals to select from (see Copymaster 42).

Plenary **5 mins**
Give 5 children a spotty number from Copymaster 11 and ask them to arrange themselves in order with largest number first. *Are they right?* Repeat with more numbers, building up until all ten numbers are put in descending order. *Who can match the correct numerals to the cards?*

Theme 7 Combining & counting on

Objectives
- Count reliably up to 15 in a variety of contexts
- Recognise numerals 1 to 5
- Begin to relate addition to combining two or three groups of objects, counting all the objects
- Begin to relate addition to counting on

Vocabulary
number names to 15, add, and, make, total, altogether, start from, count on, more, sum

Resources
Copymasters 4, 27, 33 and 34, plastic counting buttons with 1 to 5 holes, feely bag, plastic letters and numerals from 1 to 5, interlocking cubes or counters, geometric shapes, counting objects, pictures of numbers 1 to 5, small objects to count – like paperclips, marbles, centimetre cubes, matchsticks …, number tracks from Copymasters 22 and 42

Homework Copymaster 17

Mental maths starters 5, 7, 12, 19

Assessment
At the end of this theme is the pupil able to:
- Count forward to and backwards from 15 in a variety of contexts;
- Recognise numerals from 0 to 5;
- Begin to use words like more, add, total, altogether … in practical contexts;
- Say how many there are altogether by counting all the objects in two or three groups;
- Count on when adding?

Lesson 1

Introduction **10 mins**
Put your pen or chalk on the board and ask the children, *How can I draw the number 3? What shape is it? Which way do I need to move the pen?* Demonstrate how to draw the numeral 3. Repeat with other numbers to 5.

Activities **25 mins**
How many in a handful? (pairs/individuals)
Provide the children with plenty of small counting objects – centimetre cubes, matchsticks, paperclips, marbles. Ask them to take a handful of each one and count how many they can hold in their hand. *How many is a handful of paperclips? … or matchsticks? Which can you hold most of? … or least of?* Ask them to arrange their different handfuls on the table.
What does 15 look like? (pairs/individuals)
You need access to an outside area (a field or garden) for this activity. Take the children outside and ask them to collect 15 of things like leaves, blades of grass, sticks, stones. *What can they see at least 15 of, but can't collect? (e.g. bricks on the wall, roof tiles, panels in the fence …).* Make a large playground display to show what 15 looks like.

Differentiation
Low Attainers – In 'How many in a handful?' give slightly larger objects, so there are less in a handful.
High Attainers – Give smaller objects, so there are more in a handful.

Plenary **5 mins**
Use some of the small objects the children have been working with. Ask children to put 15 of each object in a row. Compare the rows. *Does 15 look more if the objects are bigger? Do 15 small objects take up the same space as 15 larger ones?* Ask them to think of 15 even smaller things. *What could they be? How much space would they take up? What about 15 very large things?*

Lesson 2

Introduction **10 mins**
Write the numerals 1 to 5 in order on the board. Tell the children you are thinking of a numeral with … a flat top, … or a flat bottom, … or no straight lines, … or 2 straight lines. *Can they guess which number it is? Can they point to the number on the board?* Demonstrate how you draw the numbers 1 to 5 and ask the children to draw them in the air with their finger.

Activities **25 mins**
How many flowers (individuals)
Give each child Copymaster 4, and a pile of plastic letters and numbers including many numerals from 1 to 5. Ask them to count the flowers, then find the correct numeral for each group. They can then draw their own sets of flowers to match each of the numerals they have found.
Touch the number (pairs/small group)
Place a number of plastic numerals from 1 to 5 in an opaque bag. Pass the bag around a small group and ask the children, without looking, to feel for and find the number 1. Pass the bag around again and the children try to find number 2, then 3 and so on. If a child pulls the wrong numeral from the bag, they replace it and wait until their next turn to look for the next number.

Differentiation
Low Attainers – Hold up the numeral they are trying to find in the bag. In 'How many flowers' exclude letters from the pile before they hunt for the numerals.
High Attainers – Put some decoy numbers from 6 to 9 in the bag, or ask them to find numbers beyond 5.

Plenary **5 mins**
You need an opaque bag and plastic numerals from 1 to 5 (plus some from 6 to 9 for the more able children). Take a numeral from the bag, hold it up and ask a child what it is. If they are correct, they keep the number. If not it is put back into the bag. Continue until every child has at least one numeral. *How do you remember which numeral is which. How are they different?*

Lesson 3

Introduction 10 mins

Hold up a counting button with 5 holes. *How many holes if there was one more? … or two more? What if there was one less? … or two less?* Repeat with different buttons. Then hold up two counting buttons and ask, *How many holes altogether?* Repeat with different pairs of buttons.

Activities 25 mins

Which button? (whole class/group)
Give each child in the class a counting button to hold. Then hold up a button with 3 holes. *Hold up your button if it is the one I need to make 6 holes altogether.* Repeat, holding up different buttons and asking for different totals. Or if in a large space, call out a number like 7, and ask the children to find other children so that the total number of holes in their buttons is 7. They could end up in a pair or a small group.

How many holes? (pairs/individuals)
Give the children a set of 5 counting buttons with 1 to 5 holes. Ask them to choose any 3 buttons, draw around them marking the holes, and count how many holes altogether. *How many different totals can you make? What happens if you use 2 buttons, or 4 buttons?*

Differentiation

Low Attainers – Use 2 counting buttons of each number from 1 to 3.
High Attainers – Could work with 2 sets of counting buttons from 1 to 5, and use more than one of each number.

Plenary 5 mins

Pick any 3 counting buttons and ask *How many holes altogether? Which button did you count first? Could we start with a different button?* Check counting, starting with each of the 3 buttons in turn. Repeat with other groups of buttons. Emphasise the fact that the order of counting does not affect the total.

Lesson 4

Introduction 10 mins

Give each child a set of digit cards from 1 to 5 only. Show the children an enlarged number card from Copymaster 27 and ask them to hold up a digit card which shows the matching numeral. Repeat with different cards, sometimes asking for a numeral which is more/less, one more/one less than the enlarged number card shown.

Activities 25 mins

Count and match (pairs/individuals)
Give the children a pile of cut up cards from Copymaster 27 and a pile of numeral cards from 1 to 5. These could be cut from Copymaster 42. Ask the children to find a numeral which matches a shape card. *How many pairs can they find?* They could record their work by sticking pairs together on paper.

Kites (pairs/individuals)
Give the children Copymaster 33 and ask them to look at the numerals and count the spots, then colour the kites according to the key at the bottom of the page.

Differentiation

Low Attainers – Provide them with a 1 to 5 number track or number line for support. Explain how they can count along to find the numeral they need.
High Attainers – May be able to write the numerals next to the shape cards in 'Count and match'.

Plenary 5 mins

Draw the colour key from Copymaster 33 on the board, underlining the colour words in the appropriate colours. Then draw a large kite shape. *If I wanted you to colour this part of the kite blue, what would I need to put on it? Could I put anything else? (e.g. 2 or two spots).* Ask a child to draw the spots or write the number. Continue until you have coded all the areas of the kite. *How many different colours have we used? Have we used every colour? How can we check?*

Lesson 5

Introduction 10 mins

Write the numbers 1 to 5 in order on the board. Hold up a square. *How many sides?* Place the square below the number 4 on the board. Hold up a row of 3 interlocking cubes. *How many cubes? Which number shall I place this next to?* Continue holding up different pictures of numbers, or real objects, placing them with the appropriate number.

Activities 25 mins

Number sort (pairs/small groups)
Give each group a wide selection of cards showing up to 5 shapes or pictures, plastic numerals from 1 to 5 and numeral cards from 1 to 5. You could even include some 2D or 3D shapes with 1 to 5 sides or edges and some real objects. Ask the children to have a number sort, finding all the things which represent each number from 1 to 5. *Why might you put a triangle with number 3?* (Many of the copymasters could be cut up for this purpose)

Count on (individuals)
Give the children Copymaster 34 and ask them to complete the number sentences, counting on from the first number. They can refer to the numbers at the bottom of the page to help them write the answers.

Differentiation

Low Attainers – May find it useful to put interlocking cubes over the squares, to move as they count.
High Attainers – Can make up some more of their own using the same starting numbers, but adding a different number of squares.

Plenary 5 mins

Depending on ability, give each child a counter and 0 to 10 number track from Copymaster 22 (spotty numbers) or Copymaster 42 (numerals). *Put your counter on number 2, count on 3 more. Which number is your counter on now?* Repeat with different numbers, including some where you count on twice before you stop.

Theme 9 Measures

Objectives
- Recite the number names to 20 in order, continuing the count forwards or backwards from a given sequence of numbers
- Recognise numerals 1 to 9
- Use language such as more or less, longer or shorter, heavier or lighter ... to compare two quantities
- Use the vocabulary of time to make comparisons
- Begin to know the days of the week in order

Vocabulary
numbers to 20, forwards, backwards, count on/back, next, before, after, more, less, long, short, heavy, light, tall, deep, shallow, wide, narrow, days of week, day, week, hour, morning, afternoon, evening, night, today, yesterday, tomorrow, before, after, quick, slow, old, new

Resources
Copymasters 37 and 38, pan scales, a variety of small objects, paper strips, plasticine or playdough, The Very Hungry Caterpillar by Eric Carle, ribbon, string, tape, a wide variety of plastic containers, water or dry sand, drum and beater, large number cards 1 to 9, digit cards

Homework Copymaster 19

Mental maths starters 4, 7, 17

Assessment
At the end of this theme is the pupil able to:
- Continue the count forwards and backwards from any number to 20;
- Recognise numerals from 0 to 9;
- Use appropriate language to compare two lengths, weights or capacities;
- Say the days of the week in order;
- Make time comparisons using words like longer, before, quicker ...?

Lesson 1

Introduction **10 mins**
Say 3 consecutive numbers from 0 to 20 and ask the children to say the next three. Repeat with different numbers, sometimes in descending order. Try only giving 2 consecutive numbers and asking for the next two in the count.

Activities **25 mins**
Count the beat (whole class/group)
Count aloud to 20, replacing any 3 consecutive numbers with 3 drum beats. *Which numbers did the drum beat for?* Repeat, but replace different numbers with drum beats, sometimes counting backwards or letting one of the children count and beat.
Digit ordering (pairs)
Give each pair a set of 1 to 9 digit cards and ask them to spread the cards face up on the table. The first child needs to look for 1 and place it at the start of a row. They then take turns to place the next numeral in the row until they reach 9. *How quickly can they do this? Can they start with 9 and take turns to find the next card in descending order?*

Differentiation
Low Attainers – Use a smaller set of cards to begin with.
High Attainers – Try spreading the cards face down. *Can the children take turns to turn one over and place it in the correct position in the number row?*

Plenary **5 mins**
Fix a set of large digit cards from 1 to 9 in order on the board, but place some of the numerals upside down, or sideways. *Can anyone spot what is wrong? Who can put it right?* Count along the row to check. Repeat the activity misplacing different numerals, or putting cards out of sequence, sometimes arranging the digit cards in reverse order.

Lesson 2

Introduction **10 mins**
Hold up a large number card from 1 to 9. *What can you tell me about this number? Is it made of straight lines or curved lines? Can you show me the same number of fingers? Which number comes before/after?* Repeat with other number cards in random order.

Activities **25 mins**
Hop, jump and step (whole class/group)
Use a large space with room for the children to move around. Hold up a large number card from 1 to 9. Ask the children altogether to do the same number of hops, jumps, large and then small steps. Repeat with different number cards, introducing some less tiring responses for the children to perform.
Balloons (individuals)
Give each child Copymaster 37 and ask them to choose a different colour for each number from 6 to 9 to complete the colouring key. They can then count the dots and colour the balloons the correct colour.

Differentiation
Low Attainers – Alter Copymaster 37 by deleting some of the dots and changing the colouring key to smaller numbers before photocopying.
High Attainers – Can add some more balloons with 10 or 11 spots and extend the colouring key.

Plenary **5 mins**
Give nine children the numerals from 1 to 9 and ask them to the front. *Can they arrange themselves in order from 1 to 9? What about reverse order from 9 to 1? Are they right?* Repeat with different groups of children, sometimes asking the observers to give instructions to the children holding the numbers, telling them how to move to get into the right order.

Lesson 3

Introduction 10 mins

Fix some strips of paper of different lengths and colours to the board so that they are parallel. Ask questions like:
Which is the longest/shortest strip?
Which strip is longer/shorter than the red strip?
Which strip is closest to the length of your finger?
Move the strips so that they are different angles and continue questioning.

Activities 25 mins

Plasticine balance (whole class/group)
Put a small object in one of the pans of some balance scales. Demonstrate how you would make a ball of plasticine or playdough, which is the same weight as the object. *If the object is lighter, do I need to add more plasticine or take some away? What if the object is heavier than the ball?*

Balance the objects (pairs/individuals)
Provide the children with a variety of small objects and ask them to make some balls of plasticine or playdough to balance the objects.

Differentiation

Low Attainers – Working with a more able child will help them.
High Attainers – Ask them if they can make two balls of plasticine, which will still balance one of the objects. *Could they make the two balls the same weight?*

Plenary 5 mins

Check some of the balls the children have made by balancing against the object. Emphasise that if the ball is too heavy, it needs to be smaller, and if it is too light, some needs to be taken away to make it balance. Reinforce the language needed to compare different masses (weights).

Lesson 4

Introduction 10 mins

Show the children some lengths of ribbon, string, tape – items which are not always straight.
Which is the longest/shortest?
How could we find out?
Can you think of things which are longer/shorter or are about the same length as each one?
Show how to compare the lengths by putting them together with the ends matching.

Activities 25 mins

Which is the same? (whole class/group)
Use four different transparent containers, two of which hold the same amount. Demonstrate, by filling and emptying, how you would find the two which have the same capacity.
Find the pairs (pairs/individual)
Provide the children with a selection of containers which include two of each capacity represented. Ask them to find the ones which are the same by filling and emptying with water or dry sand.

Differentiation

Low Attainers – Would benefit by working with a more able child.
High Attainers – Include some odd containers, which do not have a matching pair and ask them to find the odd ones out.

Plenary 5 mins

Check some of the pairs of containers the children have found, asking them to explain and demonstrate how they found the matching pairs. Reinforce the fact that containers of different shapes can hold the same amount.

Lesson 5

Introduction 10 mins

Say the days of the week in order to the children several times. Then repeat, but leave out the last day for them to add. Then leave out the last 2 days, then 3 … etc. until they are reciting them all in order.
Which day is today/yesterday/tomorrow?
Which day comes before/after Tuesday?
How many days are in the whole week?

Activities 25 mins

The Very Hungry Caterpillar (whole class/group)
Read The Very Hungry Caterpillar by Eric Carle to the children, emphasising the names of the days and what happened to the caterpillar on each day. *Can the children remember what the caterpillar ate each day?*
The caterpillar's week (pairs/individual)
Give the children Copymaster 38 and ask them to cut out the days and arrange them in order. They can draw what the caterpillar ate, or what happened to it on each day.

Differentiation

Low Attainers – Let them look at the book to help them to sort out the days, or provide them with a list of the days of the week in order.
High Attainers – Ask them to record the days of the week and draw their pictures on a blank sheet of paper.

Plenary 5 mins

Talk through the days of the week in school and ask the children to think of something different that happens on each day. *What about the weekend? How is the weekend different?* Recite the days of the week in order once more, starting from Monday, or a different day.

Theme 10 Using number

Objectives

- Recite the number names to twenty in order, continuing the count forwards or backwards from a given number
- Recognise numerals 0 to 9
- Begin to relate addition to counting on and subtraction to 'taking away' and counting how many are left
- Sort and match objects, pictures or the children themselves, justifying the decisions made

Vocabulary

numbers to 20, forwards, backwards, count on/back, next, before, after, more, less, adding, subtracting, add, more, and, make, sum, total, altogether, one more, equals, take away, leave, one less, fewer, how many? sort, match, choose

Resources

Copymasters 39 and 40, scissors, old catalogues, crayons, 0–9 digit cards, large 0–10 numbers, 10 hoops, a bean bag, small counting objects, number track and line from 1 to 10, enlarged coloured snakes from Copymaster 39

Homework Copymaster 20

Mental maths starters 10, 11, 13

Assessment

At the end of this theme is the pupil able to:

- Recite the number names in order to and back from 20;
- Continue the count forwards and backwards from any number up to 20;
- Recognise numerals from 0 to 9;
- Understand addition as counting on and subtraction as taking away;
- Sort and match objects and pictures;
- Explain their sorting criteria?

Lesson 1

Introduction **10 mins**

Ask the children to sit in a circle and count to 20 around the circle. Repeat, starting with a different child or counting in descending order. Change the way the children are seated *(e.g. into rows of 10 or 5, into pairs in a line …)* and practise counting to 20 again. *Does the way the children are sitting make any difference to the counting?*

Activities **25 mins**

Bean bag bumps (whole class/group)

Sit the children in a large circle and count to 20 using a bean bag, which the children throw to whoever they want to say the next number in the count. Repeat, counting in descending order. Then ask the child with the bean bag to choose a number and throw the bag to another child, who says the number that comes after. That child then chooses a new number before throwing the bean bag on … and so on. Repeat, asking children to say the number that comes before.

Sets of objects (pairs/individuals)

Give the children a set of 0 to 9 digit cards and ask them to make a set of counting objects to match each card. *Can they arrange the sets and cards in order? Is it easier if the objects are placed in rows? Can they check the sets that another pair have made?*

Differentiation

Low Attainers – Use 0 to 5 digit cards to start with.
High Attainers – Once they have made their sets, remove the digit cards and ask them to make their own number cards to match the sets.

Plenary **5 mins**

Give the children a set of digit cards from 0 to 9. Hold up some sets of objects, or pictures of objects and ask the children to hold up the number that matches the set. Check that they have chosen the right number by counting together along a large number track or line.

Lesson 2

Introduction **10 mins**

Hold up any numeral from 0 to 9 and ask the children to show you the same number of fingers. Repeat, but asking for one more, or one less fingers, or any number which is more or less. *Which number have you chosen? What can you tell me about the shape of it?*

Activities **25 mins**

Spot the digit (whole class/group)

Give the children a set of digit cards from 0 to 9. Ask them to hold up any number you call out. Then ask them to hold up any number which is bigger or smaller than the given one. Ask some of the children which numbers they have chosen each time, pointing to its position on a large number line to check.

Disappearing digits (pairs)

Each pair of children needs to spread a set of 0 to 9 digit cards out in order on the table. They then take turns to close their eyes, while their partner removes one (or more) of the cards. *Which one is missing? Can they guess the missing card(s) if the digit cards are in descending order?*

Differentiation

Low Attainers – Use digit cards from 0 to 5 only to start with, give them a 0 to 9 number track for support.
High Attainers – Give the children small pieces of paper, the same size as the cards. Ask them to write the missing number to complete the row.

Plenary **5 mins**

Ask a child to the front, to stand with their back to the other children. Using your finger, draw a large numeral from 1 to 9 on their back. *Can they guess which numeral you are drawing? Can the other children show you a corresponding number of fingers?* Repeat with different children and numerals. Ask the children to repeat the activity working in pairs and drawing on one another's backs.

Lesson 3

Introduction **10 mins**
Call out any number up to 19 and ask one child to count on to 20. Repeat with different numbers and children. *Can they count backwards from the number you call?* Repeat, holding up a numeral from 0 to 9 and asking the children to continue the count forwards or backwards.

Activities **25 mins**
Hoop hops (whole class/group)
Arrange ten hoops in a row with a large numeral card from 1 to 10 inside each hoop. Ask one of the children to stand in hoop 3. *If he/she made 2 jumps, which number would they be on? (e.g. 5 or 1)*. Ask the child to make the jumps to illustrate. *Does it make any difference which direction they jump?* Repeat with different starting positions and jumps. Emphasise that a movement in one direction will give a bigger number, while jumps in the other direction will give a smaller number.

Number line jumps (individuals)
Give the children Copymaster 49 showing 0 to 10 number lines. Ask them to loop a number, make 2 jumps up the line, and loop the number they land on. They can use another colour and loop 2 more numbers with a jump of 2 in between. They can to draw several jumps on each line, using the other lines to explore different jumps. *Can they explain where they started, which way they jumped, how big the jump was and where they landed?*

Differentiation
Low Attainers – May benefit from working with a more able child.
High Attainers – Could draw a longer number line to 20 and explore making jumps on this.

Plenary **5 mins**
Ask the children to explain some of their jumps. *Where did they start and land? Which way did they jump?* Model writing their jump as a number sentence.

Lesson 4

Introduction **10 mins**
Draw a small red snake, with circles down its back (see Copymaster 39) on the board.
What colour/size is the snake?
What pattern is on its back?
Draw one of the different snakes underneath.
What is the same/different about this snake?
Continue with some of the other snakes.

Activities **25 mins**
Spot the difference (pairs/individuals)
Ask the children to draw 2 snakes, making some things the same and some things different *(e.g. size, colour, pattern, shape). Can their friends spot what is the same and what is different about the two snakes?*
Snake sort (pairs/individuals)
Ask the children to use a different colour for each row of snakes on Copymaster 39. They can then cut out the rectangles with the snakes in and sort them by colour, size or pattern. *If they compare two of the snakes, can they say what is the same and what is different?*

Differentiation
Low Attainers – Will need adult support to identify sorting criteria and develop the language associated with sorting.
High Attainers – Ask them to add a further four snakes to the snake sort, using a fifth colour.

Plenary **5 mins**
Put one of the coloured snakes from Copymaster 39 on the board. *If we kept one thing the same, what could come next? (e.g. red striped snake – any red or any striped one could come next)*. Continue to build a row of snakes, asking children to select the next snake which has something the same as the last.

Lesson 5

Introduction **10 mins**
Discuss local shops with the children.
What different things to they sell?
What do greengrocers, chemists, shoe shops, garden shops, jewellers etc. sell?
What would you not find in a toy shop?

Activities **25 mins**
Which shop sells this? (whole class/group)
Draw three shop shapes, with empty windows on the board. Decide what the shops will be *(e.g. jewellers, shoes, electrical goods)*. Use some pictures cut from old catalogues, holding them up and asking the children which shop they belong in. Place them in the correct window.
A shop of your own (pairs/individuals)
Give the children an enlarged version of Copymaster 40, some old catalogues and suitable scissors. Ask them to decide what type of shop theirs will be (or allocate one) and cut out some pictures of the things they will be selling to stick in the window.

Differentiation
Low Attainers – Would benefit from working with a more able child. Give them a straightforward shop to find pictures for, like a shoe shop.
High Attainers – Give them a less well defined shop like an electrical store or gift shop, so they need to make decisions. Ask them to put an 'odd one out' in their window.

Plenary **5 mins**
Trim the shops and stick them in a row. Ask the children about the things on sale. *Are all the right things in the window? Is there anything that shouldn't be there? Why not? Do you know any shops that would sell all of these things?* Explain what department stores are.

Theme 1 Counting & ordering

Objectives
- Say and use the number names beyond 20 in familiar contexts
- Count reliably up to 20 everyday objects
- Recognise numerals 0 to 10
- Order a given set of selected numbers to 10 *(e.g. 2, 5, 1, 8, 4)*
- Begin to understand and use ordinal numbers

Vocabulary
number names to 20 and beyond, how many? compare, size, next, between, what comes next? order, first, second, third ... tenth

Resources
Copymasters 41 and 42, number cards from 0 to 10, coloured paper, counters, digit cards, number fans, a large 0 to 10 number track or line, a hundred square, 10-sided dice, teddy bears and clothes, packet of coloured sweets, playdough or plasticine in different colours, coloured paper, 5 (or more) large hoops

Homework Copymaster 21

Mental maths starters 13, 14, 15, 24

Assessment
At the end of this theme is the pupil able to:
- Say and use some number names beyond 20;
- Count reliably up to 15 objects, sounds, movements;
- Recognise counting errors to 15;
- Arrange in order a selection of small numbers;
- Begin to understand and use ordinal numbers to denote position;
- Begin to understand the relationship between cardinal and ordinal numbers?

Lesson 1

Introduction **10 mins**
Tip out a tube of Smarties or similar coloured sweets. *How many red ones are there? ... or orange? ... or pink? How many altogether? Are there more red or more purple? Are there fewer pink or fewer brown?* Sort the sweets into colours as you count and relate the numbers to a number line or track.

Activities **25 mins**
Who likes which? (whole class/group)
Ask the children to decide which coloured sweet they like the best. Ask the children to put up their hands for their favourite colour when you hold it up. Ask one of the children to count the hands and another to find a large number card to put with the appropriate coloured sweet. Ask questions like: *Which colour was no-one's favourite? Did more people like the yellow or the green colour? Which colour did more children like?*

Make some sweets (pairs/individuals)
Ask the children to make 15 play sweets for the classroom toys using playdough or plasticine in different colours. They will need to decide how many of each colour to make and which colours to make more of. They could make a paper bag for their sweets.

Differentiation
Low Attainers – Will need adult support to develop the language of comparing numbers.
High Attainers – Could make up to 20 sweets using a different number for each colour.

Plenary **5 mins**
Discuss some of the groups of 15 sweets using questions which involve counting and comparing the numbers. *Which numbers did one child use to make 15 sweets altogether?* Demonstrate by counting on the number of each colour on a number track or line. *Did anyone use different numbers to make 15?*

Lesson 2

Introduction **10 mins**
Ask the children if their house has a number. *What is it? Is it larger/smaller then 20? Can they point to it on the hundred square?* Model how to write the number on the board. Continue until you have a range of numbers beyond 20. Use some numbers from an address book if needed.

Activities **25 mins**
Number track to 10 (whole class/group)
Give each child a number track from 1 to 10 and a counter (Copymaster 42). Ask them to place their counter on ... *the number 8, ... the number 5, ... the number before/after 7, ... one more/less than 9, ... a number made from curved lines.* Continue asking similar questions, asking the children to read back the numbers they have chosen.
Random numbers (pairs/individuals)
Give the children a number track showing the numbers 0 to 10 in random order (Copymaster 42). Ask them to cut up the track, arrange the numbers in the correct order (ascending or descending) and stick them onto a sheet of coloured paper. They could also try filling in the missing numbers on the last number track on Copymaster 42.

Differentiation
Low Attainers – Just give them a number track with the numerals 0 to 5.
High Attainers – Can write numbers to extend the track.

Plenary **5 mins**
Give eleven children a large number card from 0 to 10 and ask them to stand in a row at the front in any order. Ask the rest of the class to give instructions, which will arrange the numbers in order *(e.g. Tom needs to go at the front; Jane should be after Sam, because her number is bigger)*. Continue until all the numbers are in order. Repeat with different children, or arranging the numbers in descending order.

Lesson 3

Introduction **10 mins**
Give each child a set of digit cards or number fans and ask them to show you a number which is bigger/greater than 7, or smaller/less than 7, or in between 7 and 4. *Is there more than one number that fits the rule? Which other numbers could you have shown me?* Repeat with other numbers from 0 to 10.

Activities **25 mins**
Count around (whole class/group)
Give each child a card with a number from 0 to 10. Ask them to join in counting from 0 to 10, holding up their card and saying their number when it comes in the sequence. *Can the class say the numbers faster? or in reverse order?* Ask the children to exchange cards and repeat.
Dice numbers (pairs/individuals)
Give the children a 10-sided die (with numbers 0 to 9), ask them to throw it three times and write down the numbers they throw. *Can they re-write the numbers in the correct order?* Try again. *What will you do if two of the numbers are the same?* If this is easy, ask them to order the three numbers they throw in descending order.

Differentiation
Low Attainers – Throw the die twice, write the numbers and circle the smallest. A number track may help.
High Attainers – Could throw the die more times or use a die with 12 or 20 sides.

Plenary **5 mins**
Divide the children into groups of 4 to 6, each with a 10-sided die and play a biggest number game. A child in each group throws the die and the numbers around the class are compared. *Which group has thrown the highest number?* This group wins a point. A different child in each group then throws the die and so on. Keep track of the score by modelling how to use tally marks on the board. *Who has the most points so far?* The first group to gain 5 (or 10) points is the winning group.

Lesson 4

Introduction **10 mins**
Place 5 large hoops in a row. Explain which will be the first, second … to fifth. Give children instructions to stand in a hoop. *James stand in the third hoop … Ann in the first.* When the hoops are full ask two children to exchange places (*e.g. the children in the second and fourth hoops*). Repeat, using different children, increasing the number of hoops if appropriate.

Activities **25 mins**
First, second, third (whole class/group)
Read the story of the Three Little Pigs or the Three Billy Goats Gruff ensuring that you use the words first, second and third as often as possible. Alternatively, you may have the story of Snow White, and be able to describe the seven dwarfs using first to seventh.
Race to the finish (whole class)
You need an outside space and children changed for PE for this activity. Put the children into groups of five and ask a group to run a simple race, while the others watch. *Who came first? … second? … etc. What if the slowest was the winner? Who would have been first then?* Repeat with different groups and different races. Ask similar questions.

Differentiation
Low Attainers – Should be able to listen and join in.
High Attainers – Ask them to observe one of the races and try to remember who was first to fifth at the end.

Plenary **5 mins**
Ask 10 children to the front, to make a line facing left. *Who is first? second? … etc. Can they say the ordinal numbers up to tenth?* Ask the children to turn to face the right. *Who is the first in the row now? … and the sixth?* Emphasise the need to decide which direction you should count in.

Lesson 5

Introduction **10 mins**
Ask the children to think about getting dressed in the morning. *What do you put on first? … what second?* … etc. *Does it matter which order you put things on? What about getting changed for PE?* Discuss any common classroom procedures where things are done in a specific order.

Activities **25 mins**
First to fifth (whole class/group)
Put the children into groups of five and number them from 1 to 5 in each group. Ask all the number ones to perform a simple action (hand clap) first, then the number twos can go second … to the number fives going fifth. Ask each group to make a line. *Put your hand up if you are the third child in the line … or sit down if you are the fifth child. What happens if you all face in a different direction? Who is first now?*
Dress the teddy (individuals)
Give the children a teddy or similar soft toy and 5 items of clothing. Ask them to dress the teddy and draw the clothes in the same order as they put them on. *What did they put on first? … second? … third? Did the dressing order matter? Could they have put something else on first?*

Differentiation
Low Attainers – Will benefit from working with a more able child.
High Attainers – Could use more than 5 items to dress the teddy and write first to fifth beside their drawings.

Plenary **5 mins**
Ask ten children to make a line at the front facing left. Give instructions to individuals using ordinal numbers (*e.g. I want the third child to sit down. Put your hands on your head if you are the seventh in the row*). Count along the row to check that the right child moves, making the link between counting and ordinal numbers. Ask the children to face to the right. Give similar instructions, again emphasising that the way the line is facing affects who is first.

Theme 2 More addition

Objectives
- Count reliably up to 20 in a variety of contexts
- Recognise numerals 0 to 10
- Begin to relate the addition of doubles to counting on
- Find a total by counting on when one group of objects is hidden

Vocabulary
numbers to 20, add, more, and, make, sum, total, altogether, double, count on, start with, remember, check, equals

Resources
Copymasters (42) 43 and 44, number tracks from 1 to 10, coloured counters, plastic numerals or number cards, 20 grains of rice, 20 sticks of spaghetti, 20 balls, lots of small objects, matchboxes or similar small containers, interlocking cubes, plastic 1p, 2p and 5p coins, coin stamps, pockets or purses, 6-spot dominoes, 0 to 9 digit cards

Homework Copymaster 22

Mental maths starters 6, 11, 15, 16

Assessment
At the end of this theme is the pupil able to:
- Count up to 20 objects in different arrangements;
- Recognise numerals 0 to 10;
- Match numerals to collections of objects;
- Say how many altogether in a double by counting on;
- Say how many altogether by counting on when one of the groups of objects is hidden?

Lesson 1

Introduction 10 mins
Show the children 20 grains of rice and ask the children to help you count them as you move them one at time. Count backwards to check. *Could you fit them in your hand?* Repeat with 20 sticks of spaghetti and 20 balls (or similar items which are larger than the grains of rice. Emphasise how different 20 of something can look.

Activities 25 mins
Classroom number hunt (whole class)
Tell each child a number up to 20 (if there are more than 20 children, some can work as a pair), and tell them to hunt around the classroom to find something to match that number – no more or less! They can bring it with them when they come back together, or remember it if it cannot be moved. *What did they find for each number?* They can take Homework Copymaster 21 home to try this again.

Twenty tiny things (pairs/individuals)
Give each pair or child a matchbox, or similar small container, and ask them to find 20 different things that will all fit inside it. They will need to hunt around the room for really small objects. *What did they find? How well did they fit in the box or container?*

Differentiation
Low Attainers – Give the children a larger matchbox and ask for a smaller collection.
High Attainers – Give the children two containers of different sizes and ask them to find 20 things that will fill up each container, without leaving much space.

Plenary 5 mins
Discuss some of the things the children have discovered in the number hunt. *Were there any numbers that could not be found?* Make a list of items on the board against the numbers 1 to 20. *What did the children manage to find for their matchbox or container? What was small enough to fit in?*

Lesson 2

Introduction 10 mins
Count together up to 20 saying aloud two numbers in the count, then performing an action twice (*e.g. 1, 2, clap, clap, 3, 4, clap, clap … etc.*). Repeat, performing different actions like stamping feet, punching the air above, blowing …

Activities 25 mins
1, 2, Buckle my shoe (whole class/group)
Ask the children to listen while you say the number rhyme on Copymaster 43. Then repeat it, asking the children to join in with the numbers if they can. *Can the children think up actions to go with each line?* Say the rhyme together using suitable actions.
Coloured counter count (pairs)
Give each pair of children a pile of counters or counting objects in which there are 1 of one colour, 2 of a second colour, 3 of a third … and so on up to 10. Ask the children to sort the counters into piles the same colour and match a plastic numeral or number card to each set. *Can they arrange the sets and numerals in order?*

Differentiation
Low Attainers – Use lower numbers to start with.
High Attainers – Make a mistake in the pile of counters you give the children, giving them an extra counter in one colour. *Can the children spot what has gone wrong? What will they do to sort out the mistake?* They could also be given numbers beyond 10.

Plenary 5 mins
Display the numerals from 0 to 10 at the front as number cards, or plastic numerals. Call several children to the front and ask them to show the class any number of fingers up to 10. *Who can spot the number we would need to give these children to match the number of fingers they are showing?* Ask a child to find the correct numbers to give to the children. Repeat with different children showing fingers. Recite One, two buckle my shoe once more.

Lesson 3

Introduction **10 mins**
Give each child a set of 0 to 9 digit cards and ask them to hold up the number 7, … the number 3, … the number 5 etc.
Then call out two numbers below 5 and ask the children to add the numbers together and hold up the total. Repeat, calling out different combinations of numbers below 5, sometimes including 0.

Activities **25 mins**
Domino totals (whole class/group)
Give each child a set of digit cards from 0 to 9. Hold up a domino and ask the children to hold up the 2 numerals which match the numbers on the domino. *What will they do if the domino is a double? Once you have checked these numbers, can they hold up the numeral to show the total number of spots on the domino? What happens if the total is more than 9?*

Domino totals (pairs/individuals)
Give the children a selection of dominoes and some plastic numerals or number cards (Copymaster 42). Ask them to choose some dominoes and find the 2 numerals that go with them, matching the numbers at each end. They could record by drawing the domino and writing the correct numerals at each end.

Differentiation
Low Attainers – Provide a number track with numbers 0 to 10 for support (Copymaster 42).
High Attainers – *Can they also find the numeral to match the total number of spots?* Nine-spot dominoes would also be useful if they are available.

Plenary **5 mins**
Select some of the dominoes the children have been using. *Which were the numerals that matched each end? What is the total number of spots?* Model how to write this as an addition sentence ($2+3=5$).

Lesson 4

Introduction **10 mins**
What is a double? Discuss the meaning of double in everyday contexts like twins, double burgers, double chins, double-decker buses … etc. *What would a double number be? Show 2 fingers on each hand to illustrate double 2. How many fingers is double 2?* Repeat with other numbers below 5.

Activities **25 mins**
Double towers (pairs/individuals)
Ask the children to use interlocking cubes to make 2 towers, with the same number of cubes, but in different colours. Fix the 2 towers together to make a 'double' tower. *How many bricks of each colour? How many in the 'double' tower?* Children can draw their tower and record *(e.g. double 4 is 8). How many different double towers can they make?*

Doubles (individuals)
Give the children Copymaster 44. Ask them to double the number of flowers in each row and count how many altogether, writing the number in the box. *Can they draw their own row with double 5 flowers in it?*

Differentiation
Low Attainers – In 'Double towers' ask the children to start with towers of 5 or fewer cubes.
High Attainers – Ask the children to record their 'double' towers or their double flower rows as addition number sentences.

Plenary **5 mins**
Write the numbers 1 to 20 in order on the board. *Think of a number you doubled, what was the double?* Circle this double number on the board and ask for others. *Did anyone double number 3, or number 6?* Circle all the 'double' numbers (multiples of 2) on the board. Discuss the pattern made. Say together all the numbers that are circled.

Lesson 5

Introduction **10 mins**
Show the children 2 pennies, count them together and put them in a pocket or a purse, so they are safe. Then get another 3 pennies. *How many do I have now? Count on from the 2 in the pocket.* Repeat with different numbers of coins in the pocket, counting on up to 5 more pennies.

Activities **25 mins**
How much money? (pairs/individuals)
Give the children 2p, 5p, and 4 pennies. Ask them to put any one of their coins in a pocket or purse and stamp what it is on paper to remember. They can then take up to 4 of their pennies and make more stamps to represent these. *How much altogether with the money in the pocket and the extra pennies?* Encourage them to count on from the coin in their pocket. They can try changing the coin they start with or the number of 1p coins they add.

More money game (pairs)
Each pair need 1p coins and a purse to share. One child counts up to five 1p coins and puts them into a purse. They then count up to five 1p coins again, but leave these on the table. *Can their partner work out how many coins there are altogether on the table and in the purse?* Encourage them to count on from the hidden number.

Differentiation
Low Attainers – In 'How much money?' work with 1p coins only. In the 'More money game' use up to 3×1p coins.
High Attainers – In 'How much money?' they record their choices as number sentences *(e.g. 5p + 3p = 8p)*.

Plenary **5 mins**
Ask some of the children to tell you how much money they hid. Point to the number on a large number track. *How many more pennies did you add?* Demonstrate how to find the answer by counting on from the hidden number on the number track. Repeat with different examples.

Theme 3 Shape movements

Objectives
- Use everyday words to describe position, direction and movement: for example, follow and give instructions about directions and movements in PE and other activities
- Use a variety of shapes to make models, pictures and patterns and describe them
- Make simple estimates and predictions

Vocabulary
over, under, above, below, top, bottom, side, on, in, outside, inside, around, in front, behind, back, middle, corner, left, right, up, down, next to, close, far, forwards, backwards, sideways, opposite, direction, through, towards, away from

Resources
Copymasters 45 and 46, toy cars, damp sand, small items of junk like bottle tops, matchsticks, polystyrene bits, pasta shapes, counters, small tin, items of PE equipment (cones, bean bags, hoops) interlocking cubes, small boxes

Homework Copymaster 23

Mental maths starters 18, 19, 20

Assessment
At the end of this theme is the pupil able to:
- Use simple vocabulary to describe position, direction and movement in practical contexts;
- Use 2D shapes to make pictures and patterns
- Use 3D shapes to make models;
- Begin to estimate numbers to 10 in practical contexts?

Lesson 1

Introduction **10 mins**
Ask the children to explain where they would find things around the classroom, using words describing position. *Where do we keep the glue? ... our coats? ... pencils? ... lunchboxes?*
Ask them to describe a specific location to see if the others can guess what is kept there.
What do we keep on the bottom shelf of the cupboard in the corner?

Activities **25 mins**
Which shape, where? (whole class/group)
Each child needs the shape grid from Copymaster 45 and a counter. Ask the children to put their counter on a shape which is ... next to a triangle, ... in the middle of a row or column, ... at the beginning/end of the top/bottom/middle row, ... between a star and a triangle, ... above/below, right/left of a given shape. Continue giving similar instructions involving the position of the shapes in the grid, asking the children to respond by moving their counters.

Five in a row (whole class/group, then pairs)
Give each child a blank 1×5 grid from Copymaster 45 and a pencil. Using the key vocabulary, call out instructions which tell the children where to place 5 known shapes *(e.g. draw a circle in the middle box, and a triangle in the box on the far right. In between the triangle and the circle, draw a rectangle ... etc.)*. Once they have tried this several times, they can work in pairs with one giving instructions and the other following them.

Differentiation
Low Attainers – Use a smaller grid in both activities.
High Attainers – Could give instructions to one another for placing shapes on a 2×5 grid. They can also use a wider variety of shapes.

Plenary **5 mins**
Use the shape grids and counters again. Ask the children to place their counters on the circle in the top row. Then give several instructions for moving the counter – one place right, down one row, down another row. *Which shape is your counter on now?* The children can take turns at choosing a starting place and giving instructions.

Lesson 2

Introduction **10 mins**
Ask specific children to put objects in different places while the others watch. *Did they put them in the right place? (e.g. put the book on top of the cupboard, the shoe under the chair, the pencil next to the sink, the scissors in the pot).*

Activities **25 mins**
Draw a house (whole class/group)
Draw a large rectangle on the board and ask different children to add things to it to make a house picture. Use words describing position to give instructions. *Draw 2 chimneys on the top ... a large tree on the right ... 3 windows on the upper floor ... some flowers in front of the house ... a milk bottle beside the front door ... what else?*
Draw a house together (pairs/individuals)
Starting with a basic house shape, children can draw a house together. They can take turns to describe the position of a feature for their partner to draw. *What can you draw on the house? Where could you draw it?*

Differentiation
Low Attainers – Will need support from an adult to develop the appropriate vocabulary, or may benefit from working with a more able child.
High Attainers – Encourage them to add more detail and intermittently give them some features to add *(e.g. draw a window box under the lowest window).*

Plenary **5 mins**
Look back at the house picture on the board (or use one of the houses the children have drawn) and ask the children to explain where things are. *Where is the door? What is on top of the roof? What is to the left of the house?*

Lesson 3

Introduction **10 mins**

Ask the children to think about a journey by car.
What does the car go over or under?
Which directions can it turn?
What might it need to go along, or through, or round?
Ask similar questions for journeys by sea or air.

Activities **25 mins**

Where are you going? (whole class/group)
Play a role play game in a large space. The children all need to be vehicles. Give them instructions where they must go and watch to see if they respond correctly *(e.g. the car is travelling straight, turning a corner, going under a bridge, over a river, round a roundabout).*

Traffic jam (whole class)
Enlarge the vehicles on Copymaster 46 and cut them out. Fix them to the board in a row and ask the children questions like, *What is behind/in front of the lorry? ... or in between the lorry and the bus?* Alternatively, give the children instructions where to place them in the traffic jam *(e.g. the bus was first. Behind the bus was the sports car).*

Roadways and tunnels (pairs/individuals)
Ask the children to use damp sand in the sand tray to make some roadways and tunnels for toy cars. Encourage them to include places for the cars to go uphill, downhill, over, under, round, through, along ... etc.

Differentiation

Low Attainers – Will need support from an adult to develop the appropriate vocabulary.
High Attainers – Challenge with questions like, *Is the road wide enough? Could you make the tunnel longer?*

Plenary **5 mins**

Describe in detail your journey home from school, using the vocabulary above. Ask some of the children to describe their journeys home. *What do they go past, over or under? Do they make any right or left turns?*

Lesson 4

Introduction **10 mins**

Fix some items of junk to the board, building a linear pattern – bottle top, matchstick, pasta, bottle top. *What comes next?* Build different horizontal and vertical patterns with the junk, always asking the children to predict the next item in the pattern.

Activities **25 mins**

Copy the pattern (pairs/individuals in a group)
Stick some items of junk in a linear repeating pattern across the top of a very large piece of paper. Ask each of the children to copy the pattern and make their own row underneath. Provide each group with a different pattern to copy.

Pattern making (pairs/individuals)
Provide the children with their own strips of paper and ask them to make their own repeating pattern with the junk. *Can they make a different pattern starting at the other end of the paper, or by turning the paper around and starting at the top, or bottom?*

Cube patterns (individual)
Give the children Copymaster 46 and some interlocking cubes. Ask them to make some linear repeating patterns to record on the sheet. *Can their friends make the pattern?*

Differentiation

Low Attainers – Limit the choice of junk or start the pattern off for them, so that they can continue it.
High Attainers – Make a different sort of pattern, by starting in the middle of a sheet of paper and building up, down and across. Their pattern will be a cross shape.

Plenary **5 mins**

Ask the children to describe their patterns. Ask the others to predict what would come next, if the pattern was extended in different directions. Cover up some items in the pattern and ask what is missing?

Lesson 5

Introduction **10 mins**

Put up to 10 counters in a small tin and shake it. Ask the children,
How many counters do you think there are in the tin?
Is it more than 1? ... more/less than 5 or 10?
Check by counting. Repeat using different numbers and small objects.

Activities **25 mins**

How many steps (whole class/group/pairs)
Arrange some items of PE equipment (hoops, bean bags, cones) in a large space. Ask, for example, *how many steps do you think it is from the green cone to the red cone?* Check by counting as a child makes the steps. Ask the children to work in pairs, estimating the number of steps between 2 items, then checking by counting.

Fill the box (pairs/individuals)
Give the children a variety of small cardboard or plastic boxes. Ask them to estimate how many interlocking cubes, or similar counting objects, will fit into the box, then check by counting.

Differentiation

Low Attainers – Will benefit from working with a more able child. Keep distances less than 10 steps and use boxes which hold less than 10 cubes.
High Attainers – Use longer distances or 2 distance together *(e.g. from the cone, round the bean bag to the hoop).* Use larger boxes for estimating.

Plenary **5 mins**

Discuss the '*How many steps?*' activity drawing attention to the fact that if you had larger steps, the count would be smaller. Compare your steps between two items of equipment with those of a child. *If you put larger objects to fill a box, would you fit in the same number?*

Theme 4 Comparing quantities

Objectives
- Begin to record numbers to 5, initially by making marks, progressing to simple tallying and writing numerals
- Record numbers beyond 5 by tallying
- Compare more than two quantities by making direct comparisons of lengths or masses, and by filling and emptying containers

Vocabulary
numbers to 5, flat, curved, tally, weigh, balance, heavy, light, scales, long, short, tall, full, half-full, empty, holds, container

Resources
Copymasters 47 and 48, interlocking cubes, small objects to weigh, pan scales, matchsticks, paper clips, pipe cleaners, lolly sticks, new crayons, plastic containers, small whiteboards or laminated cards, marker pens, cloths, number cards 1 to 10

Homework Copymaster 24

Mental maths starters 6, 8, 17

Assessment
At the end of this theme is the pupil able to:
- Make marks or tallies to record numbers;
- Write numerals to 5 correctly;
- Begin to use appropriate language to compare lengths, masses and capacities;
- Compare the lengths of three objects and say which is longest/shortest;
- Compare the masses of three objects and say which is heaviest/lightest;
- Compare the capacity of three containers and say which holds the most/least?

Lesson 1

Introduction **10 mins**
Draw up to 5 tally marks on the board and ask the children to show you a corresponding number of fingers. Repeat with different numbers. Show how five is often drawn as four vertical lines with the fifth line across them. *What would 6 or 7 look like?*

Activities **25 mins**
How many inside? (pairs)
Ask one child in each pair to put up to 5 small objects in a container and record by tallying (or writing the numeral if they are able) how many they have put in. The second child can then check the recording and count the objects, before having their turn.
How many? (individuals)
Give the children Copymaster 47. Ask them to count the shapes, draw the corresponding number of tally marks and write the numeral in the box. *Can they draw and count some similar or larger sets on the back?*

Differentiation
Low Attainers – Can just draw tally marks and not the numerals on the copymaster, or provide a number track for support.
High Attainers – Instead of using the copymasters, they can draw their own sets to count and write the numbers. They could design some pictures with 5 or more boxes in which to write 5 or more numerals in order.

Plenary **5 mins**
Draw up to 5 tally marks on the board and ask the children to show you a corresponding number of fingers. Sometimes add or rub out one mark and ask, *How many marks now?* Repeat using numerals instead of tally marks and include some numbers above 5.

Lesson 2

Introduction **10 mins**
Ask one of the children to choose any number up to 10, then demonstrate how you could record the number by making a row of dots or vertical tally lines on the board. *What other simple mark could be used?* Choose different numbers and ask different children to draw a corresponding number of marks on the board. All of the children can count to check.

Activities **25 mins**
Your turn to tally (whole class/group)
Each child needs a small whiteboard or laminated card, a small cloth and a marker pen. Call out a number up to 10 and ask the children to write the same number of tally marks on their board, then all show you together. Repeat with other numbers, cleaning the boards after each question. Try also asking them to draw one more/one less marks than a given number.
Out and about (pairs/individual)
Give the children Copymaster 48 and ask them to write the numerals from 1 to 5 in order in the boxes on each of the pictures. They can also copy the numerals at the bottom, starting where the spot is.

Differentiation
Low Attainers – Could just draw tally marks from 1 to 5 in order on the copymaster, or provide a number track for support.
High Attainers – Ask them to draw some taller objects with up to 10 boxes and then fill in the numerals in order.

Plenary **5 mins**
Hold up a large card showing a number from 0 to 9. *What number is this? If I was going to write it, where would I start?* Model writing the number on the board. Ask the children to draw the number in the air. Repeat with other numerals. *Which numbers have flat tops? Which are made of curved lines?*

Lesson 3

Introduction **10 mins**

Hold up five common items of different lengths (they need to be things you have plenty of in the classroom like matchsticks, pipe cleaners, paper clips, lolly sticks).
Which one is the longest/shortest?
Which is longer/shorter than the crayon?
Are any about the same length?
Put the items in order of length with the children's help – longest first then shortest first.

Activities **25 mins**

Matchstick measuring (whole class/group)
Demonstrate how you would use the matchsticks placed end to end to measure the length of a book. *How many matchsticks long is it?* Ask the children to estimate how many matchsticks wide the book is. Check with the matchsticks. Continue by measuring several different items with the matchsticks.

Out for the count (pairs/individuals)
Provide the children with 10 of one of the items used in the introduction. Ask them to use their items to measure 5 easily accessible things like the width of the table, a toy lorry, the height of a teddy bear. Give different measuring items to different children to use, but they all need to measure the same 5 things for comparison.

Differentiation
Low Attainers – Give them the matchsticks to use as in the demonstration and things which are all less than 10 matchsticks long to measure.
High Attainers – Ask them to measure the 5 things twice, using different measuring items each time.

Plenary **5 mins**

Compare the lengths of the 5 things as measured using different objects. *Why*, for example, *is the teddy bear 11 paper clips high, but only 3 pipe cleaners high?* Clarify the fact that if you use longer measuring objects, you won't need as many and if you use short measuring objects you will need more.

Lesson 4

Introduction **10 mins**

Pick two from a selection of small objects and ask the children to guess which one they think will be the heaviest or lightest. *Why do they think that?* Balance the items on the scales to see who is right. Do the same with other pairs of items, including some pairs which look the same, but are different weights *(e.g. matchboxes filled with different things).*

Activities **25 mins**

Balancing with cubes (whole class/group)
Put a small object in one of the pans of the balance scales and then add one cube at a time to the other pan, asking the children whether or not it balances after each cube is added. Continue until you find the number of cubes that best balances the object. Demonstrate with items of different weights.

How many cubes? (pairs/individuals)
Provide the children with a selection of small objects and ask them to find the number of cubes which best balances each object. They can make a tower with the cubes, to place with the object.

Differentiation
Low Attainers – Select the objects carefully so that they exactly balance a number less than 10 cubes.
High Attainers – Ask the children to try to find an object which will balance a specific number of cubes.

Plenary **5 mins**

Discuss some of the objects and their balancing towers. *How can you tell, by looking at the cubes, which object is the heaviest or lightest?* Emphasise that a good way of comparing different weights is to weigh them against uniform items like the cubes.

Lesson 5

Introduction **10 mins**

Use some common Supermarket containers *(e.g. milk/cola bottle, juice carton).* Ask questions like:
What do you think was in this container?
Have you seen these things in different containers?
Is it the same shape all the way up?
Where is it wider/fatter/narrower?
Which do you think hold the most?

Activities **25 mins**

Same or different? (whole class/group)
Use three containers which hold the same amount but look very different in shape and size. *Ask the children to guess which holds the most. Why do they think that? How could we find out?* Show by filling one and pouring into the others that they hold the same. Check by starting with another of the containers.

Which holds the most? (pairs/individuals)
Give the children three containers which hold different amounts and ask them to find out which one will hold the most water or dry sand. Vary the groups of 3 containers so that some groups include 2 with the same capacity.

Differentiation
Low Attainers – Give the children more experience of comparing the capacity of two containers.
High Attainers – Provide more than three containers for the children to compare, asking them to guess first which will hold the most.

Plenary **5 mins**

Use a yogurt pot and a bottle about three times the capacity. *How many potfuls of water will fill the bottle?* Demonstrate to check, asking the children to count as you fill the bottle using the pot. Repeat using a larger bottle. Reinforce the language of capacity.

Theme 5 Counting back & problems

Objectives
- Count in tens to 100 and backwards from 100
- Recognise numerals beyond 10
- Remove a smaller number from a larger and find how many are left by counting back from the larger number
- Solve simple addition and subtraction problems in a practical context including using 1p, 5p and 10p coins

Vocabulary
names for multiples of 10 to 100, count in tens, forwards, backwards, number names beyond 10, take away, left, count back, cost, altogether, buy, change, how much? how much left? coin, pence, pay, total

Resources
Copymasters 42, 49 and 50, plastic coins, class shop with items up to 5p (then 10p), coin stamps for 1p and 2p, number labels with numerals beyond 10 around the classroom, large 100 square, cards showing numbers beyond 10, counting objects, coloured pencils, 0 to 10 number tracks, counters, 10 plastic hoops

Homework Copymaster 25

Mental maths starters 9, 22, 23

Assessment
At the end of this theme is the pupil able to:
- Recognise some numerals beyond 10;
- Recite the multiples of 10 in order to and from 100;
- Begin to read prices such as 8p or £4;
- Count up how much two items together cost (up to 10p);
- Give change from 5p or 10p;
- Choose and use the appropriate number operation to solve simple 'story' problems involving money?

Lesson 1

Introduction **10 mins**
Show a large 100 square to the children. Count together to 20, pointing to the numbers. It would take a long time to count to 100, but we could count in tens. Point to all the multiples of 10 as you count down the row to 100. Repeat, asking the children to show you 10 fingers for each multiple of 10. Ask ten children to hold up 10 fingers to display 100 altogether. *How many fingers altogether if 4 children each held up 10?* Count in tens to check.

Activities **25 mins**
Count up to 100 (whole class/group)
Ask the children to listen carefully as you count up to 100 in tens. Then count up to 90 and ask them to say the 100 together at the end. Once they can do this, count to 80 and the children can add the 90, 100. Carry on in this way until they are able to try counting with you from 10 to 100. Allow the children to hear you repeating the counting, with them adding one or more of the last numbers in the count.

Number labels (supported small group)
Label lots of things with numbers beyond 10 around the classroom *(e.g. 15 paintbrushes, 21 pairs of scissors, 27 pencils)*. Ask the children to find the number labels and check the number of objects. *Can they find the same number on the 100 square?*

Differentiation
Low Attainers – Just use numbers up to 20.
High Attainers – Could make a copy of the labels they find and make some new ones for additional items.

Plenary **5 mins**
Ask the children to tell you about the labels they found. *Did they recognise the numbers? Can they say them? Where were they on the 100 square?* Count up to 20 together again asking one of the children to point to the numbers on the square as you count.

Lesson 2

Introduction **10 mins**
Show a large 100 square to the children. Point to all the multiples of 10 as you count up the row from 100. Ask 10 children to hold up 10 fingers to display 100 fingers altogether. Then ask one child at a time to put down their fingers as you count backwards from 100 in tens. *If I count backwards in tens what would come after 70? or 40?*

Activities **25 mins**
Count back from 100 (whole class/group)
Ask the children to listen carefully as you count back from 100 to 0 in tens. Then count back to 20 and ask them to say the 10, 0 together at the end. Once they can do this, count back to 30 and the children can add the 20, 10 and 0. Carry on in this way until they are able to try counting back with you from 100 to 0. Allow the children to hear you repeating the counting, with them adding one or more of the last numbers in the count.

Number find (pairs/individuals)
Position and/or hide some cards showing numbers beyond 10 around the classroom. Ask the children to find the numbers and blu-tak them to the same number on the 100 square. *Can they read the numbers they find? Are they more or less than 20?*

Differentiation
Low Attainers – May benefit from using numbers to 20 only or working with a more able child.
High Attainers – *Can they write the numbers they find or look at the 100 square to see what would come before and after?*

Plenary **5 mins**
Ask the children to show some of the number cards they found around the classroom. *Which number is it? Can you find it on the 100 square? How do you know it is the right number?* Point out how easy it would be to get the digits in the wrong order and choose the wrong number *(e.g. mixing 12 with 21)*. Emphasise the order of the digits.

Lesson 3

Introduction **10 mins**
Show the children 7 counting objects, count them to check how many, then remove 3. *How many are left?* Work out by counting back from 7, using fingers to keep track of the count. Repeat, using different numbers of counting objects and removing different numbers. Always count back from the number of objects you started with to find out how many are left.

Activities **25 mins**
Number track jumps (whole class/group)
Give each child a number track from Copymaster 42 and a counter. Ask them to put their counter on number 6 to start with. Now make 2 jumps back. *What number are you now on? (e.g. cover up 6, count back 5, 4).* Model how you could write this as a number sentence on the board, 6 – 2 = 4. Repeat using different starts and different sized jumps.
Number line jumps (individuals)
Give the children Copymaster 49. Ask them to draw a coloured ring around a number, count back 3 by drawing the jumps as loops, and ring the number they land on. *What number did you start with? How many jumps back? What did you land on?* They can then choose a different colour to use, a different number to start with and how many jumps back they are going to make.

Differentiation
Low Attainers – A moveable counter may be useful to them when working with the number lines.
High Attainers – Could write the number line movements as number sentences above the lines.

Plenary **5 mins**
Draw a number line from 0 to 10 on the board and circle number 8. *If I made 2 jumps back, where would I be? Do I count the number I started on?* Emphasise that it is the jumps the children should be counting. Repeat with different numbers. This could also be demonstrated by using 10 plastic hoops, labelled with large number cards. Children can be asked to stand in a numbered hoop and make some jumps backwards along the line.

Lesson 4

Introduction **10 mins**
Hold a real coin in your hand. The children can ask three yes/no questions about it before they all try to guess what it is *(e.g. Is it round? Is it bronze? Is it small?)*. Try with different coins.

Activities **25 mins**
How much altogether? (whole class/group)
Show the children two real coins, both less than 10p in value, and ask how much money you have altogether. Encourage them to use the addition strategies they have learned, counting on from the highest value coin, using a number line or fingers to support. Try with different pairs of coins.
Buying for two (pairs/individuals)
Set up the class shop with items priced from 1p to 5p and ask the children to buy two items the same. *Can they record the items and the total cost, using drawings and/or coin stamps? Would the cost of a different 2 items be the same?*

Differentiation
Low Attainers – Use items up to 3p only or pay only using 1p coins.
High Attainers – Can buy any two (or three?) items at the shop. *How many different combinations can they find?*

Plenary **5 mins**
Go through working out the cost of two items the same from the shop with the children, encouraging them to use their fingers to check, and relating the totals to doubles of the numbers up to 5. Discuss the different ways the children have recorded their purchases.

Lesson 5

Introduction **10 mins**
Give the children a 1p, 2p, 5p, 10p and 20p coin each.
Can they hold up the coin worth the same as 5 pennies?
Try with the other exchange values.
Can they hold up coins worth 3 pence?
What would 1p more than 5p, or 10p be?

Activities **25 mins**
How much change? (whole class/group)
Show the children a 2p coin and ask how much change they would have if they spent 1p in the shop.
Try similar questions with change from 5p or 10p.
Encourage them to use the subtraction strategies they have learned, counting on from the price or back from the coin value, using a number line or fingers to support.
Don't forget your change! (pairs/individual)
Set up the class shop with items up to 10p. Ask the children to go to the shop with a 5p or 10p coin, buy an item and record what they bought and how much change they received. They can try buying different items with the same amount. Alternatively, use Copymaster 50.

Differentiation
Low Attainers – Use a 5p coin for shopping, give all change in 1p coins.
High Attainers – Could try going to the shop with different amounts up to 10p and working out their change from this.

Plenary **5 mins**
Go through working out some examples of change with the children. Extend with some short one, or even two step oral problems like: *I bought two toffee bars, which cost 2p each. How much change did I have from 5p?*

Theme 6 Estimating & comparing

Objectives
- Estimate a number in the range that can be counted reliably, then check by counting
- Write numerals to 10
- Begin to understand and use ordinal numbers in different contexts
- Use language such as more and less, greater or smaller to compare two numbers up to 20 and say a number which lies between two given numbers

Vocabulary
guess, estimate, count, check, numbers to 10, first, second, third … tenth, more/most, less/least, larger(est), bigger(est), greater(est), fewer(est), smaller(est), compare, size, next, between, what comes next?

Resources
Copymasters 51 and 52, plastic numerals, large number cards to 10 or 20, digit cards, small red and green cards, cards with up to 10 thick black stripes or stars on, large number line or track, flash cards showing words of different lengths, Ten in the Bed by Penny Dale, small whiteboards/laminated card, marker pens, crayons

Homework Copymaster 26

Mental maths starters 8, 13, 14, 24

Assessment
At the end of this theme is the pupil able to:
- Estimate numbers within the range that can be counted reliably;
- Check an estimate by counting;
- Write numerals to 10 correctly;
- Use ordinal numbers in different contexts;
- Recognise which is more/less, greater/smaller than two numbers to 20;
- Give a number that lies between 2 numbers up to 20?

Lesson 1

Introduction **10 mins**
Briefly show the children a flash card with one word on it. *How many letters long do you think the word was?* Count to check. Repeat, showing different words. *How many letters? What would a good guess be? Are there more or less than the last word?*

Activities **25 mins**
Seeing stripes or stars (whole class/group)
Use some cards with up to 10 thick black stripes or black stars on. Show one to the children briefly. *How many stripes? Were there more or less than 5?* Count to check. Show 2 cards briefly one at a time. *Which had the most stripes, the first or the second card? Can anyone guess how many?* Repeat with different cards.
Guess first (individuals)
Give each child Copymaster 51 and allow them a short, fixed time to guess how many pictures in each group and write their guess in the first box. Stress that they will not have enough time to count the pictures properly. Then allow them more time to count carefully and compare the real count with their guess. *Did you guess the same number? Did you guess too many, or too few?*

Differentiation
Low Attainers – Provide then with a 0 to 10 number track for support.
High Attainers – Can draw some more groups of objects on the back of the page and ask their friends to guess how many and check by counting.

Plenary **5 mins**
Go through the 'Guess first' sheet with the children. *What was the biggest guess for each group of pictures? What was the smallest?* Use a large number line or number track to compare some of the children's guesses with the actual number. *What would a good guess be?*

Lesson 2

Introduction **10 mins**
Each child needs a small whiteboard or a piece of laminated card and a marker pen. Write any number up to 10 on the board and ask the children to copy it on their board. *Which number is it? Where did you start to write it?* Repeat with the other numbers up to 10.

Activities **25 mins**
Ten in the Bed (whole class/group)
Write the number 10 on the board. Read Ten in the Bed by Penny Dale to the children. Every time someone falls out of the bed ask, *Who was the first (or second, or third …) to fall out? How many are left in the bed? Who can write the number left?* One of the children can cross out the number on the board and write one less. Children could use their fingers to keep track of how many are left in the bed.
Writing numbers (supported group)
An adult working with a group of children shuffles a set of digit cards and then calls out the numbers in random order. The children need to write down the numbers in the order they are called out. The cards can then be shown to the children, one at a time in the same order, and they can check to see which ones they were able to write. Discuss the shape of any they found difficult. Repeat, with the cards in a different order.

Differentiation
Low Attainers – Use digit cards 1 to 5 only, or provide support with a number track to start with.
High Attainers – Use number cards beyond 10.

Plenary **5 mins**
Use the white boards again, asking the children to write any of the numbers up to 10 that were causing difficulties. Discuss any reversed numbers that were written. If the children are comfortable with writing these, extend to numbers beyond 10. You could also explain how to write the multiples of 10 to 100.

Lesson 3

Introduction — 10 mins

Draw a 0 to 10 number line on the board and ask the children to count from 0 to 10 as you point to the numbers. Then point to numbers at random and ask what they are. Tell the children to close their eyes while you rub out one or more numbers. *Which ones are missing? Who can write them in?*

Activities — 25 mins

Green for yes (whole class/group)

Give each child pieces of red and green card to hold. Say a statement which compares or orders numbers and ask the children to hold up the green card if it is true and the red one if it is false *(e.g. 3 is more than 7, 6 is between 5 and 8, 9 comes before 12, 4 is one less than 5)*. Repeat with different statements.

Fill in the numbers (pairs/individuals)

The children need a set of 1 to 9 digit cards and a blank number line from 0 to 10. They then need to turn over the digit cards one at a time, marking each number on the line as they turn it over. If working as a pair, they can take turns to write the next number.

Differentiation

Low Attainers – In 'Fill in the numbers' mark the line to show how to space the numbers. They may need a 1 to 10 number line for support.

High Attainers – Could extend their number lines beyond 10, but they will need additional number cards.

Plenary — 5 mins

Draw a blank number line on the board, marking 0 at the beginning and 10 at the end. Mark where 5 would be. *Which number would come here?* Write it in. *Where would number 9 go?* Continue asking questions until the numbers 0 to 10 are all on the line. Repeat, asking for the numbers in a different order and allowing the children to write the numbers.

Lesson 4

Introduction — 10 mins

Draw a 10 to 0 number line on the board (note reverse order) and ask the children to count from 10 to 0 as you point to the numbers. Then point to numbers at random and ask what they are. Tell the children to close their eyes while you rub out one or more numbers. *Which ones are missing? Who can write them in?*

Activities — 25 mins

Which number where? (pairs)

Give each pair a large sheet of paper and some crayons. Ask them to take turns to call out a number up to 10 for their partner to write anywhere on the paper. They can use different colours and write them different sizes, making sure they include at least one of each number. When their page is really full, they can take turns to point to a number and ask their partner which number it is.

Fill in more numbers (pairs/individuals)

Give the children a set of 1 to 9 digit cards and ask them to draw a blank number line from 10 to 0 (note reverse order). They then need to turn over the digit cards one at a time, marking each number on the line as they turn it over. If working as a pair, they can take turns to write the next number.

Differentiation

Low Attainers – In 'Fill in more numbers' mark the line to show how to space the numbers. They may need a 1 to 10 number line for support.

High Attainers – Could begin their number lines with 15 or 20, but they will need additional number cards. In 'Which number where?' they could use numbers beyond 10.

Plenary — 5 mins

Draw a blank 0 to 10 number line on the board. Mark where 9 would be. *Which number would come here?* Write it in. *Where would number 2 go?* Continue asking questions until the numbers 10 to 0 are all on the line.

Lesson 5

Introduction — 10 mins

Hold up a large number card and ask the children what comes before and what comes after. Use numbers up to 10 at first and up to 20 if appropriate. Repeat with different numbers. Hold up two cards. *Which is the larger/smaller number? Which numbers would come in between them?*

Activities — 25 mins

What comes before and after? (pairs/ individuals)

Give the children a set of plastic numerals from 0 to 9. Ask them to select any one and write it down. *Can they write the number that comes before (in front) and the number that comes next (after it)?* Mix the numerals and pick a different one.

Curly caterpillars (individuals)

Give the children Copymaster 52 and ask them to write the numbers in order on each caterpillar. *Which is the highest /lowest number? Which numbers are missing?*

Differentiation

Low Attainers – Provide them with 5 counters, so they can find the numbers at the bottom of the page before writing them in order on the caterpillar.

High Attainers – Give them any five or more number cards from 0 to 10 and they can draw their own caterpillar and write the numbers in order.

Plenary — 5 mins

Draw a caterpillar with only three sections on the board and have any 3 cards from 0 to 10 in your hand. Show one of the numbers and ask the children where they would like you to write it on the caterpillar. The aim is to get the 3 numbers in order, but each one has to be written, before the next is shown. Show, and write the second, then third number in the spaces left. If the numbers are in ascending order, the children win, if not you win. Repeat with different groups of 3 numbers.

Theme 7 Patterns & problems

Objectives
- Count in twos to 20 and backwards from 20
- Write numerals to 10 and beyond
- Select two groups of objects to make a given total
- Separate (partition) a given number of objects into 2 groups

Vocabulary
count in twos, numbers to 20, together, make, sum, total, add, and, separate, split, parts, equals, group

Resources
Copymasters 5 and 54, interlocking cubes, coloured counters, large number line/track to 20, a large hundred square, slider cards showing addition sentences with a total of 10

Homework Copymaster 27

Mental maths starters 9, 10, 16

Assessment
At the end of this theme is the pupil able to:
- Count in twos to twenty;
- Count in twos back from 20;
- Write numerals to 10 correctly;
- Write some numbers beyond 10;
- Find different ways of separating a number up to 10 into two groups?

Lesson 1

Introduction **10 mins**
Ask first 5 and then 10 children to the front, stand them in a line and use them as models to count in twos. The children can together count their feet, legs, arms, hands, eyes, ears … anything that there are 2 of. *Can the children in the row count along, saying the next even number?*

Activities **25 mins**
Twos of cubes (whole class/group)
Make a row of 20 interlocking cubes, with 10 pairs of colours along the row. Use this to count in twos, to and back from 20. Break the row along its length where the colours change. *How many in each piece?* Count in twos to check. Continue, breaking the row in different places. Try breaking the row so that a pair of one colour is split. The children can then count the pieces in twos, with one more at the end making an odd number.

Make a twos track (individuals)
Give the children an empty number track made from 20 squares – 2 cm squared paper is ideal. Ask them to colour the squares, changing the colour after every 2 have been coloured. *Can they use their number track to count in twos?*

Differentiation
Low Attainers – Provide them with a row of interlocking cubes, with the colours in pairs, for support.
High Attainers – Could write the even numbers on the track, on the second square of each colour. *Could they continue their track beyond 20?*

Plenary **5 mins**
Refer to a large hundred square as the children count to 20 in twos. Circle the multiples of two or mark them in some way. *Can the children count in twos around the class, or on their own? How could the hundred square help us to count in twos beyond 20?* Put two of the children's coloured tracks together and use them to count beyond 20 in twos.

Lesson 2

Introduction **10 mins**
Recite the numbers to 20 altogether, saying odd numbers quietly and even numbers loudly. Point to the numbers on a larger number line or track as they are spoken. Repeat, but clapping as the even numbers are spoken. Then try clapping for the odd numbers, and only saying the even numbers out aloud. Try similar counting from 20 backwards to 1 or 0.

Activities **25 mins**
Big steps (whole class/group)
You need to be in a large space for this activity. Ask the children to make a row on one side of the room, facing the space. All count as the first child takes 2 big steps, then stops and sits down. Then count as the next child takes 4 big steps and sits down. Continue with each child taking two more steps than the one before. *What happens? Can the children remember the number of steps they took and say them aloud along the line? If they take the same number of steps back, will they end up where they started?*

Count in twos (pairs/individuals)
Give the children the two different 1 to 20 number grids from Copymaster 54. Ask them to count in twos and colour all the even numbers. Discuss the patterns made.

Differentiation
Low Attainers – Provide the children with 2 counters of different colours, so they can move them along the rows in the grid to identify the numbers they need to colour. Use a crayon the same colour as the second counter. In 'Big steps' give them the lower even numbers to count.
High Attainers – Could try colouring all the even numbers on a 1 to 20 number grid with the numbers arranged as 4 rows of 5 numbers, or 5 rows of 4 numbers. *What patterns do the twos numbers make?* In 'Big steps' give them the higher even numbers to count.

Plenary **5 mins**
Count to 20 in twos again, this time nodding or clapping on all the odd numbers instead of saying them aloud. Discuss the different patterns made when the even numbers were coloured on the different number grids. Relate the position of the numbers on one grid to the other.

Lesson 3

Introduction **10 mins**

Ask the children to show you 3 fingers on one hand and 2 on the other. *How many altogether?* Model how to write this as a number sentence ($3 + 2 = 5$). *Could we make 5 using our fingers in a different way?* Record the different possibilities including $5 + 0 = 5$ and $1 + 4 = 5$ as they are suggested. Continue making different totals up to 10, using some fingers on one hand and some on the other.

Activities **25 mins**

Groups of children (whole class/large group)

Put the class into groups of between 1 and 5 children, with at least one group to match each number. Ask them to sit with their group with a clear space between each group. *If I only wanted 5 children (to fit in the car, or go to a party …), which groups could I take? Are there any other choices?* Ask groups to stand up, as different possibilities are discussed. Explain, for example, that 5 could be made with a group of 5, 4 and 1, or 3 and 2. Repeat for different given totals.

Making totals (pairs/individuals)

Give the children towers made from 1 to 5 interlocking cubes of the same colour *(e.g. 1 blue, 2 red, 3 white …)*. Ask them to select any two towers to make a total of 6. *How many are in each tower? Could you make the same total in a different way? How could you write this as a number sentence? Which other totals can you make using two towers?*

Differentiation

Low Attainers – Give the children towers made from 1 to 3 cubes only. Ask them to record by drawing the cubes, counting them and writing the total as a numeral.

High Attainers – Could also make totals using more than two of their towers.

Plenary **5 mins**

Discuss some of the totals made by the children, drawing attention to pairs of numbers added in a different order to make the same total *(e.g. $4 + 3 = 7$ and $3 + 4 = 7$)*.

Lesson 4

Introduction **10 mins**

Use a row of interlocking cubes, with 5 of one colour at one end and 5 of another at the other end. Break the row into two pieces. *How many cubes in each piece?* Model writing the number sentence on the board. Repeat, breaking the row in different places.

Activities **25 mins**

Show a cube (whole class/group)

Ask 10 children to the front and give them two cubes each, one of each of 2 colours *(e.g. red, blue)*. When you say 'show a cube', each child needs to hold up any one of their cubes. *How many red cubes are showing? How many blue?* Explain how the two numbers together make 10. Repeat, so that different bonds to 10 are displayed.

Break up 10 (individuals)

Give the children Copymaster 54 and ask them to find different ways of splitting the arrays of ten into two (or more) parts. *Can they record the two parts, which make 10 as a number sentence?*

Bonds to 10 (pairs/individuals)

Give the children a two-colour row of 10 interlocking cubes, as used in the introduction. Ask them to break the row in different places and write the two parts and the total as a number sentence. *How many different ways can they find of breaking the row of 10 cubes into two pieces?*

Differentiation

Low Attainers – Could record their pieces by drawing and writing the numerals under each piece.

High Attainers – Could try breaking the row in two places.

Plenary **5 mins**

Ask the children for all the pairs of numbers that make ten and record them on the board. Then re-write them in order *(e.g. $9 + 1$, $8 + 2$, $7 + 3$, $6 + 4$ … etc.)*. *Can anyone spot a pattern?* Draw attention to the way the first number decreases as the second one increases.

Lesson 5

Introduction **10 mins**

Ask the children some simple word problems involving two groups which add to make a given number *(e.g. If you had 3 sweets, how many more would you need to make 5? I have 2 short pencils and 4 long ones, how many altogether?)*. Model the problems with real objects if possible.

Activities **25 mins**

Stand up, sit down (whole class/group)

Ask 6 children to make a line at the front. When you say 'stand up, sit down', they can choose to sit down or remain standing. *How many are standing? How many are sitting?* Explain that these 2 numbers together make 6. Repeat several times to get different pairs of numbers that make 6, then try with 7, 8 or 9 children in the line.

Coloured counters (pairs/individuals)

Give the children four groups of coloured counters representing the numbers 1 to 4 *(e.g. 1 green, 2 blue, 3 yellow, 4 green)*. Ask them to separate one coloured group from the others. *How many in the separate group? How many are left?* Record the numbers as a number sentence with a total of 10 *(e.g. separate 2, write $2 + 8 = 10$)*. *What happens if you separate a different group, or separate two groups? How many different number sentences can you write?*

Differentiation

Low Attainers – Use 3 groups of coloured counters showing numbers from 1 to 3 only. Groups will then total 6.

High Attainers – Could experiment with different numbers of counters in the groups *(e.g. 1, 2, 3, 3 or 2, 3, 4, 4)*.

Plenary **5 mins**

Use slider cards showing addition sentences with a total of 10 (these have a moveable loop which slides to cover up different numbers). Cover up one of the numbers in one of the sentences and ask the children if they know what it is. *How could they use their fingers to work out the covered number?* Repeat with the other slider cards.

Theme 8 Shape & space

Objectives

- Talk about, recognise and recreate patterns: for example, simple repeating or symmetrical patterns in the environment, or patterns from different cultures
- Solve simple problems or puzzles in a practical context, and respond to 'What could we try next?'

Vocabulary

pattern, shape names, size, big(ger), large(r), small(er), repeat, turn, move, next to, close, space, along, direction, up, down, left, right, before, after, position, over, under, middle, edge, corner, between, top, bottom

Resources

Copymasters 55 and 56, thick paint, crayons, large mirror, small mirrors, small objects, counters, 2 cm squared paper, large paper capital letter shapes, familiar 2D shapes, multilink cubes, patterned fabric/wallpaper

Homework Copymaster 28

Mental maths starters 18, 21, 23

Assessment

At the end of this theme is the pupil able to:

- Use a mirror to explore patterns;
- Talk about and recreate a simple pattern;
- Find half of paper shapes by folding them;
- Solve simple problems or puzzles in a practical context;
- Talk about and record in their own way how a problem was solved;
- Suggest what to try in response to 'What could we try next?'

Lesson 1

Introduction **10 mins**

Use some pieces of fabric or wallpaper with clear repeating patterns. Show them to the children and ask them to spot parts of the pattern which are repeated. *Where does the repeat start/end? How many times is the pattern repeated? Where else might they see repeating patterns?*

Activities **25 mins**

Reflections (whole class/group)

Use a large mirror and place it up against different surfaces, so the children can see things reflected. *What do you see in the mirror? Where are things reflected in the mirror? Do you see different things if the position (angle) of the mirror is changed?* Place some mirrors around the room for the children to look in throughout the week.

Paint blobs (pairs/individuals)

Provide the children with some large sheets of paper and thick paint in different colours. Demonstrate how to put paint blobs on one side of the paper, fold it in half and press hard. Open it out and discuss what happens. Allow the children to make reflective paint blobs of their own. *Can they identify the matching halves of the symmetrical pattern?*

Differentiation

Low Attainers – Use paper, which has already been folded to make a crease along the middle.
High Attainers – Try putting paint blobs on a quarter of the page and folding it in half in two ways. *What happens?*

Plenary **5 mins**

Discuss some of the children's work, identifying where different blobs have been reflected on the other half of the page. Point out that some colours are reflected close to the fold and others farther away. Put half of the pattern close to the mirror, to see if the pattern is reflected in the same way.

Lesson 2

Introduction **10 mins**

Put one small object in front of a large mirror. *How many can you see altogether?* Continue with other numbers of objects up to 5, relating the images to doubles of the numbers. *What happens if you use 2 mirrors angled to meet one another on one side?*

Activities **25 mins**

How many counters? (pairs/individual)

Give the children 5 counters and a small mirror. Ask them to spread the counters in a group (or line) and put the mirror in different places in relation to the counters, sometimes to the side of the group and sometimes cutting across it. *How many counters can you see altogether? Can you put the mirror in the right place to double each of the numbers? Can you put the mirror so that you can see 3 counters altogether? … or 5? What happens if you use 2 mirrors?*

Reflecting squares (pairs/individuals)

Give the children 3 colours and some 2 cm squared paper and ask them to colour nine squares in a 3×3 grid. Each square needs to be all one colour. *Can you put a mirror along each side of the grid and see the squares reflected? Do you always get the same pattern? Can you spot the reflections of some of the individual squares?*

Differentiation

Low Attainers – Provide 3×3 grids that are already cut out for them.
High Attainers – Could try different sized grids and more or fewer colours.

Plenary **5 mins**

Ask some of the children to show their patterns. Check that the reflection contains all the squares in the original coloured grid. Draw attention to the fact that the distance between squares close to the mirror and their reflections, is less than with those farther away from the mirror.

Lesson 3

Introduction **10 mins**

Cut out some large capital letter shapes including some which are symmetrical and some which are not (E, H, T, X, P, J, Z). Show the children a shape. *Can I fold this letter in half, so that both sides match? Can I do it any other way?* Demonstrate folding the letters to check.

Activities **25 mins**

Mirror images (whole class/group working in pairs)

Ask pairs of children to face each other and imagine there is a mirror in between them. One needs to move part of their body, and the other needs to copy as if they were the reflection in a mirror. They can take turns to be the first to move.

Shape folding (individuals)

Provide the children with a selection of familiar 2D shapes (square, rectangle, circle, triangle, star) and ask them to try folding the shapes in half to see if both sides match. *Which ones will/won't fold exactly in half? Can you fold some of them in half in different ways?*

Differentiation

Low Attainers – May need adult support with the folding.
High Attainers – Can draw around shape templates and cut out their own shapes before folding. They can also use a wider variety of shapes.

Plenary **5 mins**

Discuss some of the shapes the children have folded and whether they found any different ways of folding them in half. Emphasise that a circle can be folded in half in lots of places, and that both sides of the shape need to match if it is really a half.

Lesson 4

Introduction **10 mins**

Ask the children how they could make 6, using fingers on both hands (1 + 6, 2 + 4 ...) *If you use 4 on one hand, how many do you need on the other? What happens if you use one less on this hand? Are there any other ways?* Ask similar questions involving different ways of making any number up to 10.

Activities **25 mins**

Who goes first? (whole class/group)

Choose 3 children and ask them to stand in a line. *Who is first, in the middle, last? How could we arrange them so that someone else was first? Can you think of any other possible order they could be in?* Move the children around. *Who is first now?* Continue with 3 or 4 different children, looking to find all the different orders they could stand in.

How many different squares? (pairs/individuals)

Give the children multilink cubes in only 2 colours and ask them how many different squares they can make, by fixing 4 together. They could be all one colour, or both colours. Each 4-cube square must be different, whichever way it is turned or moved. *Can they record the ones they find by drawing?*

Differentiation

Low Attainers – They could start with the 4-cube squares, which are all one colour.
High Attainers – Could also try making 6-cube rectangles, or making making squares with 3 colours.

Plenary **5 mins**

Discuss the squares the children have found and ask them to describe them (there are 6 possibilities – e.g. *all red, all blue, 3 red/1 blue, 3 blue/1 red, 2 different arrangements of 2 red and 2 blue*). Show them the complete set, ask them to close their eyes and remove one. *Which one is missing? How many of each colour were in it? How were they arranged?*

Lesson 5

Introduction **10 mins**

You need two different hats and two different scarves *(e.g. red/blue hats, green/orange scarves). Ask the children what choices they would have, if they went out with a hat and a scarf.* Demonstrate the different possibilities by dressing one of the children *(e.g. red hat, green scarf). What would happen if they only wore one item?*

Activities **25 mins**

Buckets or spades (whole class/group)

Draw a seaside bucket, with three stripes across it on the board and ask the children how they would colour the bucket, if they only had red, yellow and blue paint. Ask three children to colour a stripe each. *How else could they colour it using the same colours? Do they need to use all 3 colours? Could some of the colours be used for 2 stripes?* Draw some alternatives, using top, bottom and middle to explain the position of the stripes.

Sandcastles (pairs/individuals)

Give the children Copymaster 56 and ask them to find different ways of colouring the stripes using only two colours for the whole sheet. When they have done one or two, they need to look at these carefully to make sure they don't repeat them. There are 8 different possibilities.

Differentiation

Low Attainers – Provide a few clues like: *Could you colour all the stripes the same colour? What happens if the one in the middle is different?*
High Attainers – Could return to the buckets puzzle and see how many different ways they can find of colouring the buckets using 3 colours.

Plenary **5 mins**

Ask one of the children who has discovered all 8 possibilities to explain how they did it. *How did they know they had all the different ones? Did anyone work them out differently?*

Theme 9 Time

Objectives
- Count to 20 and beyond, forwards and backwards
- Count reliably up to 20 everyday objects
- Begin to recognise numerals to 20
- Begin to understand and use the vocabulary of time
- Begin to read o'clock time

Vocabulary
numbers to 20, forwards, backwards, time, day, morning, afternoon, evening, night, bedtime, dinner time, playtime, before, after, early, late, takes longer/less time, o'clock, clock, days of week, hour, today, yesterday, tomorrow,

Resources
Copymasters 57 and 58, 4 of each of 4 different containers – margarine cartons, plastic bowls, boxes, sticky shapes, interlocking cubes, construction bricks, 1 minute timers, large hoop, number cards 1 to 12, large geared clock, small clock faces with moveable hands, circle templates, long and short arrows, number cards to 20, 100 square

Homework Copymaster 29

Mental maths starters 1, 4, 5, 6

Assessment
At the end of this theme is the pupil able to:
- Recite the numbers to 20 and backwards from 20;
- Count reliably up to 20 objects;
- Begin to understand and use the vocabulary of time;
- Begin to know key times of the day;
- Begin to read the time to the hour on a clock?

Lesson 1

Introduction **10 mins**
Recite the numbers to 20 and beyond. *How far can the children count? Can they count from 20 to 30? … or from 15 to 25? … or from 22 to 32?* Encourage them to think of their own starting and stopping numbers.

Activities **25 mins**
Stick counting (pairs)
Write the numbers 10 to 20 – one each at the end of long, wide sheets of coloured paper. Give each sheet to a pair of children, who need to stick some sticky shapes in a group on the paper, counting to check they have the same number as shown. They then pass the sheet to another pair and try a different number themselves. Encourage the children to stick the shapes in an arrangement that will make counting easy. Make a numbers from 10 to 20 display at the end.
Container fill (pairs/individuals)
Show the children a plastic mug or beaker and some interlocking cubes or small building bricks. *How many do you think I can fit in the mug?* Fill the mug and count. Give the children some containers and some bricks or uniform objects to fill them with. Use a limited number of containers, so comparisons will be possible, and different sets of objects for filling. *How many cubes can you fit in? Can you fit in more lego bricks?* Encourage the children to estimate before they fill the container.

Differentiation
Low Attainers – Use smaller containers and/or larger objects, so the count is lower.
High Attainers – Use larger containers and/or smaller objects, so the count is higher.

Plenary **5 mins**
Choose a container which will hold more than 20 cubes. *How many cubes will it hold?* Ask the children to help you count and demonstrate. Emphasise the numbers beyond 20. *Will it hold a different number if we use a different object?* Fill the container several times with different objects, count and compare the numbers of objects. *Why does the container hold more of some things?* Try different containers.

Lesson 2

Introduction **10 mins**
Hold up a large number card from 0 to 20. *Which number is it? Is it more or less than ten? How many digits in the number? Can anyone point to it on the hundred square? Can anyone write it on the board?* Repeat with different numbers to 20.

Activities **25 mins**
Tidying up time (pairs/individuals)
Give the children some real life counting activities around the classroom and ask them to match a number card or make a number label for the things they count. Choose counting where there are between 10 and 20 items. *How many paintbrushes? … pairs of scissors? … felt pens? … newspapers? … coat hooks? … tables?*
How many faces, how many hats? (pairs/individuals)
Give the children Copymaster 57 and ask them to count the number of faces and the number of hats. *Can they write the numbers from 1 to 20 beside the faces? How many more hats are needed so that everyone has a hat? Can they draw the missing ones?*

Differentiation
Low Attainers – Provide them with a 1 to 20 number track for support.
High Attainers – Draw seven (give different numbers to different children) extra faces and four extra hats. *How many faces and hats now?*

Plenary **5 mins**
Hold up ten fingers and ask the children to show you how many more they would need to make 16. Write the number 16, emphasising that it is ten and six more. Repeat with other numbers. *If I had ten and four more, how many would I have?* Discuss the counting around the classroom the children did. *How many of each thing did they count?*

Lesson 3

Introduction 10 mins

Discuss how long it might take to perform actions – clean your teeth, wall to the gate, get dressed, write your name, paint a whole house, build a house. *What could you do in one minute? … or one hour? … or one day?*

Activities 25 mins

Take a minute (whole class/group)

Ask the children to watch a minute sand timer so they know about how long a minute is. Then ask them to stand up, start timing and they can sit down when they think a minute is up. *Who made a good guess?* Repeat, asking the children to try different things for a minute – close their eyes, cover their faces, hold up their arm. *Do they get better at guessing how long a minute is?*

Take another minute (small groups/pairs/individuals)

Give the children a minute timer and ask them to see what they can do in one minute. *How many times can they write their name? How many cubes can they fit together? How many times can they write the number 8? How many squares can they draw?*

Differentiation

Low Attainers – Ensure that they are given straightforward things to do in a minute.

High Attainers – Allow them to choose their own one minute challenges.

Plenary 5 mins

How many times did you write your name in one minute? Why did some children manage to write their name more times? Can they write more quickly, or do they have shorter names? Discuss the other things the children tried and compare the results.

Lesson 4

Introduction 10 mins

Show the children a large clock face and ask them to count the numbers from 1 to 12 on the clock as you point to them. *Which way round did we count? Which number is at the top/bottom? Which is on the right/left side?* Point to different numbers and ask what they are. Cover one up and ask which one is missing.

Activities 25 mins

The giant's clock (whole class/group)

Sit the children in a semi-circle with a large hoop in the middle. Give out large cards showing the numbers 1 to 12. *Who has got the number 1? Where would it go?* Ask the child to place it in the correct position on the edge of the hoop. Continue with the other numbers until they are all in place around the hoop. Repeat, using different children and asking for the numbers in a different order. *Who has the number that goes at the bottom of the clock? … or the number that goes in between the 3 and the 5?*

Draw a clock (individuals)

Give the children some circle templates and ask them to draw some clock faces, writing in the numbers up to 12. *Can you fit on all the numbers? Can you write them in order? Can you space them out around the clock face?*

Differentiation

Low Attainers – Give them a number line with the numbers for support, provide them with a numbered clock face or write some of the numbers on to get them started.

High Attainers – Give them some square or hexagonal shapes to make clock faces and write the numbers on.

Plenary 5 mins

Draw a large circle on the board and ask some of the children to write in the numbers to make a clock face. Rub a number out and ask what's missing. Try drawing a clock face which is a different shape. *Where would the numbers go on this clock?*

Lesson 5

Introduction 10 mins

Show the children a large geared clock face. *What time does school begin?* Show the children the time to the nearest hour. Repeat with other hour times in the day. *What would you be doing at 12 o'clock? … or 3 o'clock?* Explain where the two hands would go and demonstrate how the small hand moves to the next number every time the long minute hand moves all around the clock. Also how we count to 12 hours from midnight to midday and then count to 12 again from midday to midnight.

Activities 25 mins

The giant's day (whole class/group)

Sit the children in a semi-circle with a large hoop in the middle. Place the numbers around the edge to make a clock as in lesson 4. Tell a story about the giant who likes to keep to time. At 8 o'clock he eats breakfast. Explain how to put the hands (long and short arrows) in the right places on the hoop clock. At 9 o'clock he digs his garden … and so on through the day.

Show me the time (pairs/individuals)

Each pair or individual needs a small clock face with moveable hands. Tell the children things about the giant again and ask them to put the hands of their clocks in the correct places to show different hour times as they are mentioned. They can use Copymaster 58 to draw the times that the giant performs each activity.

Differentiation

Low Attainers – Would benefit from working with a more able child.

High Attainers – Can draw an additional picture to illustrate a time in the giant's day.

Plenary 5 mins

Go through some of the times in the giant's day again, comparing it with what the children might be doing at the same time. *Would it be the same at the weekend?* Make some hour times on the large geared clock and ask the children if they can tell you what they are.

Theme 10 Using number

Objectives

- Count in tens and twos, forwards and backwards
- Begin to write numerals to 20
- Begin to find out how many have been removed from a larger group of objects by counting up from a number
- Work out by counting how many more are needed to make a larger number
- Use developing mathematical ideas and methods to solve practical problems involving counting or comparing

Vocabulary

count in twos/tens, numbers to 20, multiples of 10 to 100, forwards, backwards, take (away), leave, how many are left/left over, how many have gone? one less, enough, how many more? more, less, count on/back

Resources

Copymasters 59 and 60, 5 popular real fruits, large 100 square, cocktail sticks, sticky labels, squared paper or blank 100 squares, interlocking cubes, 10 bundles of 10 straws, large paper pet shapes, drum and beater, crayons, puppet, biscuits, plate, shoe box, small soft toys

Homework Copymaster 30

Mental maths starters 9, 10, 23

Assessment

At the end of this theme is the pupil able to:

- Recite multiples of 2 forwards to and backwards from 20;
- Recite the multiples of 10 forwards to and backwards from 100;
- Find how many have been removed by counting up to the larger number;
- Find by counting up, how many more will make a given number;
- Solve practical problems involving counting or comparing?

Lesson 1

Introduction **10 mins**

Use a puppet who is trying to learn to count to 100 in tens, but can't quite get it right. The puppet can count part way and get stuck, miss a number out, get two in the wrong order. *Can the children put the puppet right? Can then demonstrate counting in tens, forwards and backwards?*

Activities **25 mins**

Counting in tens (whole class/group)

Ask 10 children to make a line at the front so that everyone can count in tens to 100, with the children in the line showing their fingers as the count moves along. Then they can show all of their fingers, with 10 going down each time as everyone counts back to 0. Stop at times and ask what comes next. Repeat with children holding up bundles of ten straws or rows of ten interlocking cubes as the count proceeds.

Ten in a row (individual)

Give the children a blank 100 square and ask them to colour each row of 10 squares in a different colour. *Can they use their coloured square to count in tens, pointing to one row at a time?*

Differentiation

Low Attainers – Could just colour 5 rows of 10 squares and count in tens to 50.

High Attainers – May be able to write the multiples of 10 in order on the squares at the end of each row.

Plenary **5 mins**

Use one of the coloured 100 squares. Fold it along one of the horizontal lines and count together in tens to see how many squares are on each side of the fold. Repeat, folding along a different line. Count in tens once more pointing to the multiples of ten on a large hundred square as the children count.

Lesson 2

Introduction **10 mins**

Altogether count in twos to twenty and back again. Count in twos again, beating a drum for the odd numbers and all saying the even numbers aloud. Repeat several times allowing different children to beat the drum.

Activities **25 mins**

Quick count (whole class/group)

Use a large hundred square to count in twos to 20 and back (or beyond). Highlight the multiples of 2 in some way (turning 2 colour numbers around, circling, marking with a coloured counter ...). *If we count in twos, which number comes after 4? ... before 10? ... between 12 and 16?* Call out different numbers up to 20 and ask if we would use them if we were counting in twos.

Patterns of twos (individuals)

Using Copymaster 59, ask the children to fill in all the numbers up to 20 on the 3 different grids. Ask them to colour all the multiples of 2 (the numbers they have been counting) in a light colour. *Do you see any patterns?*

Differentiation

Low Attainers – Provide them with a 1 to 20 number track for support.

High Attainers – Could try writing the numbers 1 to 20 on different sized grids with 3 or 6 numbers in a row. *What happens? Why do you think you get different patterns?*

Plenary **5 mins**

Look at the number grids the children have written numbers on. *What patterns did you spot? Where are 10 and 20 on each grid? On the first grid, what do you notice about the numbers that are above and below each other?* Use the grids to count in twos to 20 and backwards from 20, with the children pointing to the numbers as they say them.

Lesson 3

Introduction **10 mins**

Show the children 5 biscuits on a plate and tell them you started with 8! *How many have been eaten? How could we find out?* Demonstrate by counting up from 5 to 8 on a number track, putting up one finger for every one counted. Repeat with different numbers.

Activities **25 mins**

How many in the box? (whole class/group)

You need some small soft toys and a shoe box. Ask one of the children to count any number of toys up to 10 to start with. All the children then close their eyes while a second child hides some of these toys in the box. *How many did we start with? How many are left? How many must be hidden?* Count up from the number left to work it out. Count on from the same number as toys are taken from the box. Repeat with the children choosing different numbers.

How many more? (individuals)

Ask the children to draw on Copymaster 60 to make the numbers shown. *How many did you start with? How many did you draw? How many are there altogether?*

Differentiation

Low Attainers – Numbering the shapes on the copymaster may help them to make sure they have enough. They may need a 1 to 10 number track for support.
High Attainers – May be able to record the additions on Copymaster 60 as addition sentences.

Plenary **5 mins**

Start with a plate of biscuits with one for each child. Count them altogether. Ask the children to close their eyes, then give out some of the biscuits. *How many are left? How many have gone?* Count up from the number left to check, pointing to the numbers on a large 100 square. Repeat the activity until there are no biscuits left. (It is the last week of term!)

Lesson 4

Introduction **10 mins**

Show the children 5 popular fruits. Identify their names. *Do you like any of these fruits? Why do you like them? Which is your favourite?* Ask the children to choose just one as their favourite and to put up their hand when you hold up the fruit. Count the hands, demonstrate counting to the same number on the 100 square and mark it in some way to record which fruit the count was for. *How can the 100 square tell us which the most popular fruit was?*

Activities **25 mins**

Make a label (whole class/group)

Give each child a cocktail stick and a sticky label. Ask them to make a flag type label with their name on. They can then stick it in one of the 5 fruits above, choosing their favourite. All 5 fruits can be displayed for comparison.

A different display (individuals)

Each child can draw a picture of their favourite fruit, selecting from the 5 above. Fruit pictures can be named, cut out and displayed in groups, so that it is easier to count how many of each there are, and easier to make comparisons.

Differentiation

Low Attainers – May need help to make their labels.
High Attainers – Can have the task of sorting the fruit pictures and sticking them in similar groups.

Plenary **5 mins**

Discuss the different ways of showing favourite fruits. *Is it easy to count how many chose each one?*
Which way is the clearest? Which one was the most/least popular? Can you put the fruit in order from the least to most popular?

Lesson 5

Introduction **10 mins**

Discuss the different pets the children have. *What are they? How many? What are their needs? If you had a pet shop, what sort of things would you sell?* Pose the problem – they are going to start a new pet shop and need to know what to sell in it.

Activities **25 mins**

Playful pets (whole class/group)

Display a large shape for each of the pet groups (*e.g. dog, cat, fish …*) represented in the class. Ask each child with a pet of that type to make a name label to stick on the shape of the pet they have. Some will need to make more than one label, some will have no pets. Work in small groups to find out what different pets eat and what they like to play with. *Who can they ask?* (This could run into a homework activity.)

How many pets? (pairs/individuals)

Ask the children to draw their pets, using a separate piece of paper for each. Any child without a pet can help those with more than one. Some children could visit other classes to ask how many of each different pet those children have. Pet drawings can be displayed in horizontal or be vertical rows for comparison. *Which is the most popular? Which animals do no children have?*

Differentiation

Low Attainers – Will benefit working with a more able child.
High Attainers – Challenge them to find out the information from other classes and write a list of how many different pets the children have.

Plenary **5 mins**

Discuss the different representations of the children's pets. Draw all the information together and look back at the original problem. *What have we found out? Does the information help us? Which pet foods and toys would we need to sell more of in our shop? What else might we sell?*

Two by two

Funny faces

Draw a nose on each face.

... 2 eyes

... 2 ears

... 1 mouth

... a hat?

Turtles

Colour the turtles, 3 of each colour.

How many flowers?

Count the flowers in each group.

Count out the same number of counters.

Check by placing the counters on the flowers.

Shape hunt

Colour the same shapes the same colour.

2D shapes

Teacher's resource sheet – templates

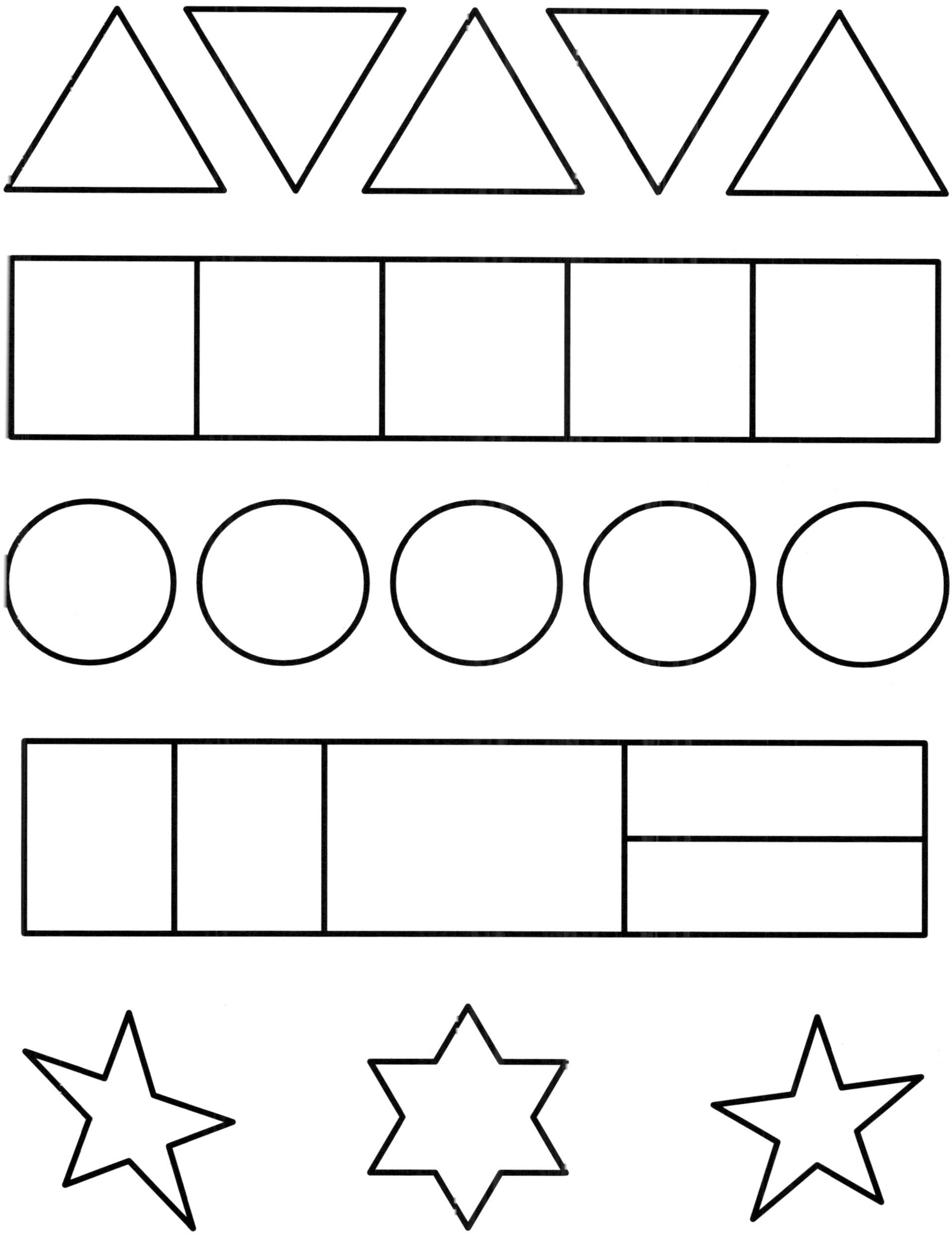

Humpty's wall

How many cubes can you fit on each brick?

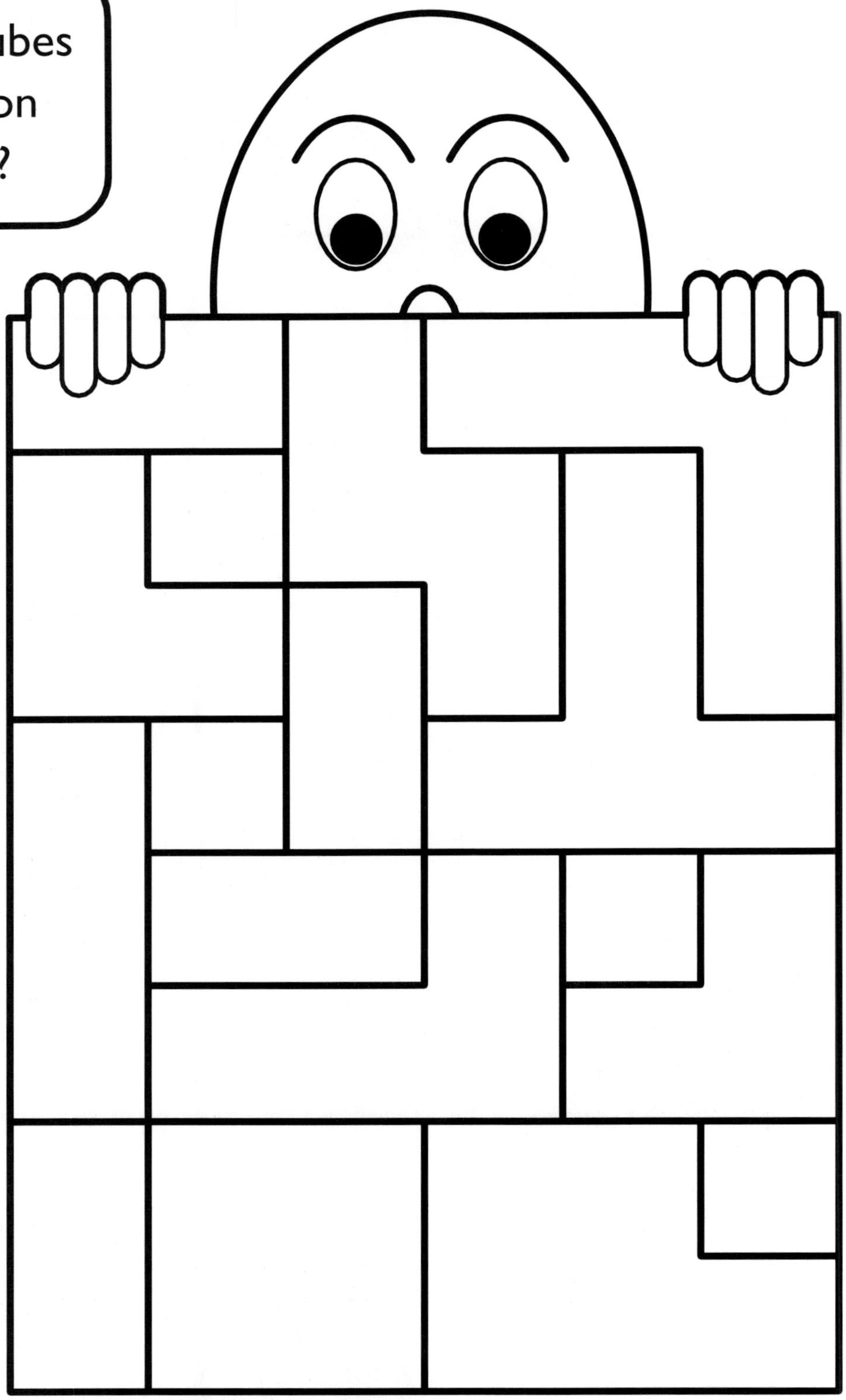

1 green
2 blue
3 yellow
4 orange
5 red

Match the lengths

Make a row of cubes the same length as each object.

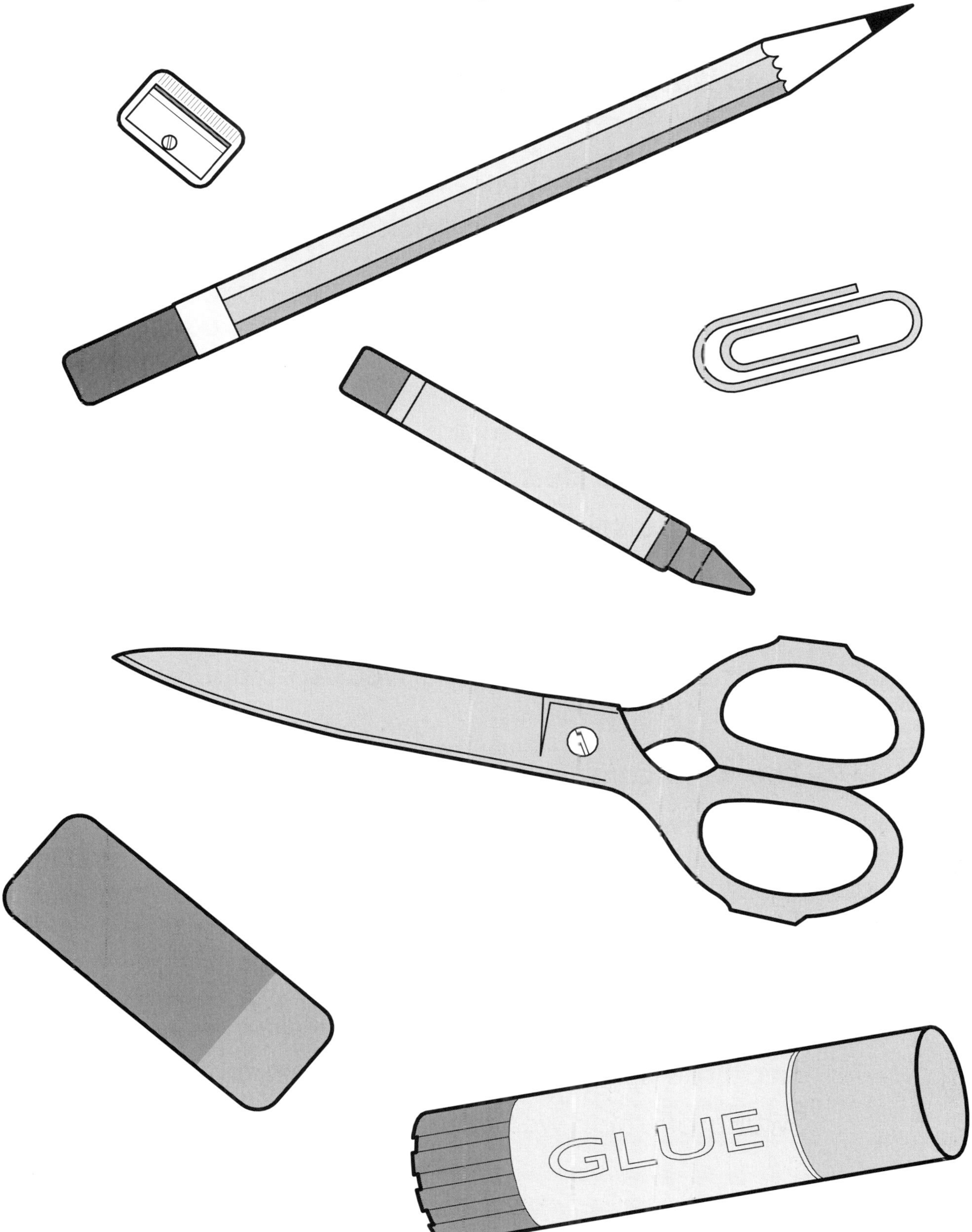

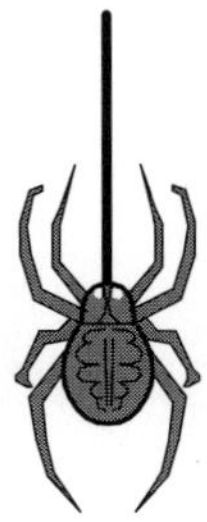

Spiders at play

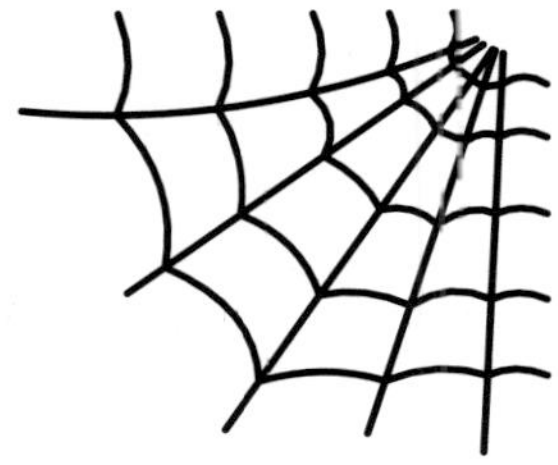

Ten little spiders one sunny day,
Went out on their silvery webs to play.

Down flew a blackbird and gobbled up three,
Seven little spiders ran back to the tree.

Seven little spiders one sunny day,
Went out on their silvery webs to play.

Along came a duster and flicked away four,
Three little spiders fell down to the floor.

Three little spiders one sunny day,
Went out on their silvery webs to play.

The wind came up and hard it blew,
One blew right away and that left two.

Two little spiders one sunny day,
Went out on their silvery webs to play.

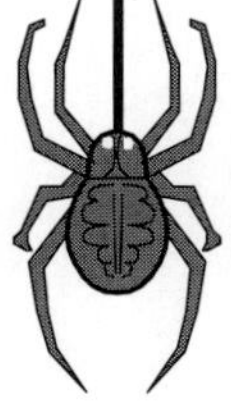

Two little spiders swinging in the sun,
Swung off their webs and then there were none!

Use your fingers to keep count of the spiders.

One more

Draw one more and count.

1 2 3 4 5

Copymaster 11

Teacher's resource sheet
Enlarge and cut out dotty numbers

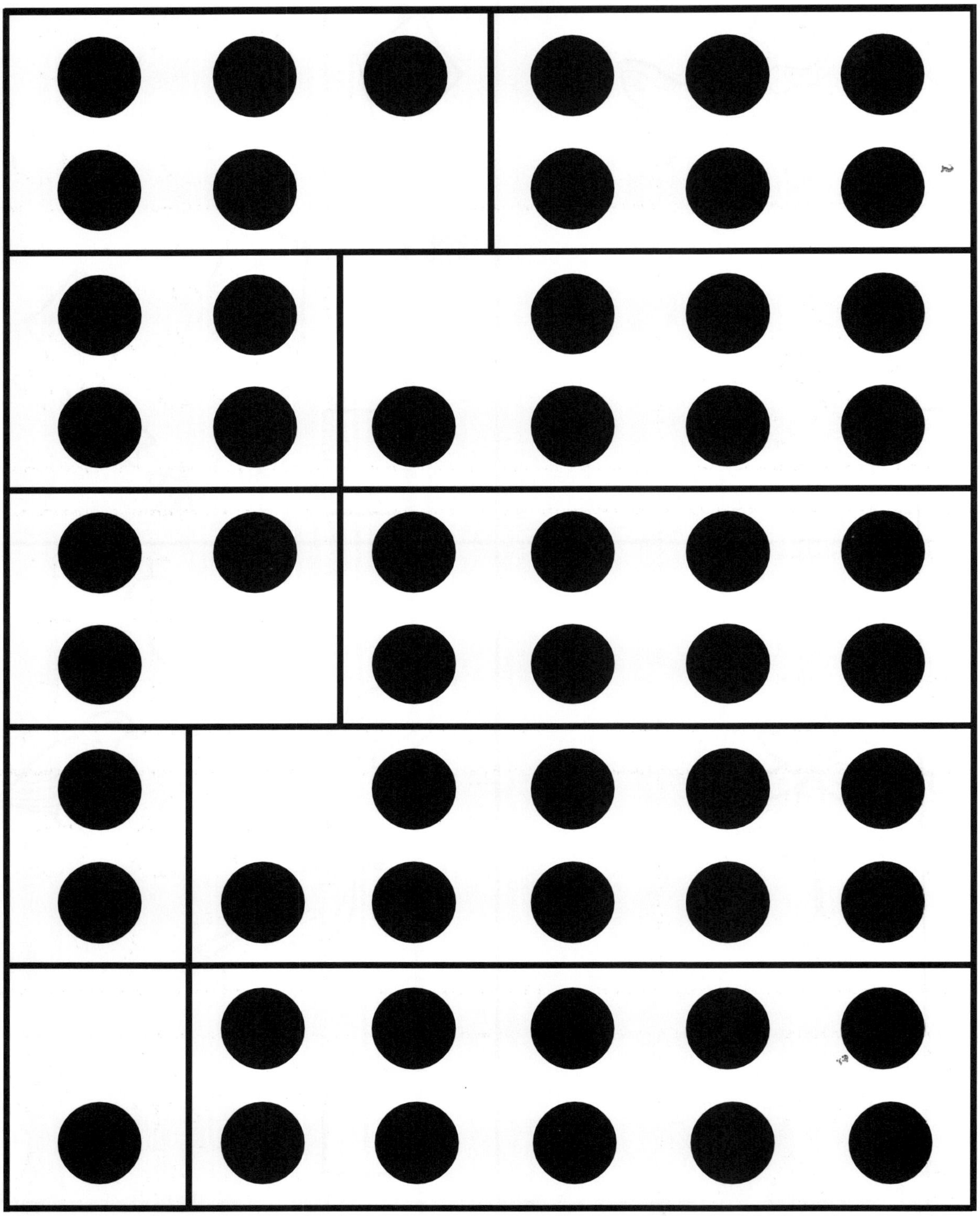

What comes in between?

Draw the missing number of objects.

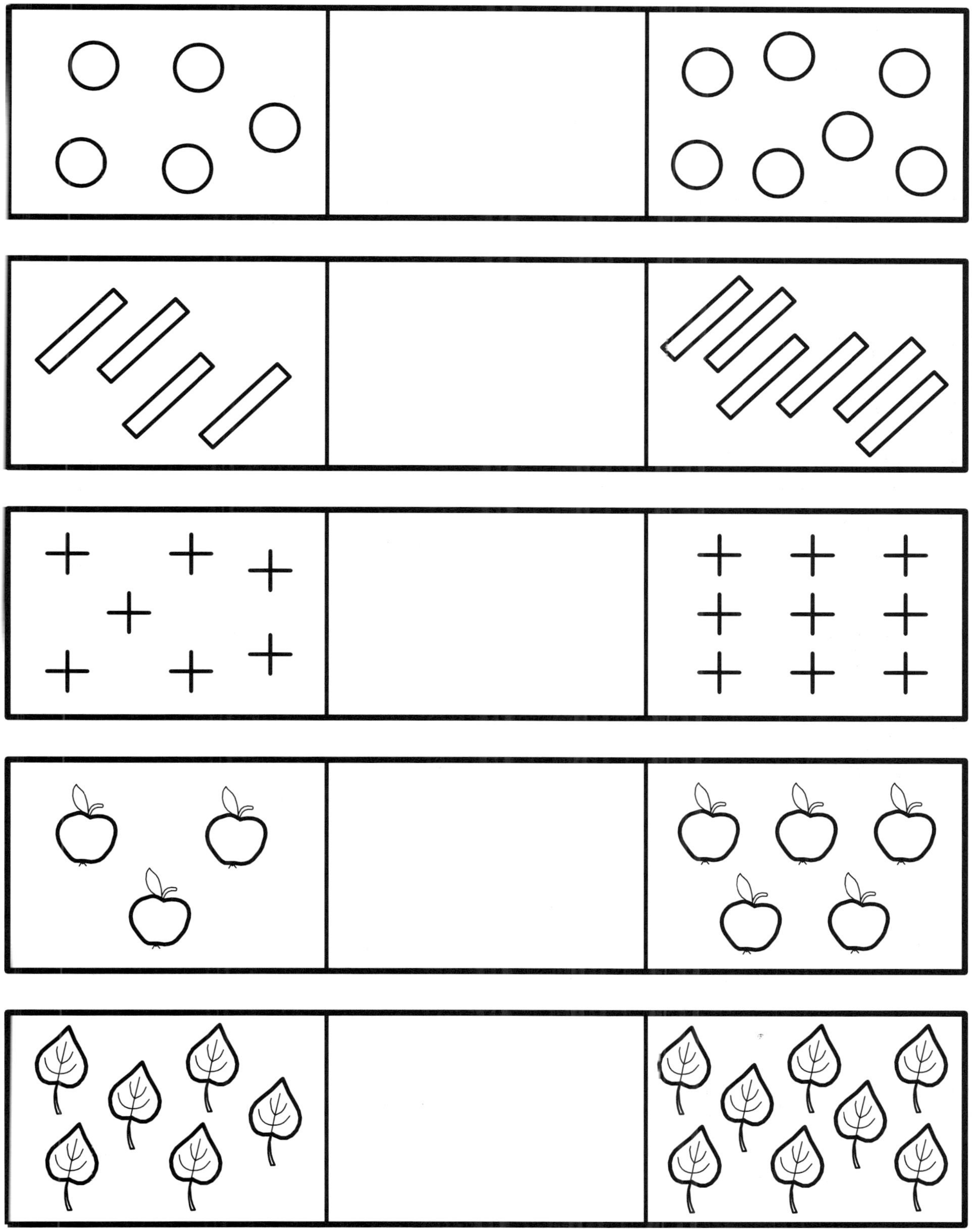

More or less

Draw 1 more and 1 less in the boxes.

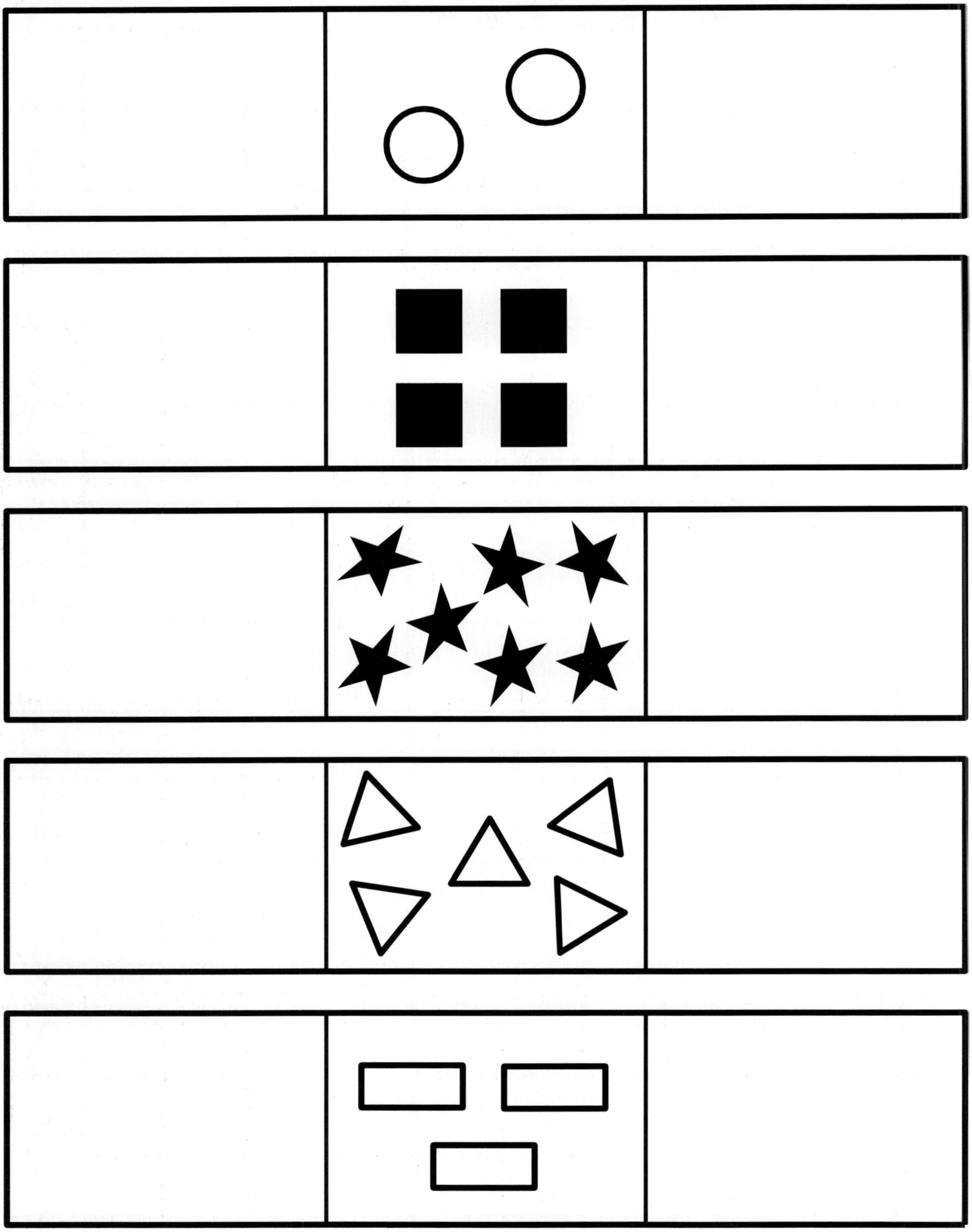

Lucky sevens

Colour the groups of 7 red. If there is 1 more use yellow, if 1 less use green.

Spot the shapes!

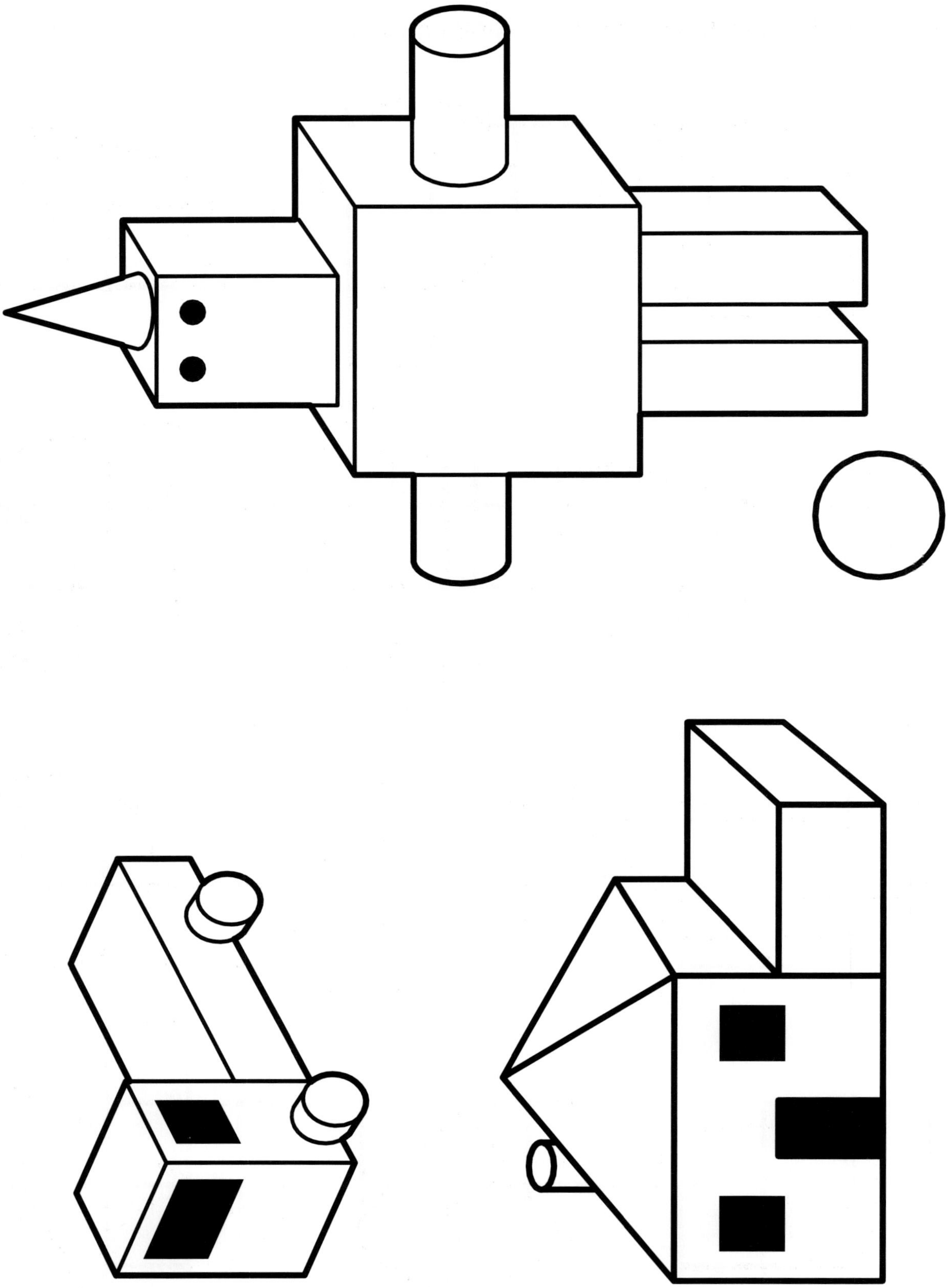

Solid shapes

Colour the same shapes the same colour.

Teacher's resource sheet

light	heavy
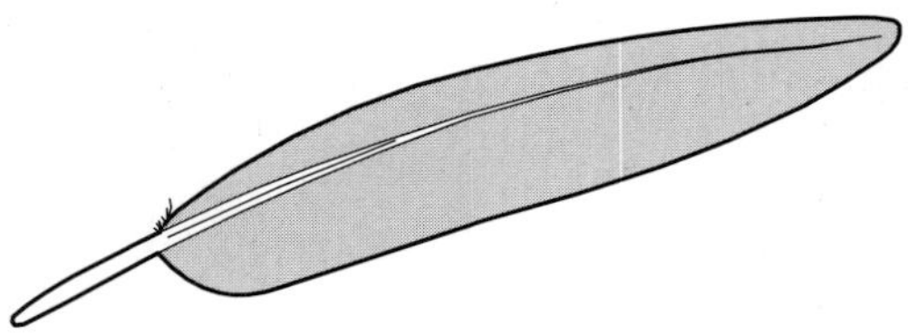	

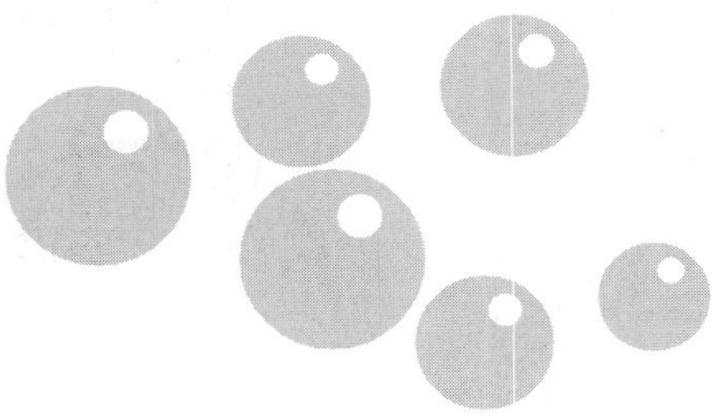	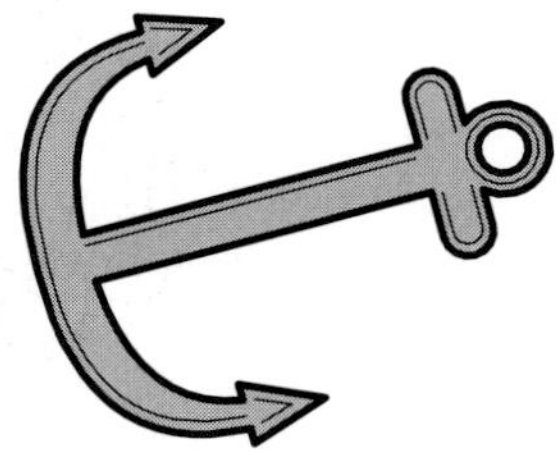
	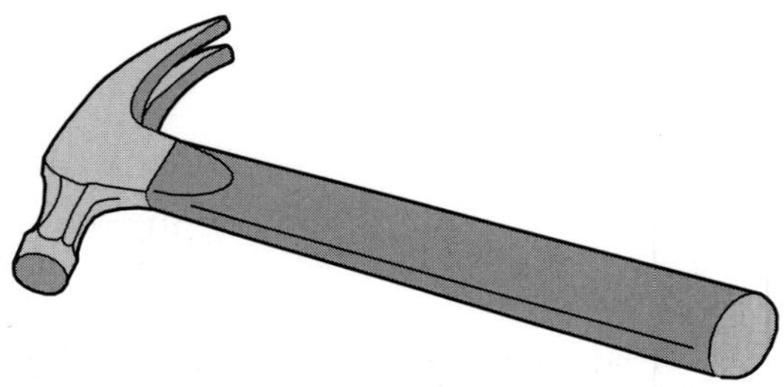
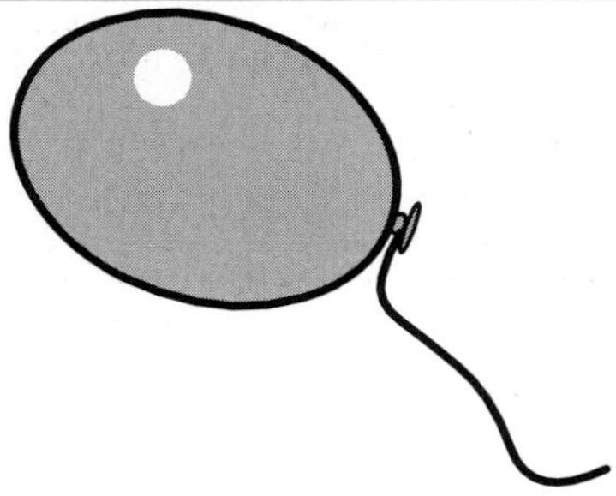	

Sort out the day in order

Purse full of pennies

Colour the odd one out in each line.

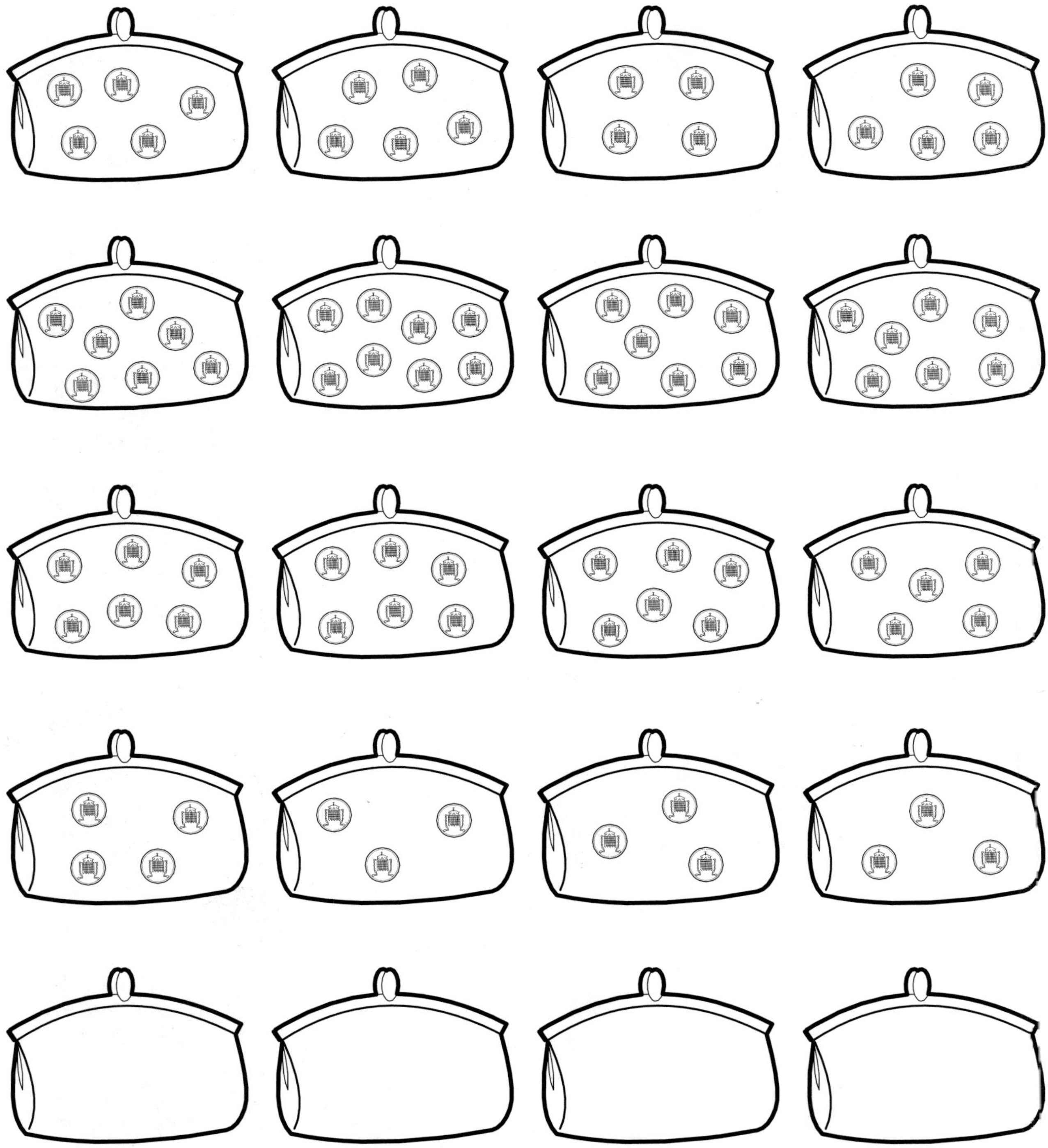

Draw your own odd one out on the last row.

Buy a snowman

Throw the dice and collect the pennies.

Domino count

Draw more dominoes with the same number of spots.

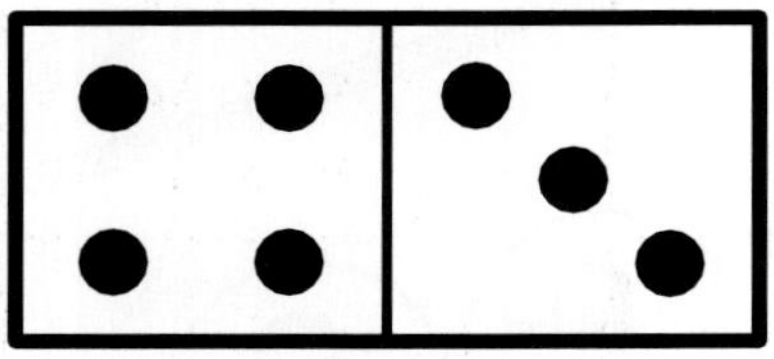

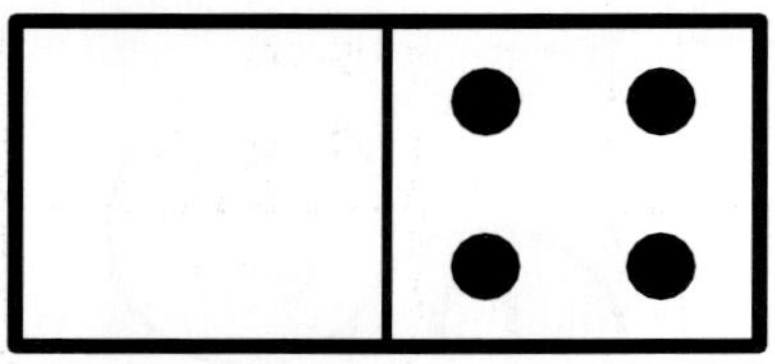

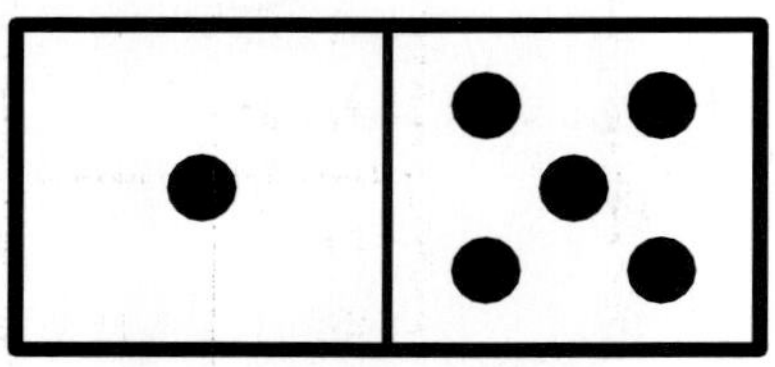

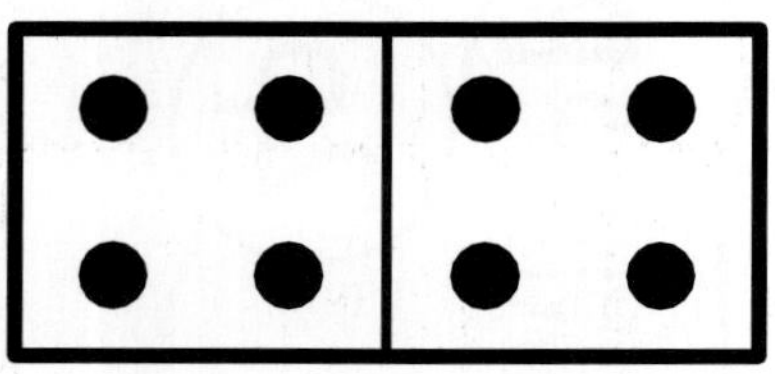

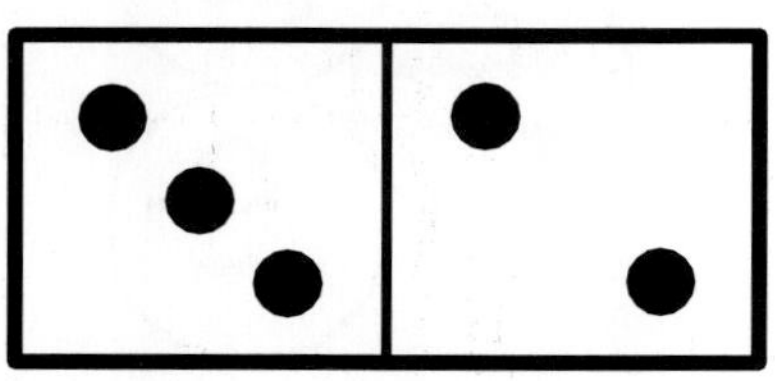

Spotty number tracks – enlarge for whole class use

Ascending order

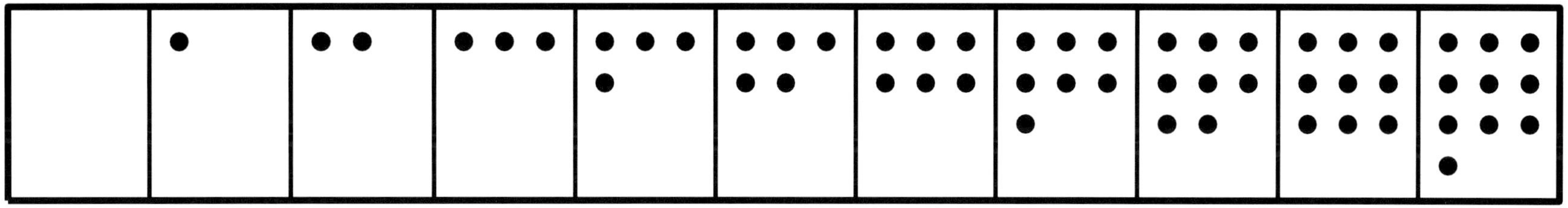

Random order

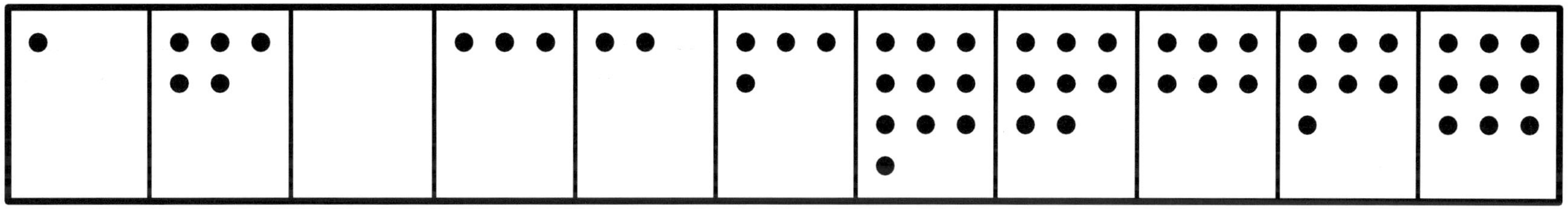

Descending order

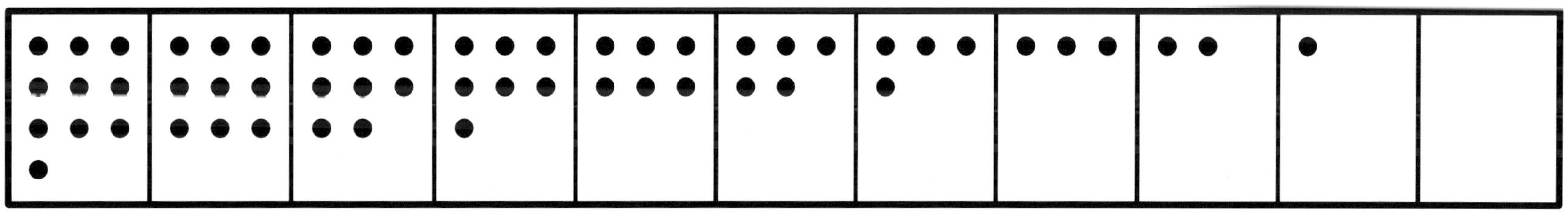

Missing numbers

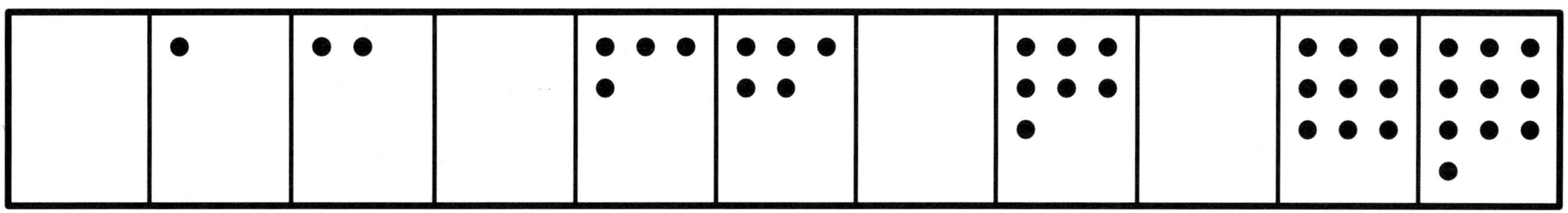

It's raining!

Throw the die and put counters on the raindrops.

Cross country

Throw the die and run the race.

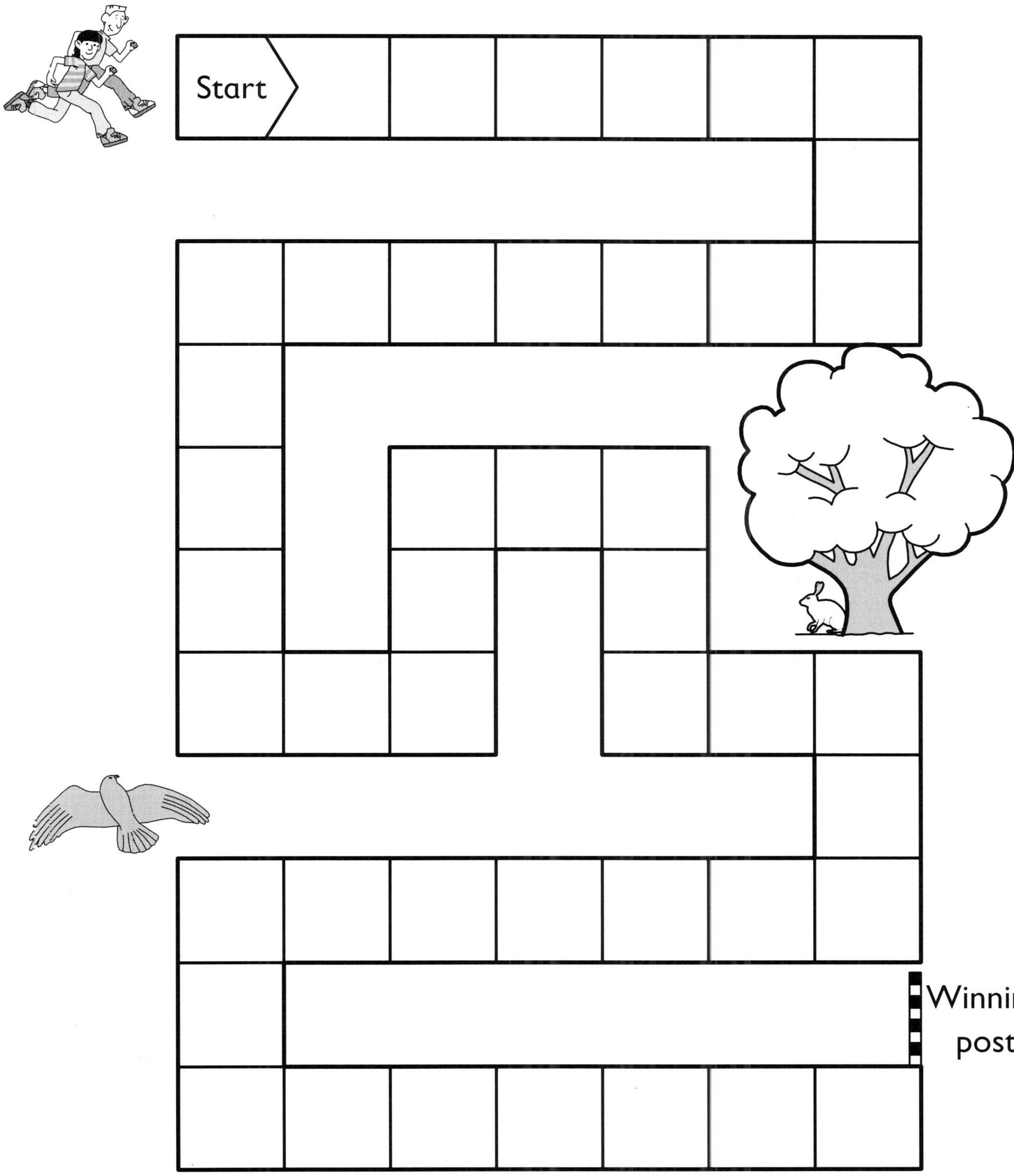

Cube patterns – colour a different pattern on each row

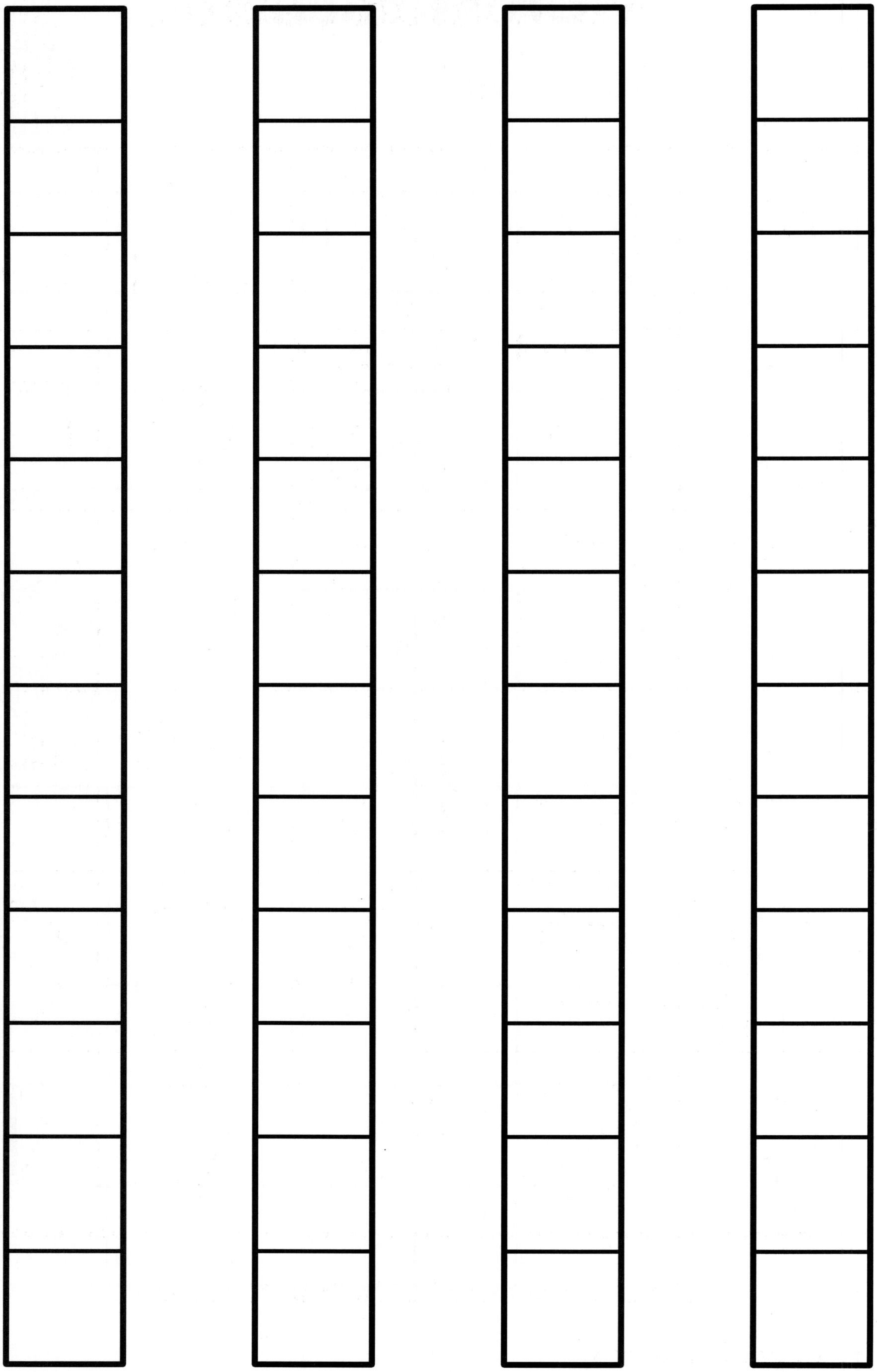

How many sides?

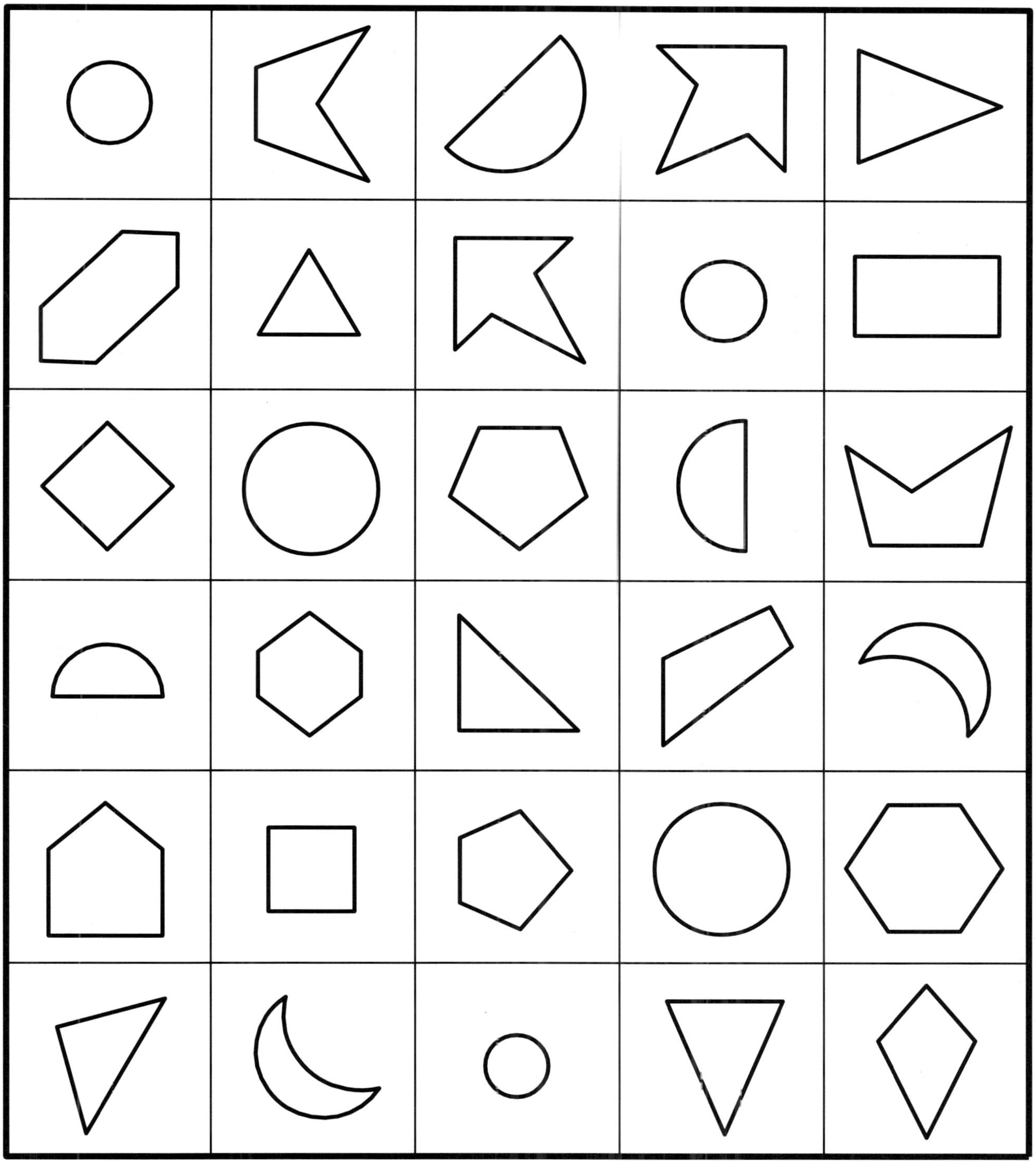

Throw a die and count the sides to find the right shape.

Try to get 3 in a row.

Teacher's resource sheet – recognise small numbers without counting (enlarge to A3)

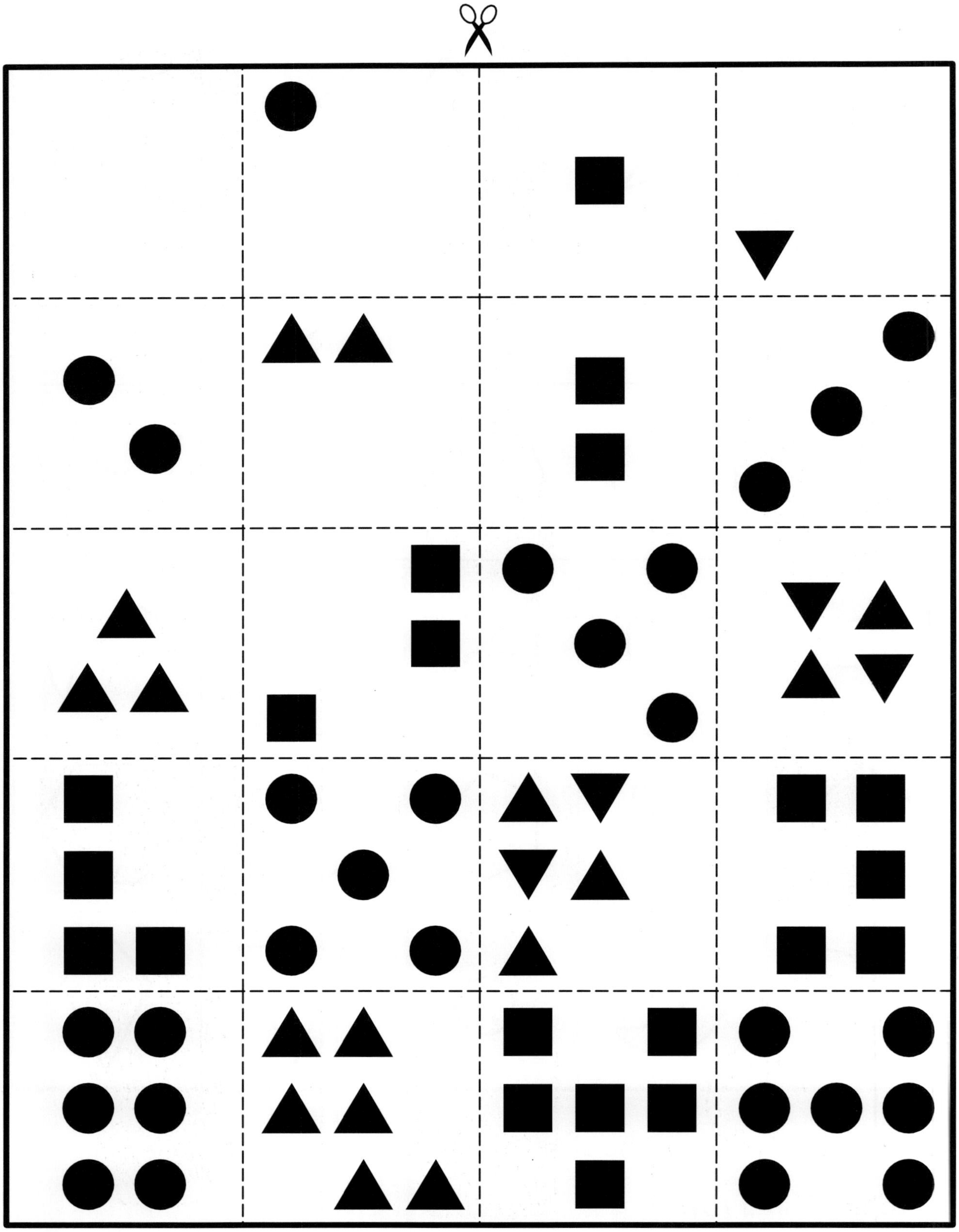

Full, empty or half-full?

Count the grapes

Colour bunches with the same number of grapes the same colour.

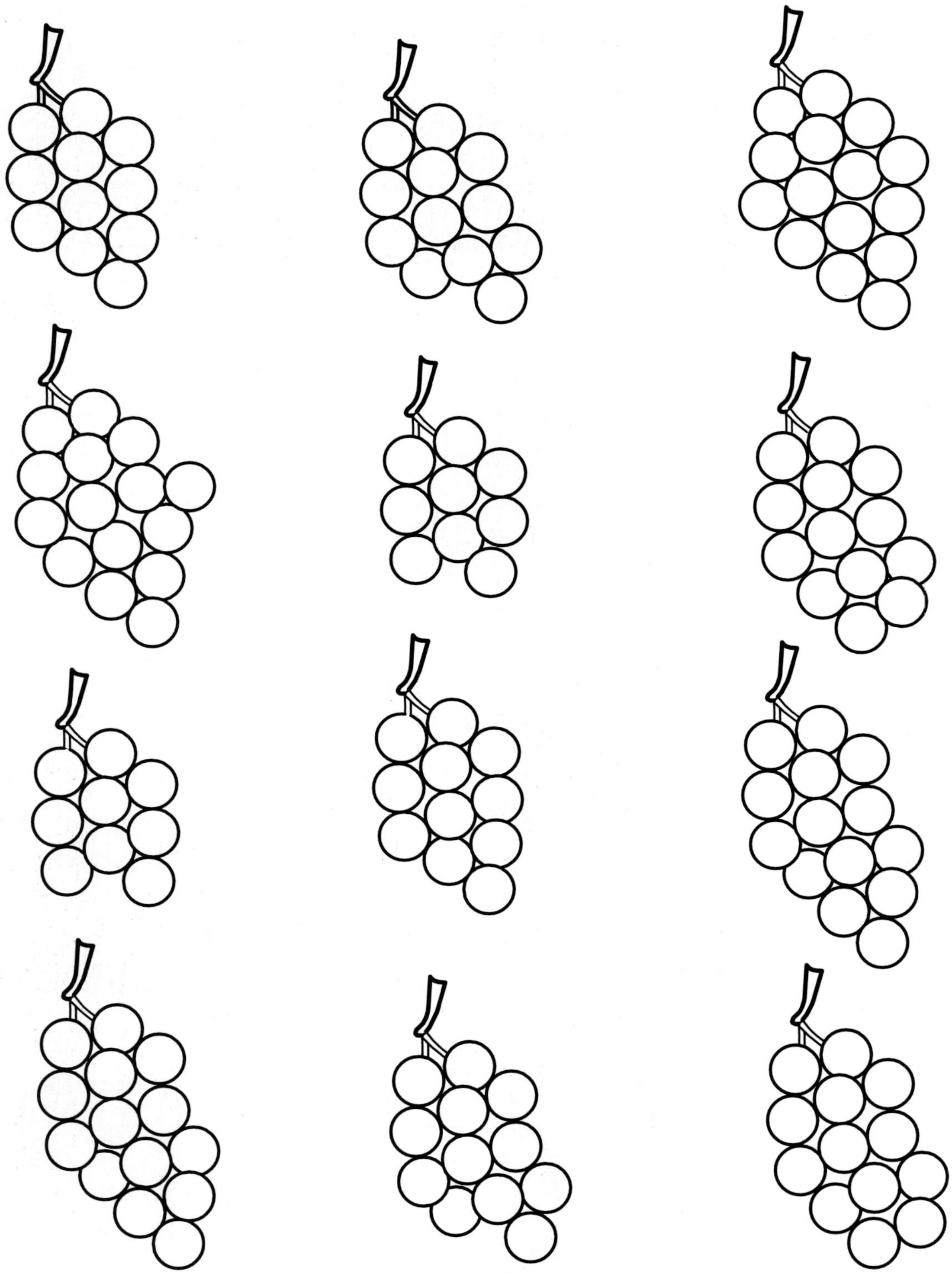

How many would be left if 2 grapes were eaten from each bunch?

Buy a scarecrow

Throw the dice and collect the coins.

Wobbly worms

Fill in the missing spots and count the numbers forwards.

0 1 2 3 4 5 6 7 8 9 10

Smart snakes

Fill in the missing shapes and count the numbers backwards.

10 9 8 7 6 5 4 3 2 1 0

Kites

Objective
* To recognise numbers to 5.
* To count reliably objects to 5

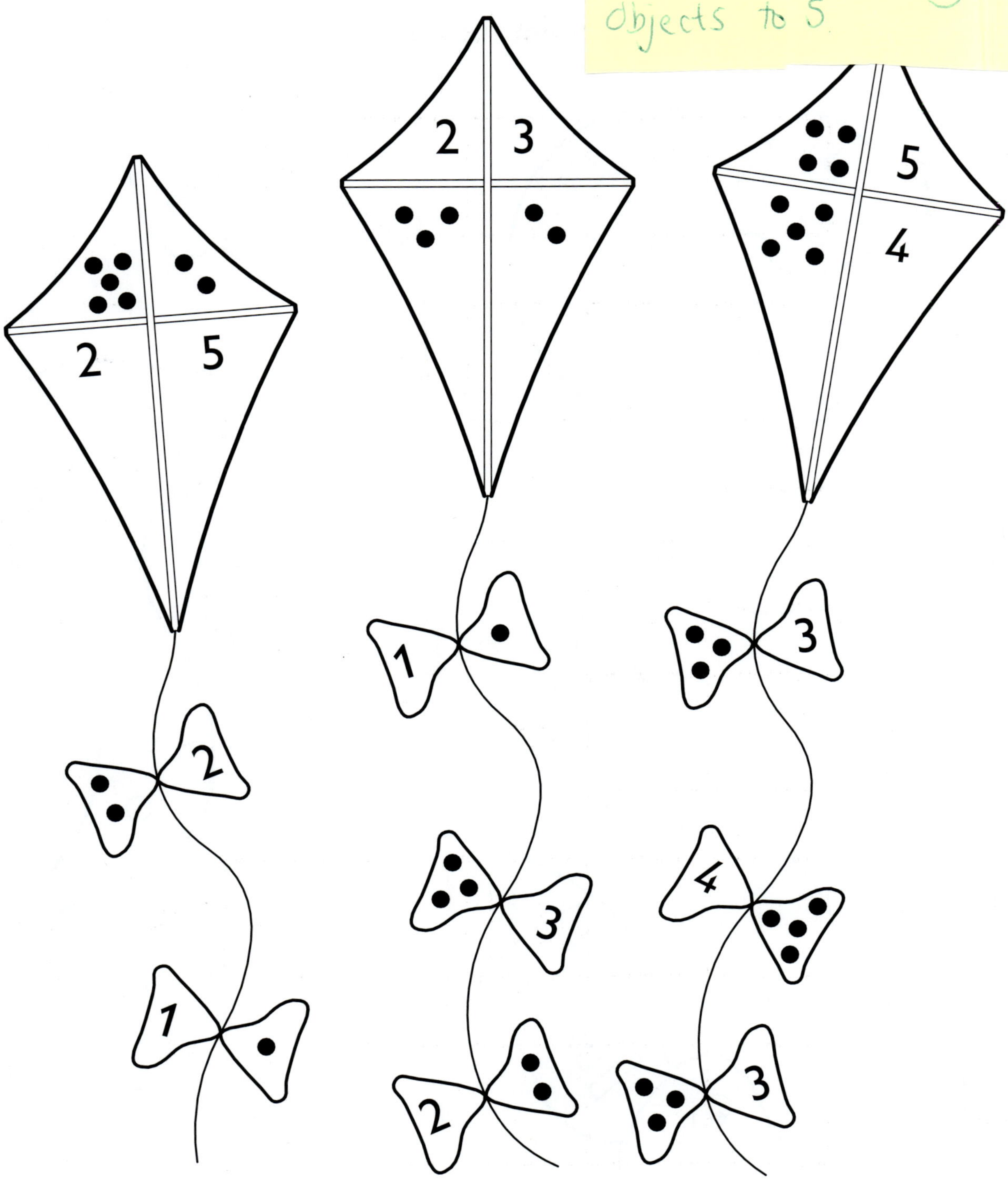

1 •	2 ••	3 •••	4 ••••	5 •••••
yellow	blue	green	orange	red

Count on

Start with the number and add the squares.

3 + ☐☐☐☐ =

2 + ☐☐☐ =

5 + ☐ =

0 + ☐☐ =

1 + ☐☐☐☐☐ =

4 + ☐☐☐☐ =

Make up some more of your own.

0 1 2 3 4 5 6 7 8 9 10

Bright and beautiful

... but what's missing?

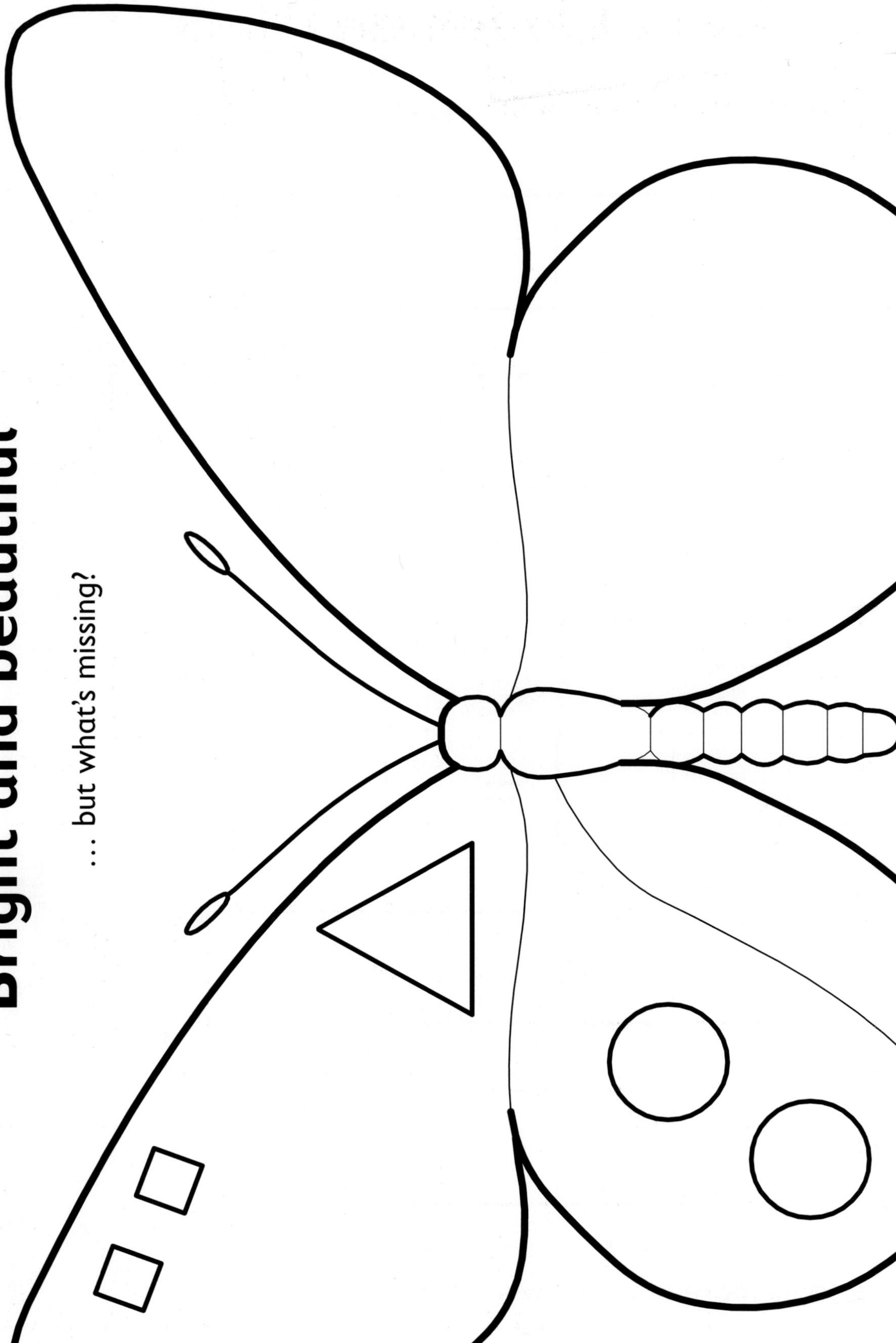

Beautiful butterflies

Colour each column a different colour, cut out and sort.

Balloons

Objective
* To count reliably objects to 9
* To recognise numbers to 9

5	red
6	
7	
8	
9	

Choose a colour for each number. Count the dots and colour the balloons.

Hungry caterpillars

Monday

Sunday

Wednesday

Saturday

Friday

Tuesday

Thursday

Slippery snakes

Colour each column a different colour, cut out and sort.

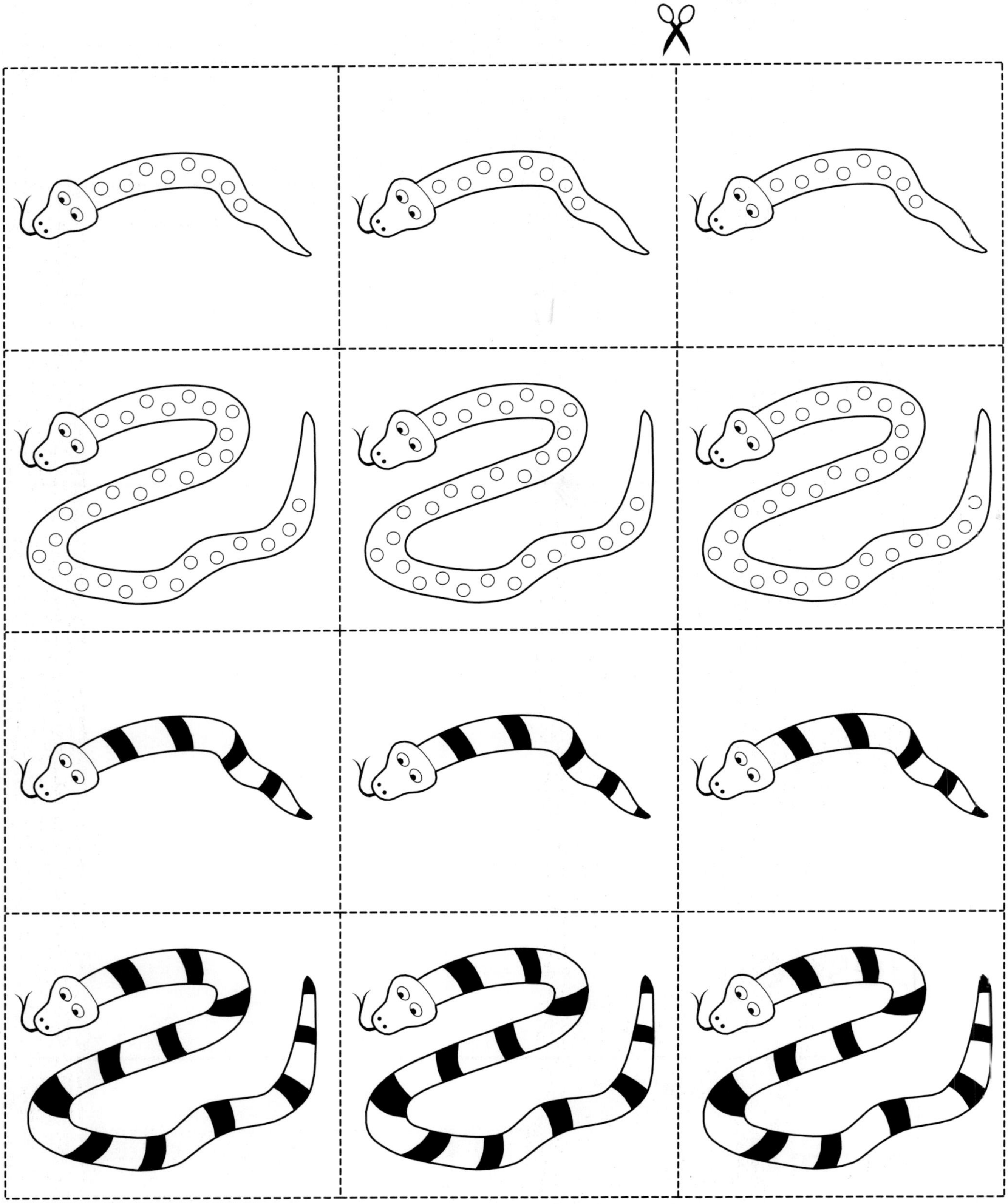

Shops

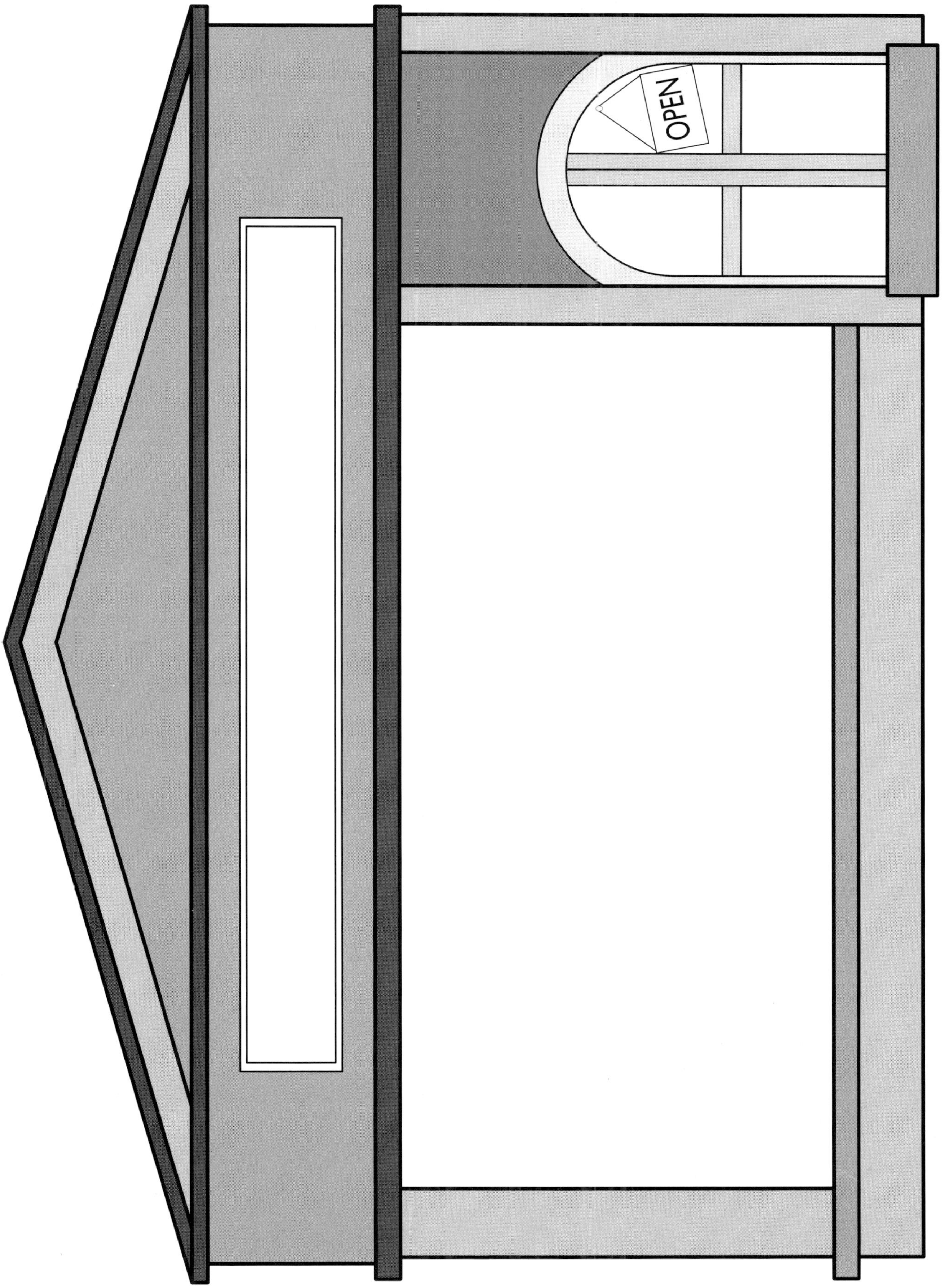

Fishy numbers

Colour the smallest number in each group orange …

… and the biggest number green.

Number tracks – enlarge for whole class use

Ascending order

0	1	2	3	4	5	6	7	8	9	10

Random order

1	5	0	3	2	4	10	8	6	7	9

Descending order

10	9	8	7	6	5	4	3	2	1	0

Missing numbers

0	1		3	4		6	7		9	10

One, two, buckle my shoe

1 2

One, two, buckle my shoe.

3 4

Three, four, knock at the door.

5 6

Five, six, pick up sticks.

7 8

Seven, eight, lay them straight.

9 10

Nine, ten, a big fat hen.

11 12

Eleven, twelve, dig and delve.

13 14

Thirteen, fourteen, maids a-courting.

15 16

Fifteen, sixteen, maids in the kitchen.

17 18

Seventeen, eighteen, maids in waiting.

19 20

Nineteen, twenty, my plate's empty!

Doubles

Double the number of flowers and count on.

2 □

4 □

1 □

3 □

Which shape where?

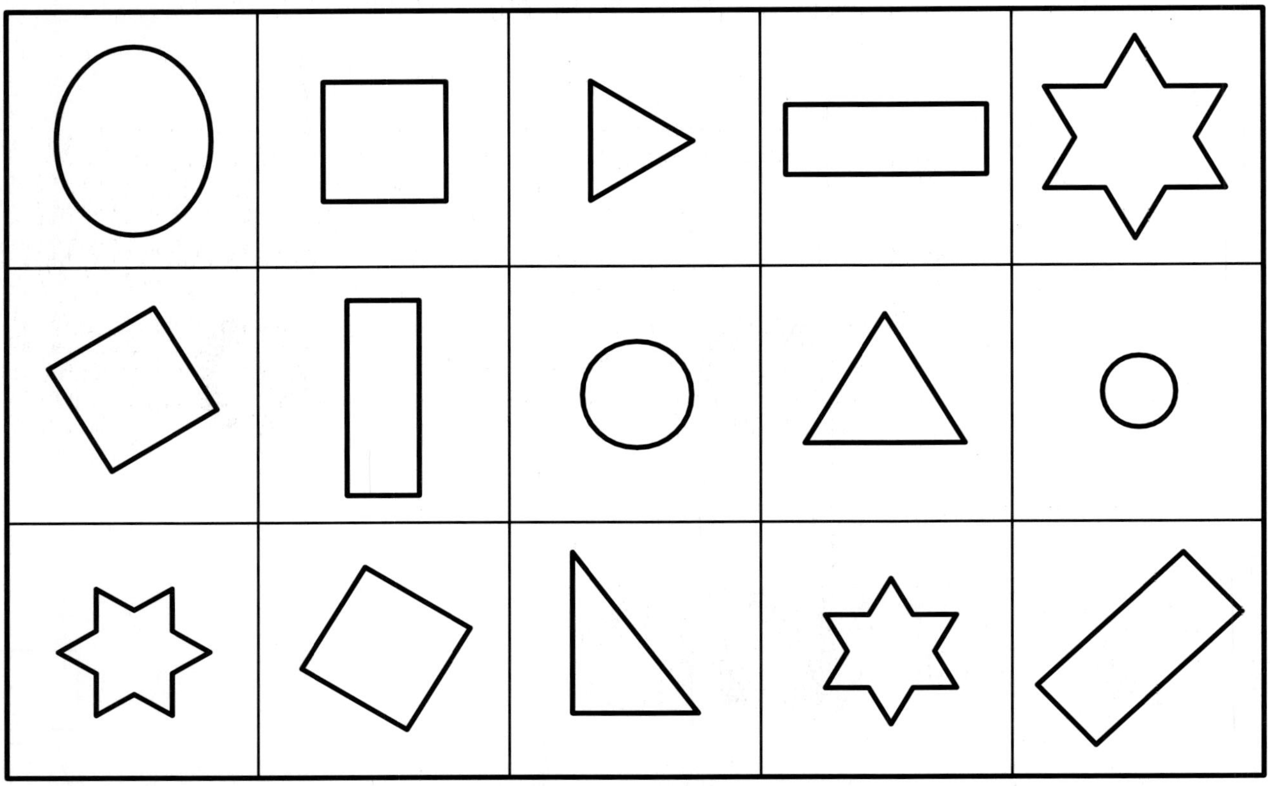

Five in a row

Traffic jam

Teacher's resource sheet

Objective
* To recognise numbers to 5.
* To count reliably objects to 5.

How many?

Draw the same number of tally marks and write the number in the box.

1 1 2 2 3 3 4 4 5 5

Out and about

Write the numbers 1 to 5 in order.

1 1 2 2 3 3 4 4 5 5

Number lines

0 1 2 3 4 5 6 7 8 9 10

0 1 2 3 4 5 6 7 8 9 10

0 1 2 3 4 5 6 7 8 9 10

0 1 2 3 4 5 6 7 8 9 10

0 1 2 3 4 5 6 7 8 9 10

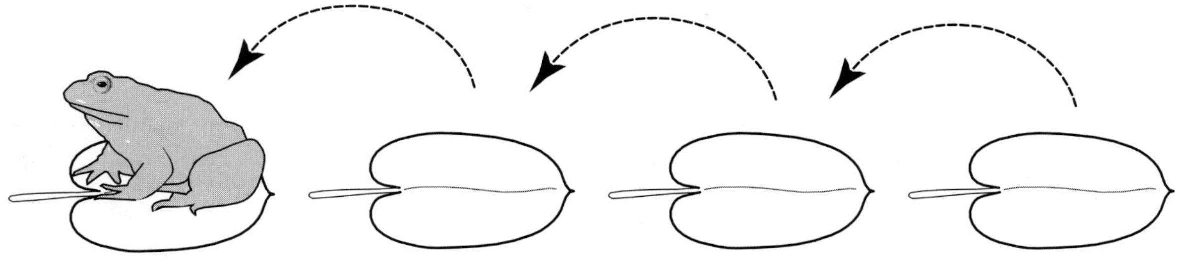

5p to spend

How much change do you get?

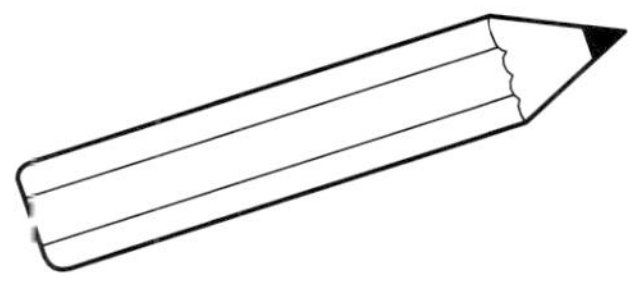

pencil 2p

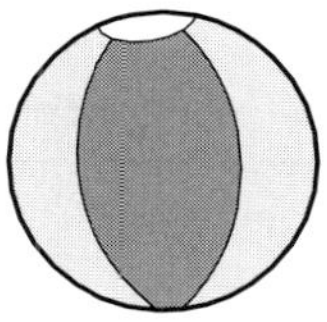

ball 5p

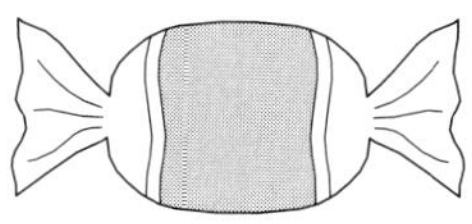

toffee 1p

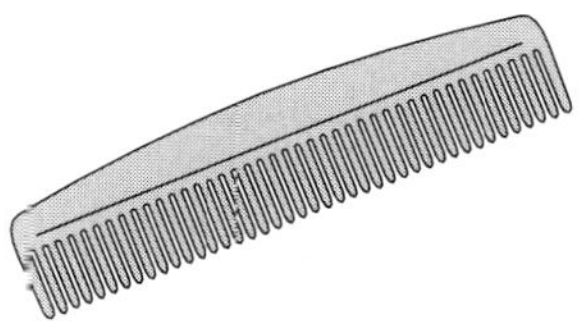

comb 4p

apple 3p

Guess first!

How many? Guess first then count.

guess

count

---

guess

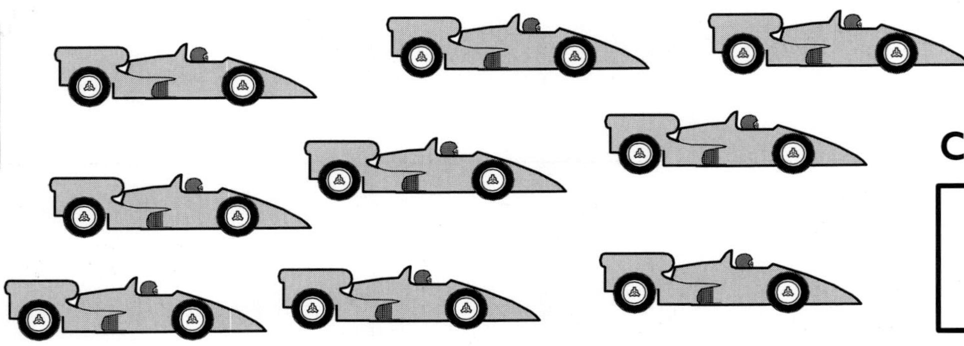

count

---

guess

count

---

guess

count

Curly caterpillars

Write the numbers in order on the caterpillars.

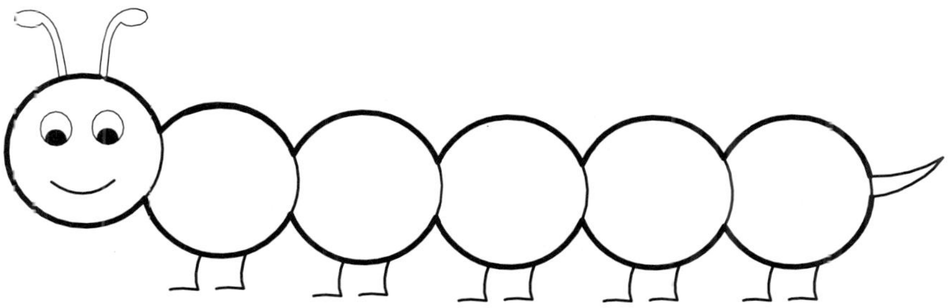

4 6 8 1 2

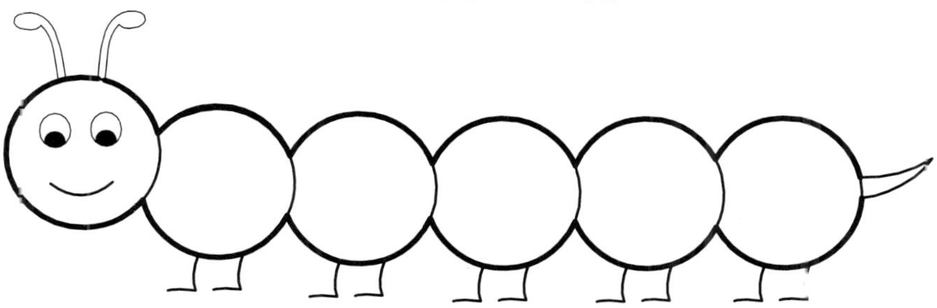

3 7 10 5 1

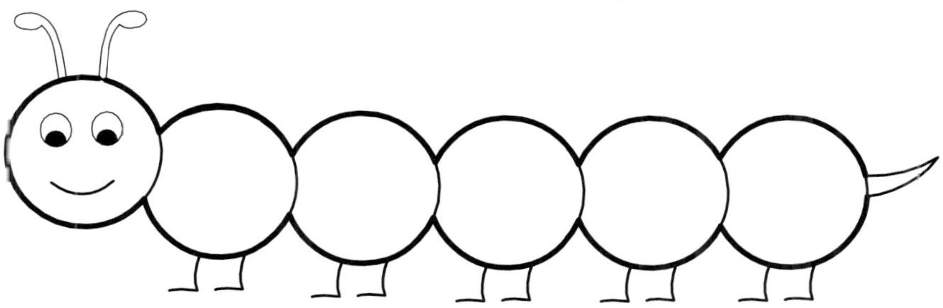

2 0 9 6 3

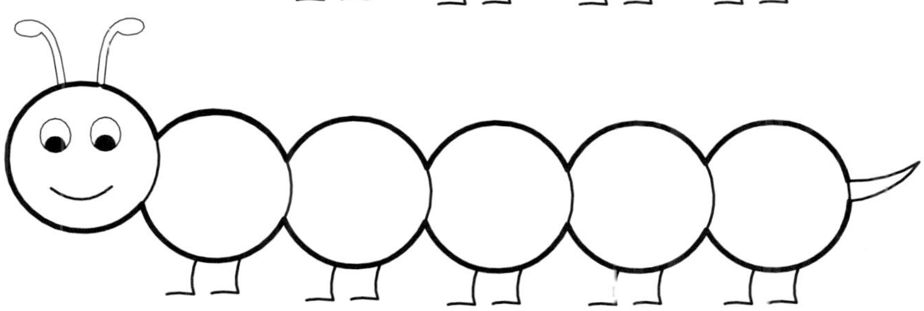

9 6 4 2 7

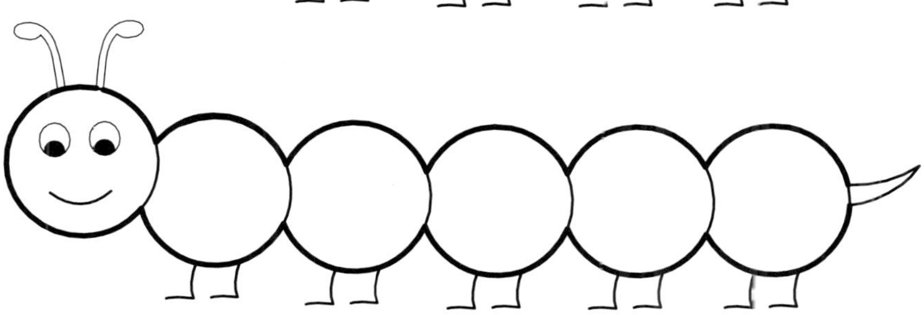

3 10 5 0 8

0 1 2 3 4 5 6 7 8 9 10

Count in twos – Colour the even numbers.

1	2	3	4	5	6	7	8	9	10
11	12	13	14	15	16	17	18	19	20

1	2
3	4
5	6
7	8
9	10
11	12
13	14
15	16
17	18
19	20

Colour the even numbers.

1	2	3	4	5	6	7	8	9	10
11	12	13	14	15	16	17	18	19	20

1	2
3	4
5	6
7	8
9	10
11	12
13	14
15	16
17	18
19	20

Break up 10

Break 10 into two parts in different ways.

Square patterns – what comes next?

Sandcastles

Use two colours to colour the flags in different ways.

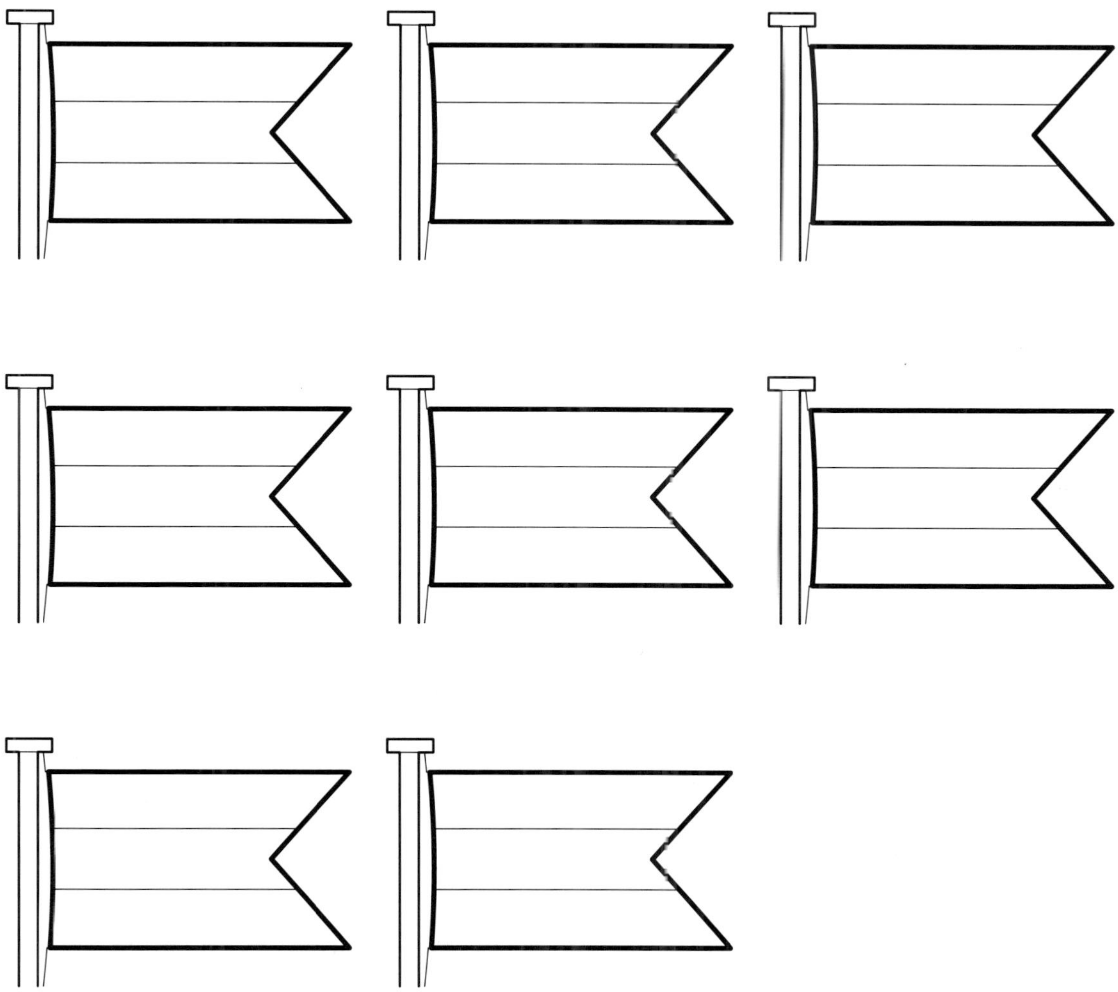

How many faces? How many hats?

The giant's day

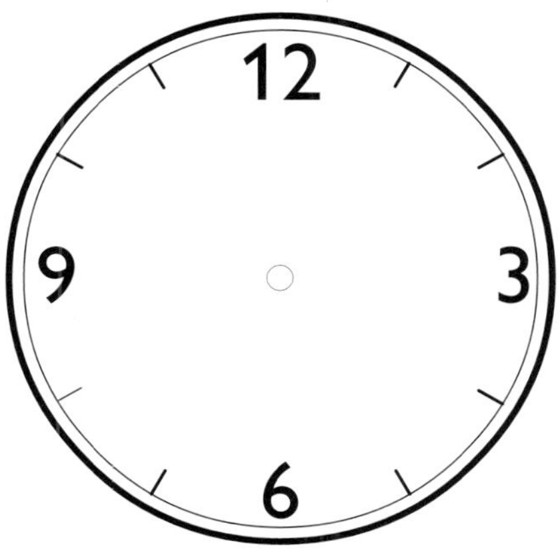

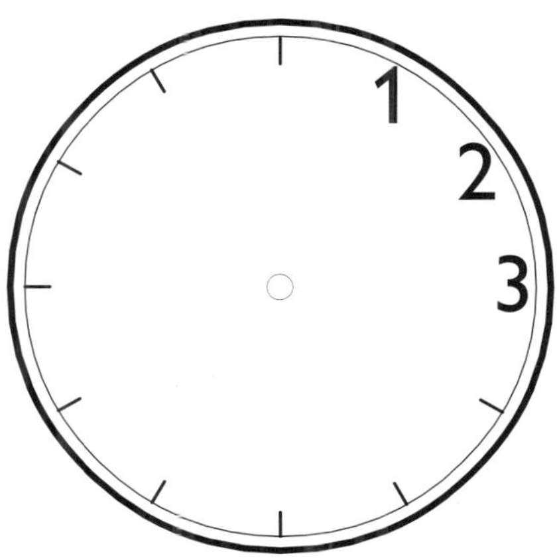

Draw the times and numbers on the clocks.

Patterns of twos

Fill in the numbers to 20 and count in twos. Colour the numbers you count.

1	2			5				9	
11			14			17			20

1		3		
	7			10
11			14	
		18		20

1	2		
5		7	
			12
13		15	
	18		20

How many more?

Draw more to make the numbers. How many more did you draw?

make 7

I drew ☐

make 9

I drew ☐

make 4

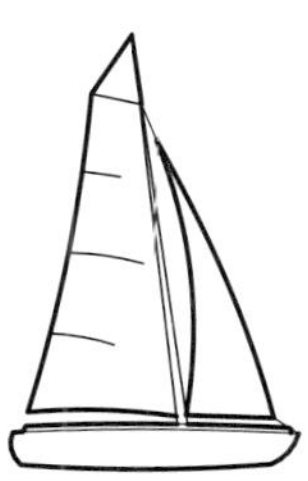

I drew ☐

make 6

I drew ☐

Homework 1

Learn this number rhyme with your child. Encourage them to point to the different parts of the body as they say it.

Me and you

I've got one head
One nose too
One mouth, one chin,
So have you.

I've got two eyes
Two ears too
Two arms, two legs,
So have you.

I've got two hands
Two thumbs too
Four fingers on each hand,
So have you.

Learn this number rhyme with your child. Encourage them to think of some actions to match the rhyme.

Busy people

1 busy person sweeping up the floor,
2 busy people oiling the door,
3 busy people washing baby's socks,
4 busy people winding up the clocks,
5 busy people mowing the grass,
6 busy people dusting very fast,
7 busy people cleaning in a rush,
8 busy people shaking out the brush,
9 busy people stirring the stew,
10 busy people with nothing left to do.

Help your child to count up to 10 and back again.

Shape sort

Colour the shapes the right colour.

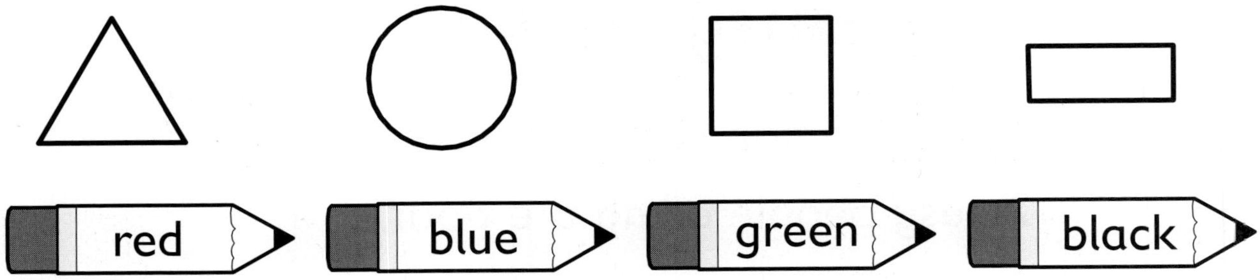

Help your child to find some things which are the same shapes.

Crazy characters

Count the squares to find the colour for the character.

•	red
••	yellow
•••	blue
••••	orange
•••••	green

Underwater count

Count the things in the picture with your child. Check by counting backwards.

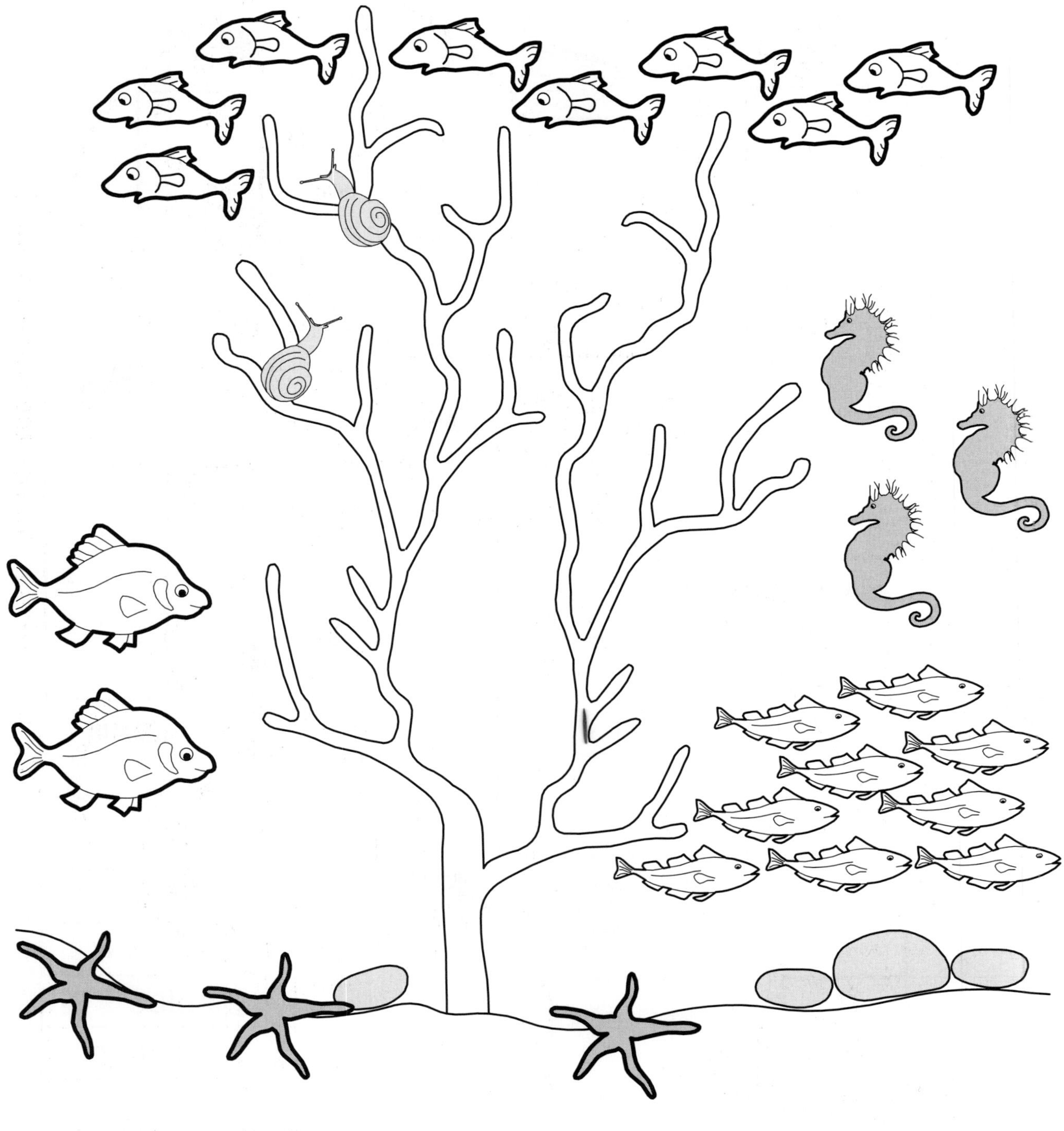

Help your child count to 10 and back.

Spotty butterfly

Count the spots and colour the butterfly using a different colour for each number.

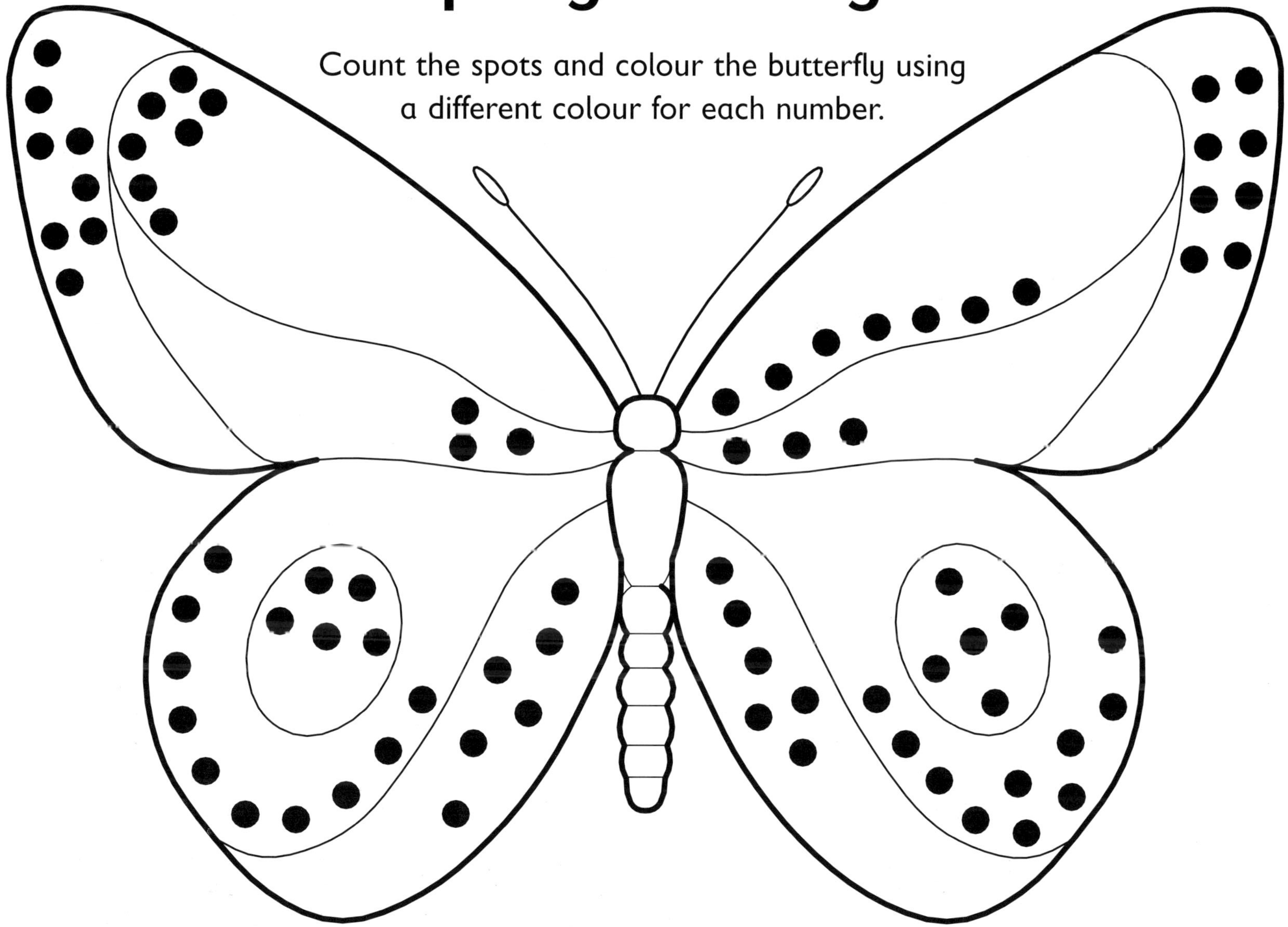

Will your friends choose the same colours?

Beetle friends

Put the beetles into groups of 8.

Your child could colour each group of 8 a different colour, join them with a line or draw a loop around them.

Packages

You need some small cardboard boxes.

Try these activities with your child.

- Draw around the boxes using different sides as a base. What shapes do you get?
- Count the numbers of faces and corners.
- Look at the boxes from different sides, or from above.
- Undo the boxes to see how they were made.

Useful words: shape side rectangle triangle circle square straight curved corner face cube cylinder flat

Homework 9

Fruit and vegetables

You need a medium sized potato and some other pieces of fruit and vegetables.

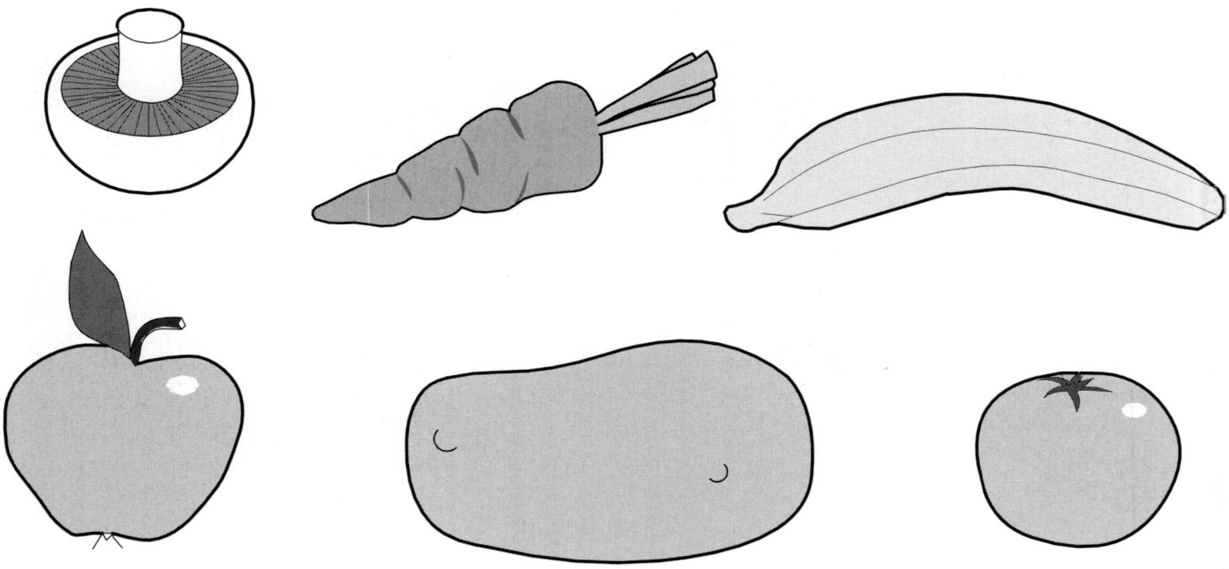

Start with the potato and then help your child to decide which of the other fruits and vegetables are heavier and which are lighter. Sort them:

Useful words: heavy light heavier lighter weigh balance more less

Coin sort

You need some real coins, one of each value.

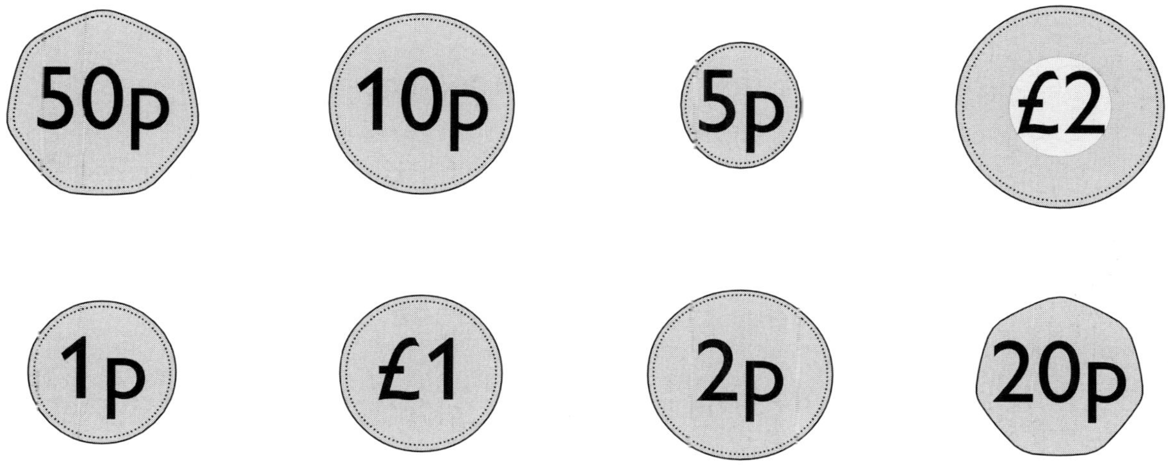

Help your child to make some coin rubbings by placing thin paper over a coin and rubbing gently with a crayon.

Pick two coins and talk about what is the same, or what is different.

Take turns to hide one of the coins and try to guess what is missing.

Useful words: thick thin round money coin penny pence size silver copper big(ger) small(er) edge same different

Ordering numbers

Cut out the dotty number cards at the bottom of the page and try these activities with your child.

more

less

before

after

bigger

smaller

next

- Count the dots on each one.
- Put them in order with the biggest (or smallest) first.
- Spread them in order and turn 2 or 3 face down. Ask your child which numbers are missing.
- Put 3 cards in a row *(e.g. 3, 4, 5, ?)* and ask your child to find the next one.
- Find 2 cards with one missing in between *(e.g. 7, ?, 9)*. Ask your child to find the missing number.

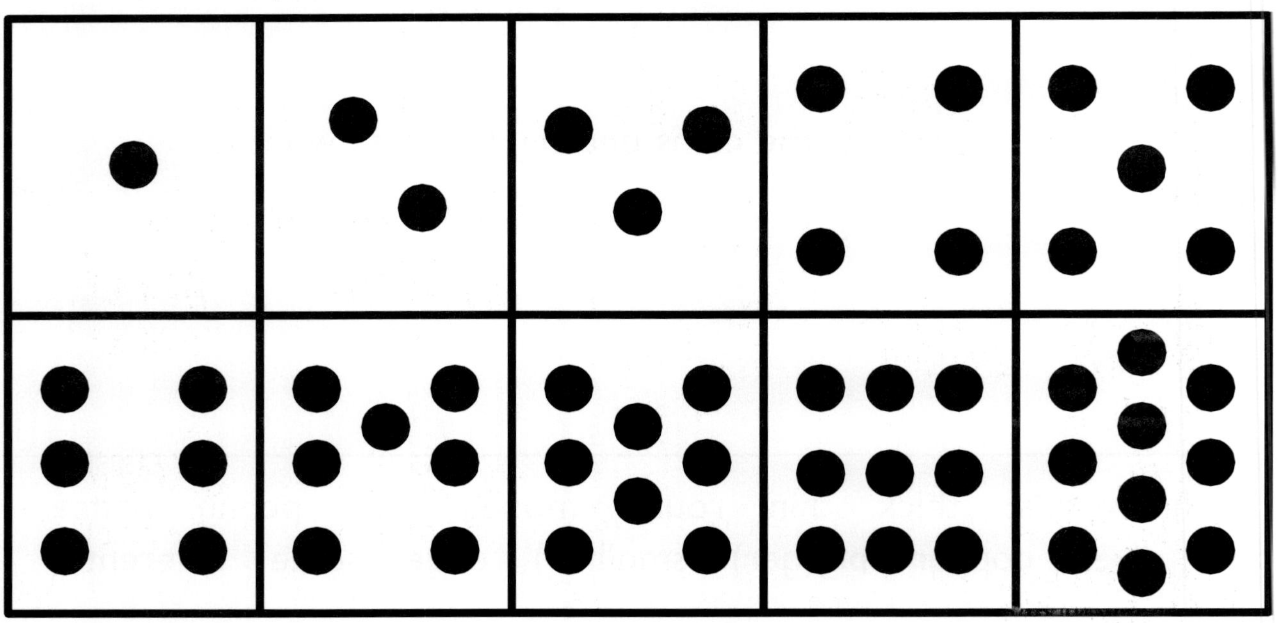

Transport trails

Count how many in each group.

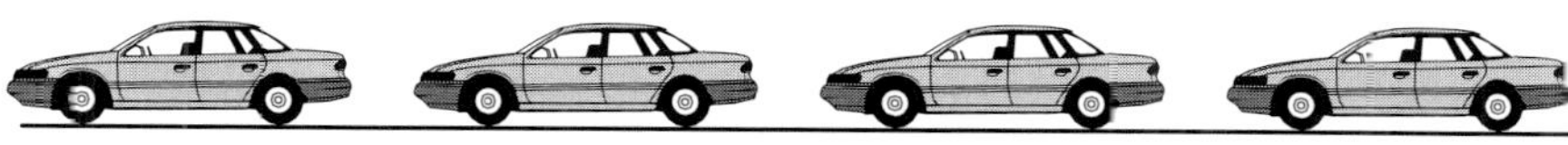

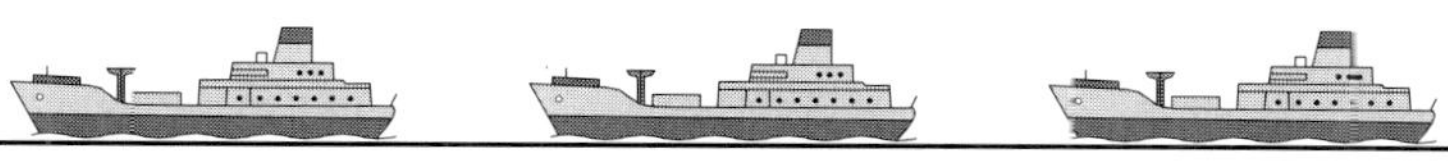

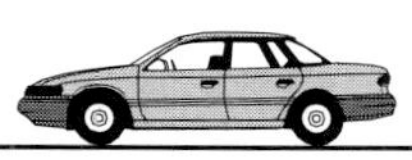

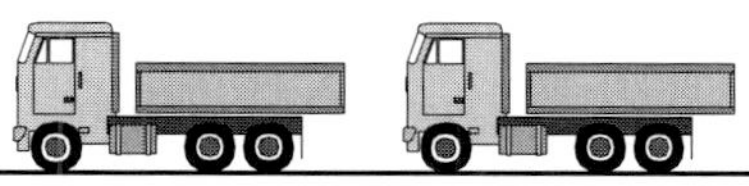

How many altogether?

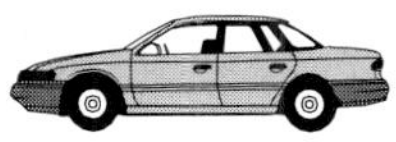

cars?

trains?

boats?

lorries?

Shape patterns

Help your child to colour and continue the patterns. Use the same colours for the same shapes.

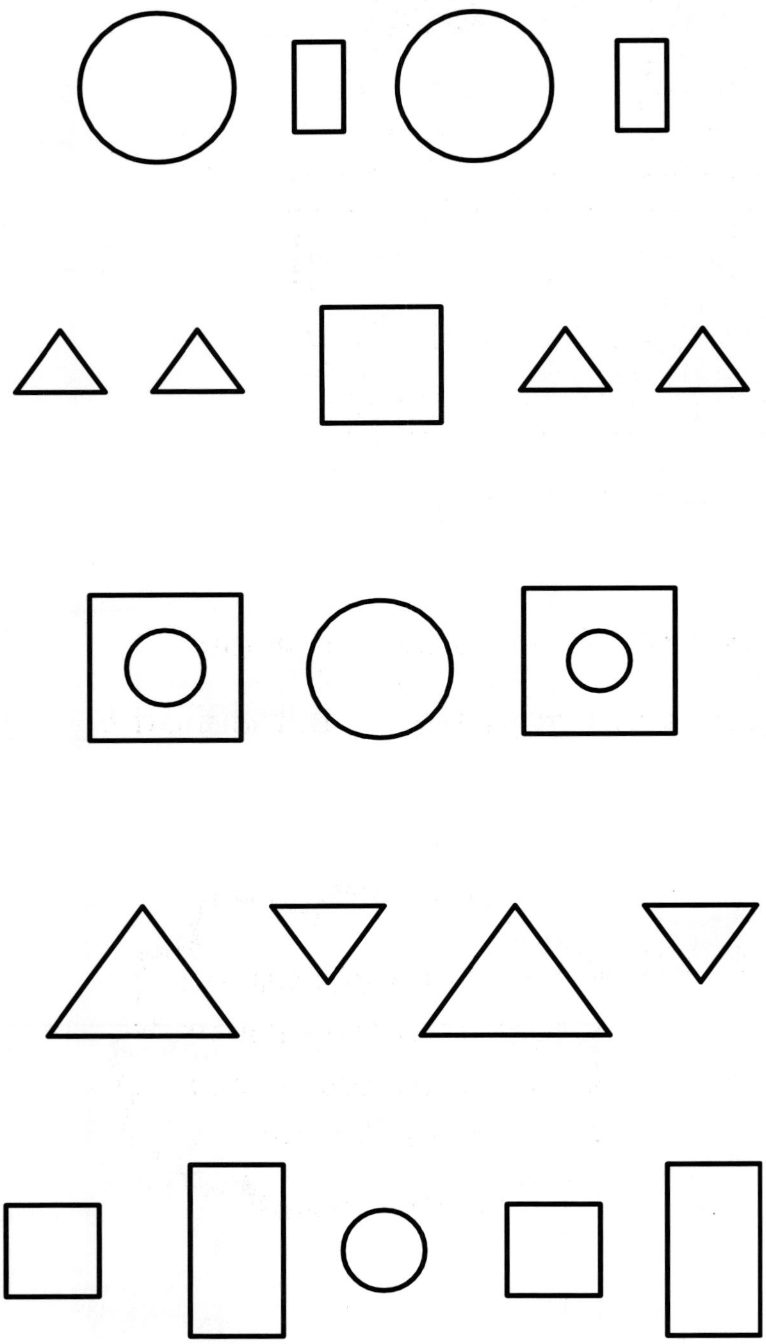

Make up some patterns of your own.

Bathtime fun

You need some plastic containers of different sizes and water.

Encourage your child to find out which containers hold the most by filling and emptying.

What happens when you pour water from a small pot into a bigger one?

What happens when you pour water from a big container into a smaller one?

Useful words: full empty holds enough too much too little more less half-full just over just under compare

Homework 15

Action counting

Try these things with your child ...

clap 8 times

jump 13 times

blink 10 times

hop 6 times

wave 14 times

Change the numbers and try again!

Ladybirds

Count the spots and colour the ladybirds the right colour.

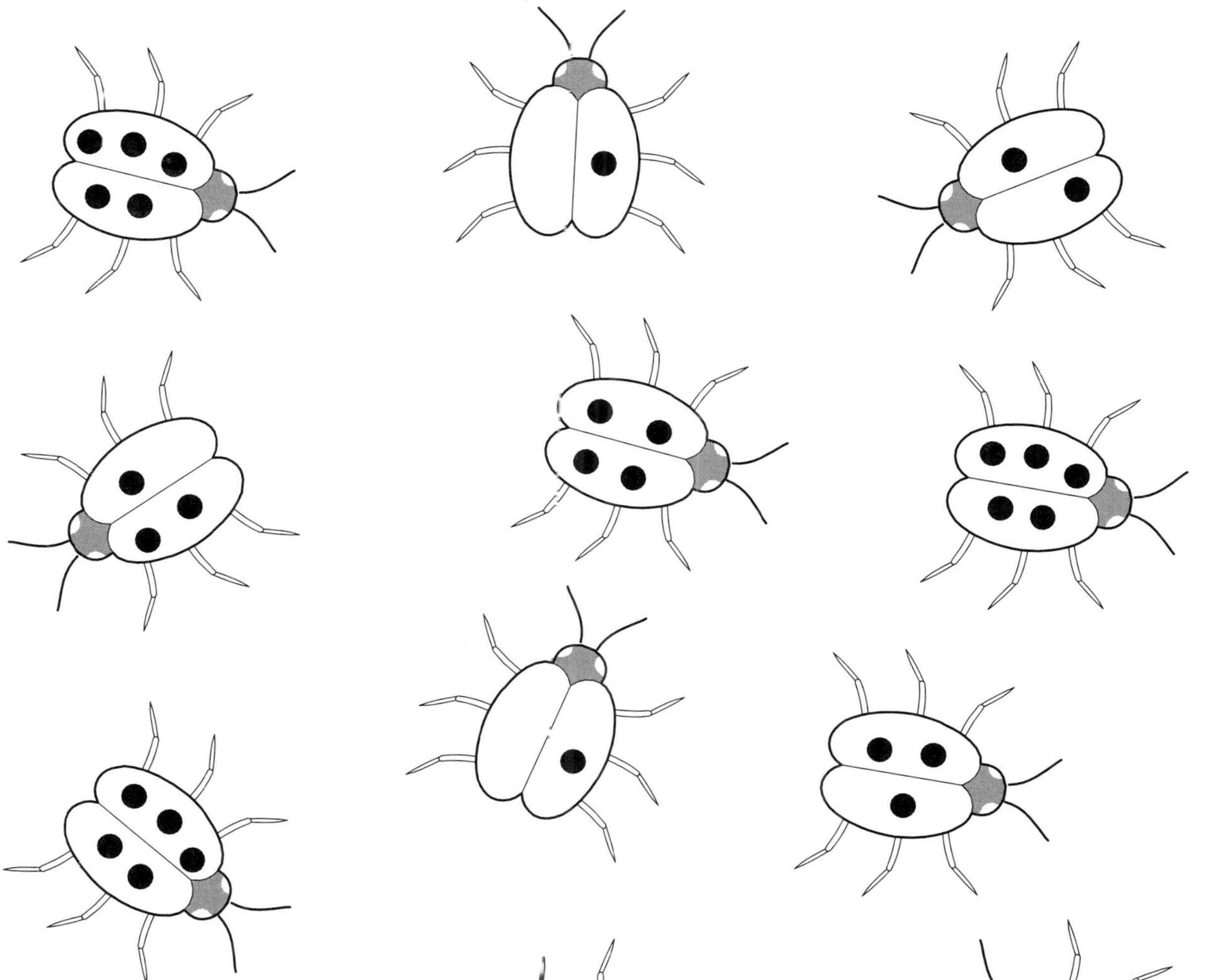

1	yellow
2	green
3	red
4	blue
5	orange

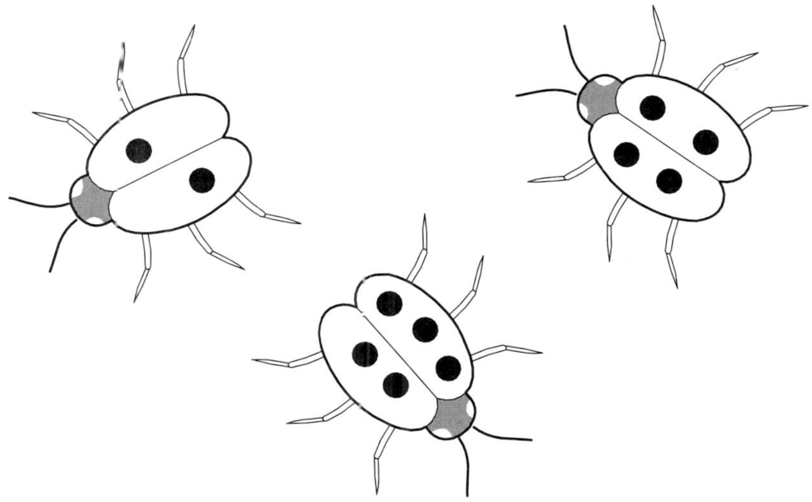

Whose birthday?

Draw the candles on the cakes.

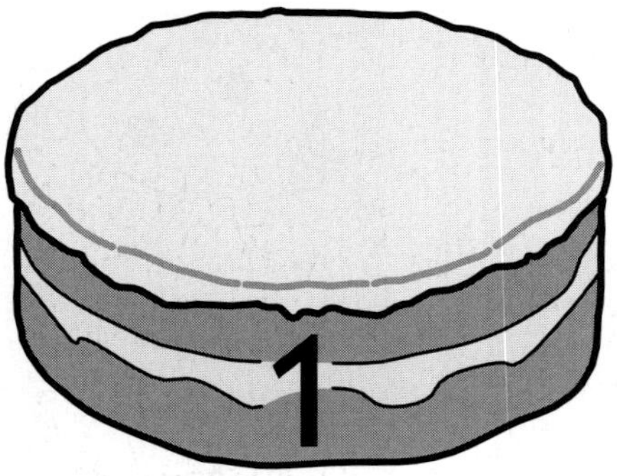

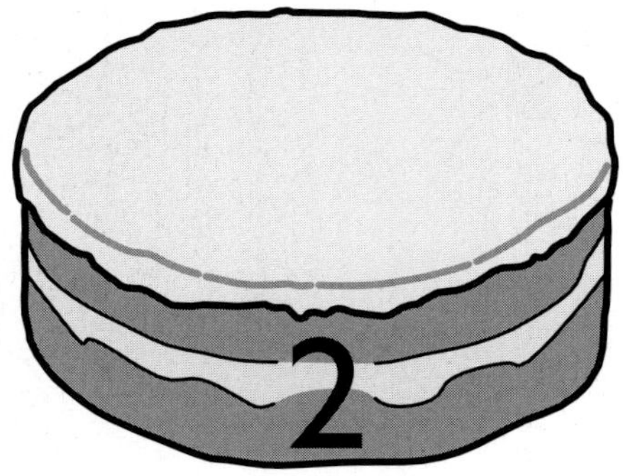

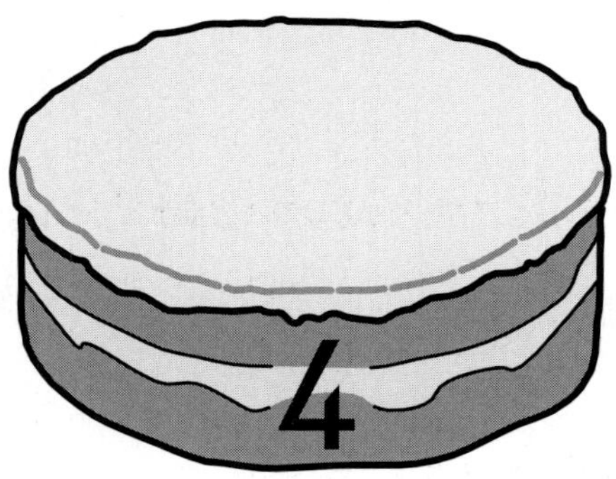

Help your child to recognise the numbers to 5. Point to the cakes in any order and ask them to tell you the numbers.

Tin can time

You need some different sized tins of food.

Help your child to put the tins in order:

- with the tallest first.
- with the widest first.
- with the biggest last.
- with the heaviest first.

Talk about how you decide the order.

Useful words: big(ger/gest) small(er/est) large(r/est) cylinder tall(er/est) short(er/est) heavy(ier/iest) light(er/est) size first next last

Homework 19

Passing the time

Three activities to try with your child.

1. Help them to learn to say the days of the week in order, starting with any day.

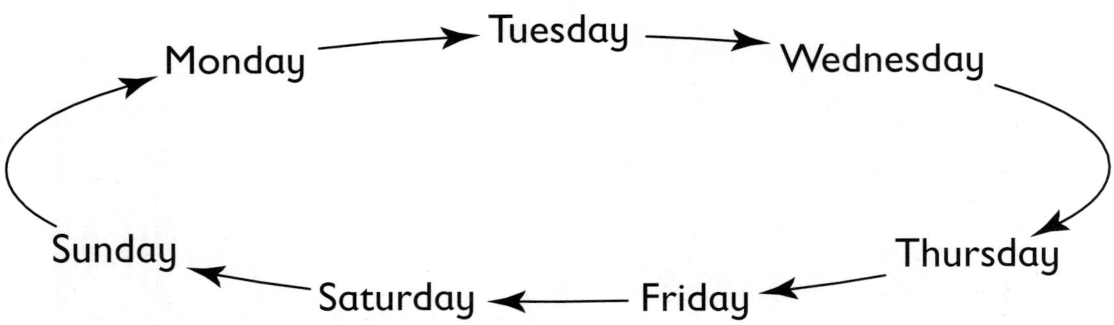

2. Talk about what takes longer.

having a bath

eating breakfast

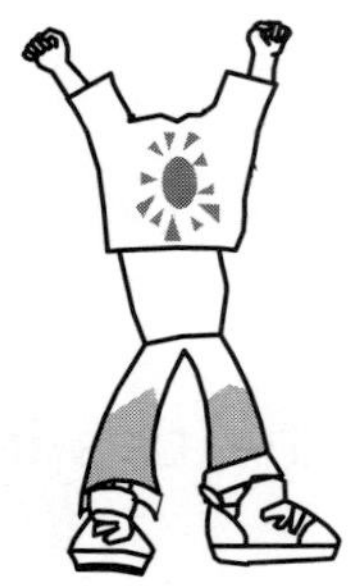

getting dressed

cleaning teeth

3. Try to do some things for a whole minute.

stand on one leg

sit still

run

balance a book on your head

Join the dots

Join the dots in order to finish the picture.

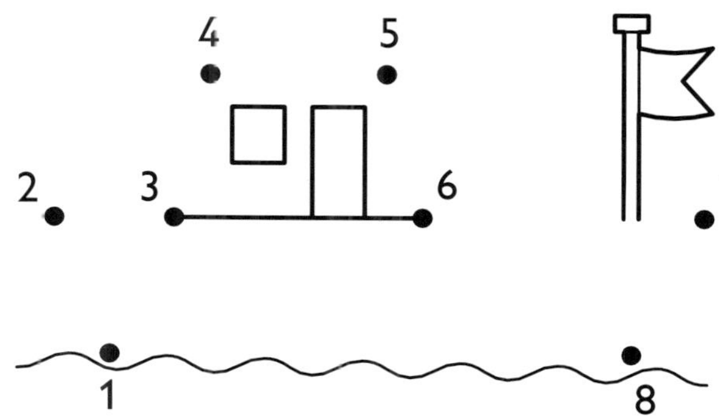

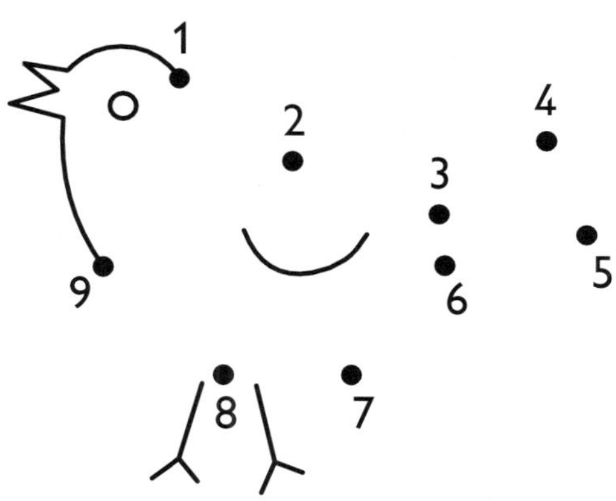

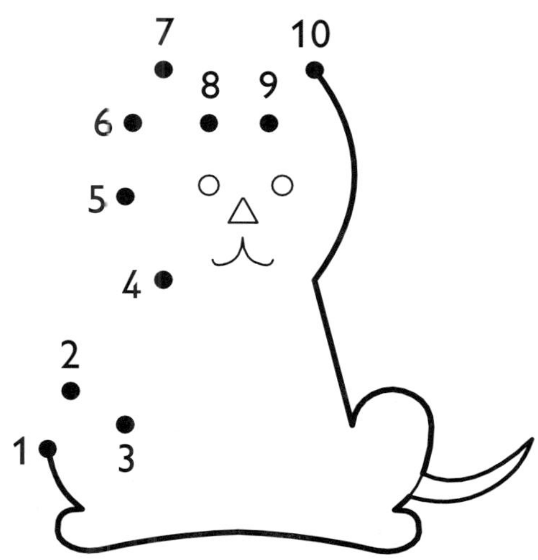

Help your child to make their own join the dots picture.

Homework 21

Number hunt

You and your child will need to work really hard to finish this activity.

Find something around the house to match every number up to 20.

1

2 — apples in the bowl

3

4

5 — eggs in the fridge

6

7

8

9

10

11

12

13 — stairs

14

15

16

17

18

19 — leaves on the plant

20

Make 10

Draw more to make 10.

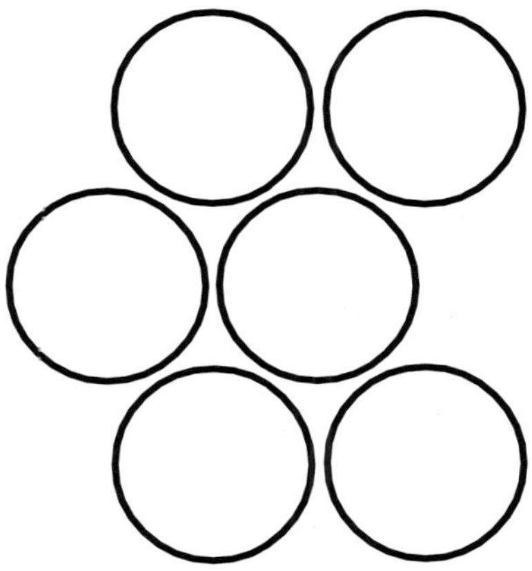

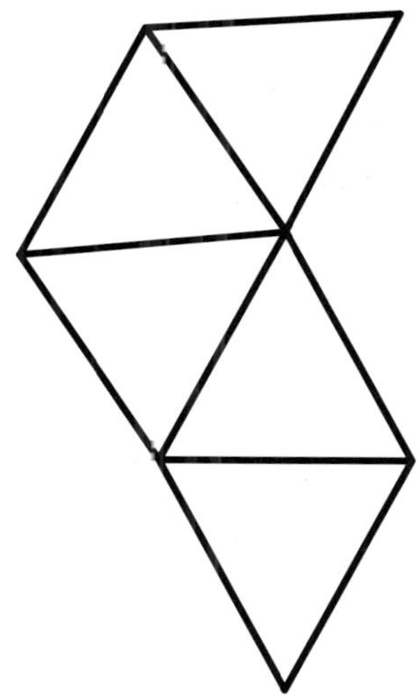

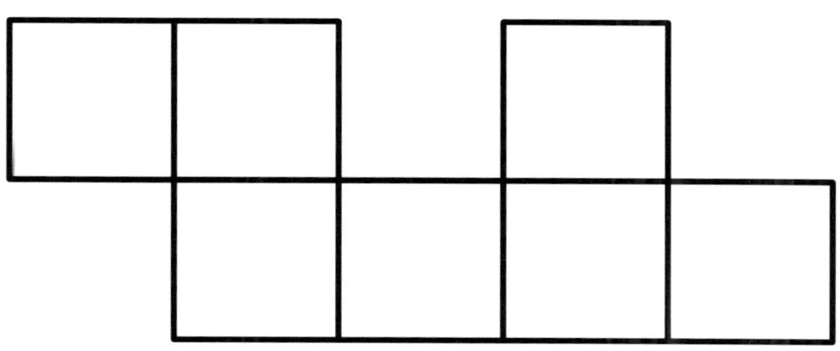

Count and write how many you started with.

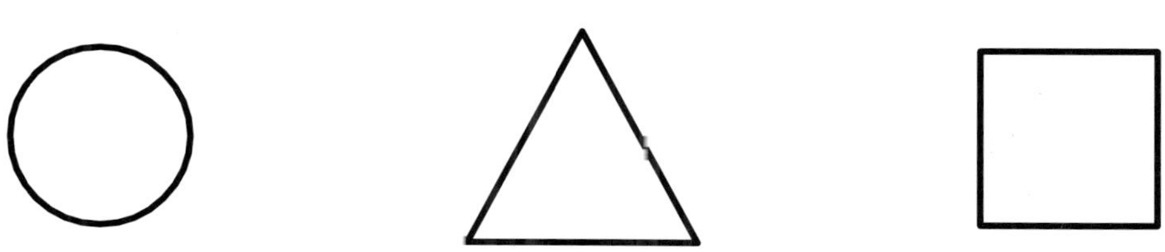

1 2 3 4 5 6 7 8 9 10

Blind man's bluff!

Stand at one side of the room and close your eyes. Ask your child to give you instructions to get to the other side of the room without bumping into anything.

Now swap places … or put more things in the way … or start from a different place … or try a different room.

Useful words: forwards backwards right left over under around to the side in front behind between next to corner

Longer or shorter?

Look for two objects the same and colour the longer one.

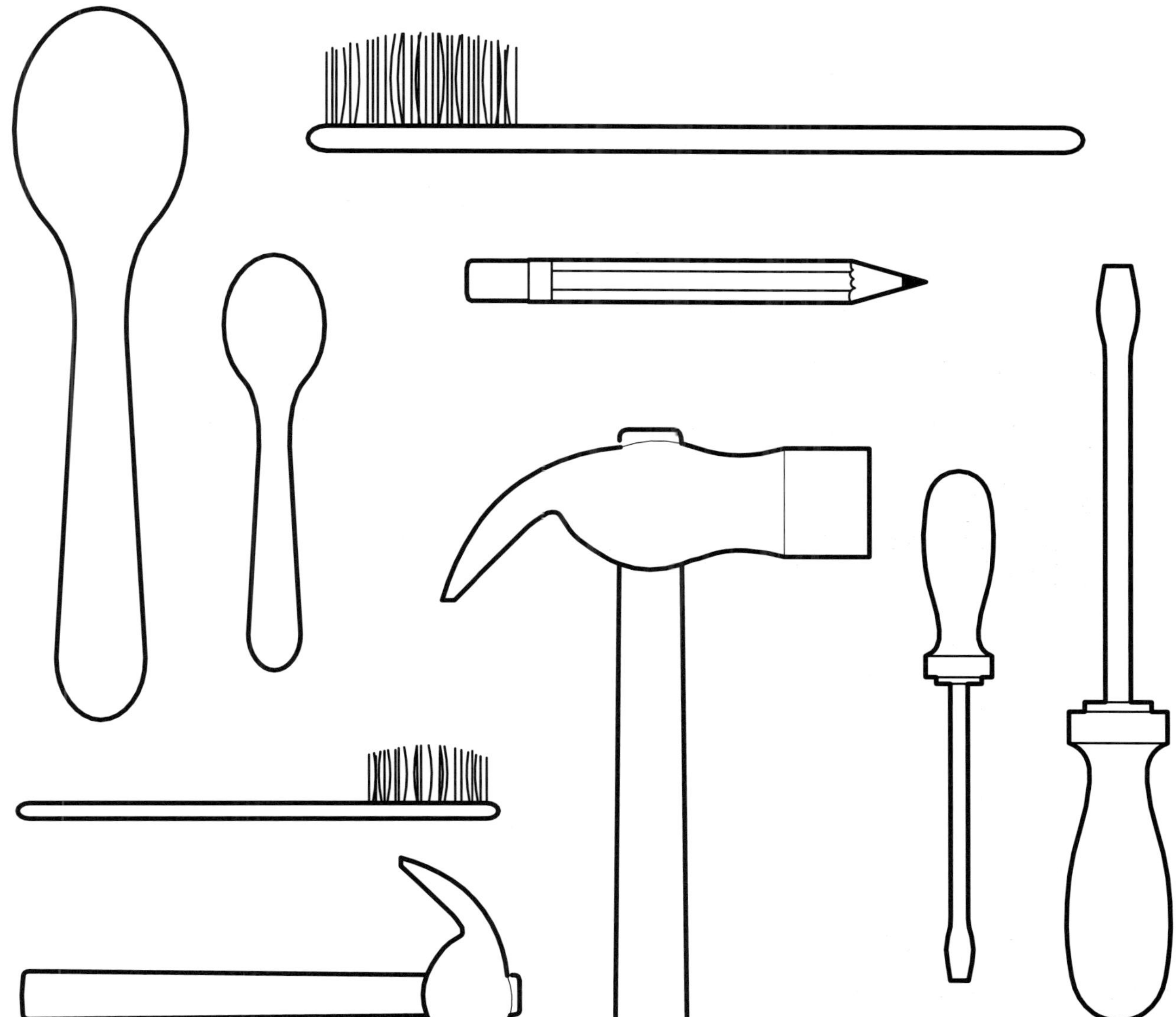

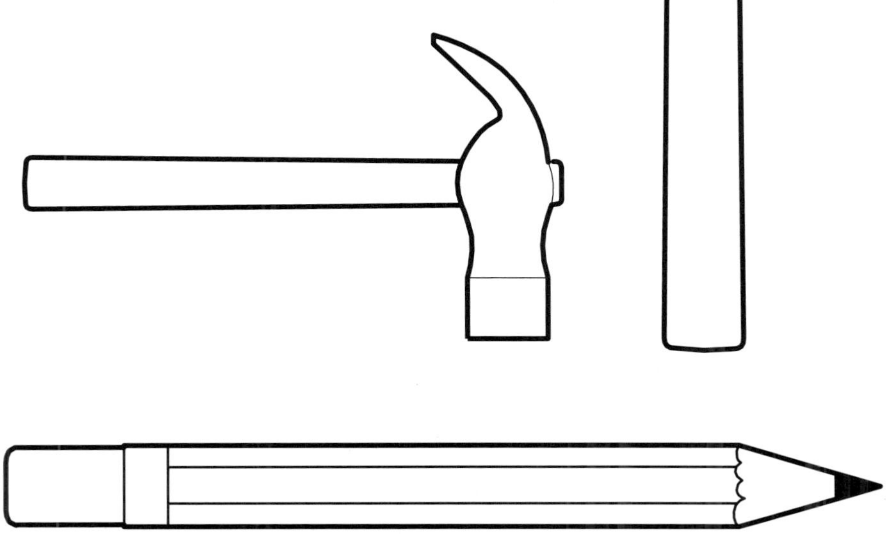

Look around to find some long things and some short things.

Count in tens

Count in tens and join the dots.

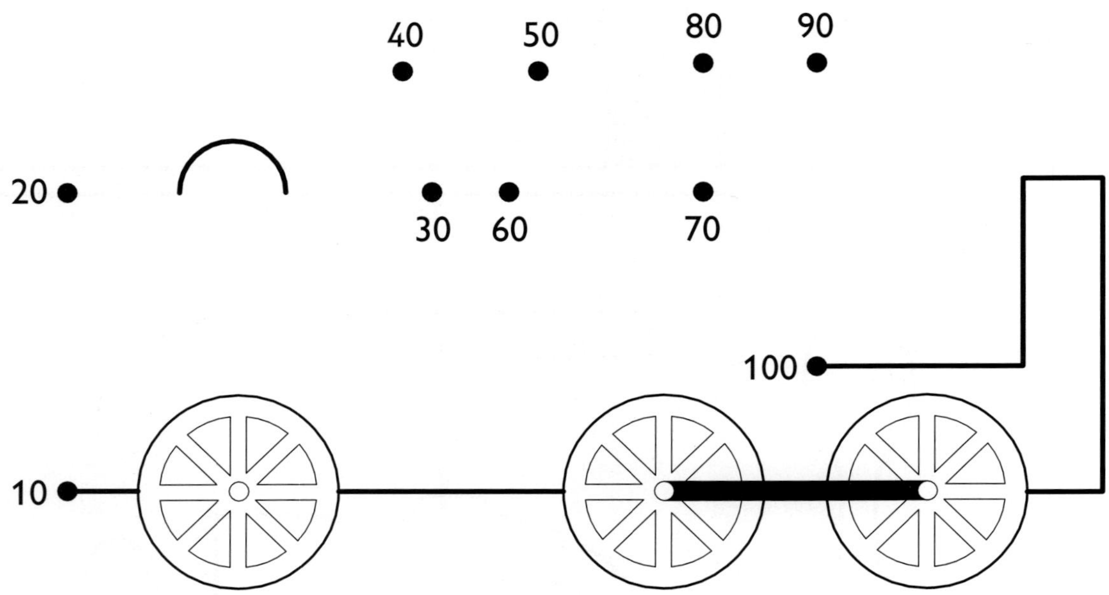

Now try backwards …

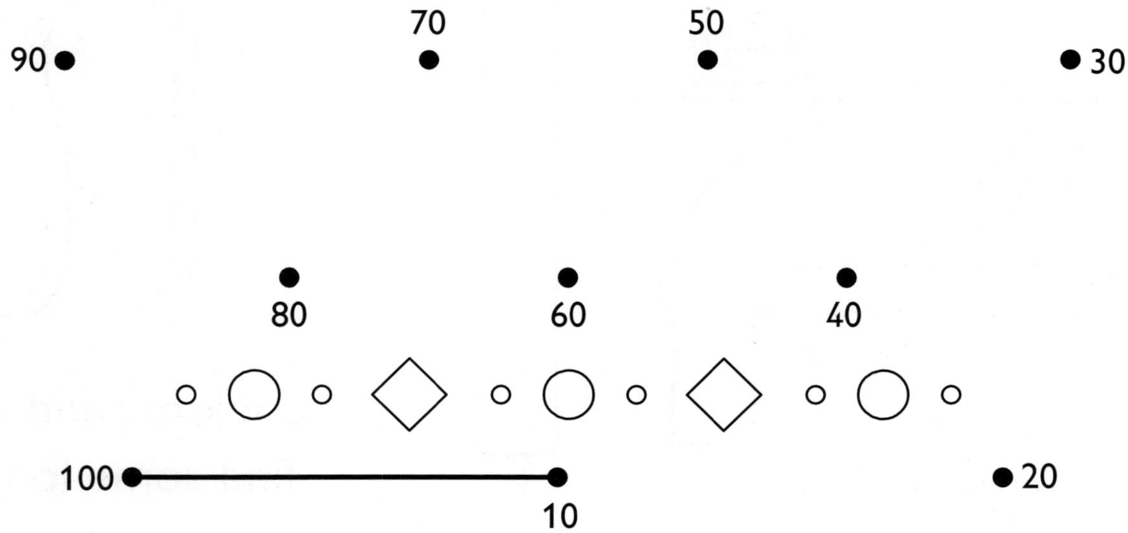

10 20 30 40 50 60 70 80 90 100

Blowing bubbles

Count the bubbles and write the numbers as you count.

1 2 3 4 5 6 7 8 9 10

What's missing?

Fill in the missing numbers.

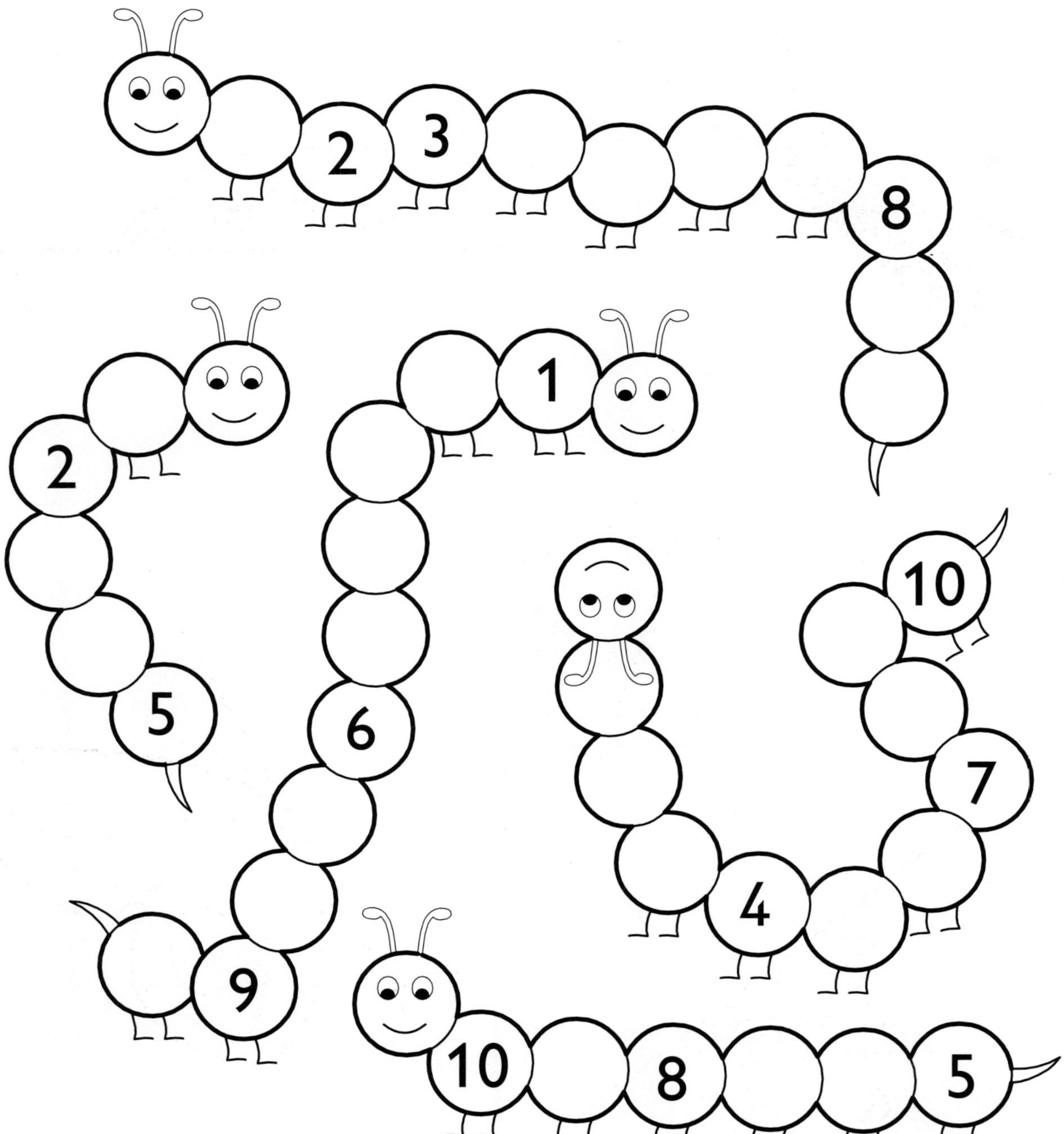

1 2 3 4 5 6 7 8 9 10

Mirror magic

Use a mirror to see the whole.

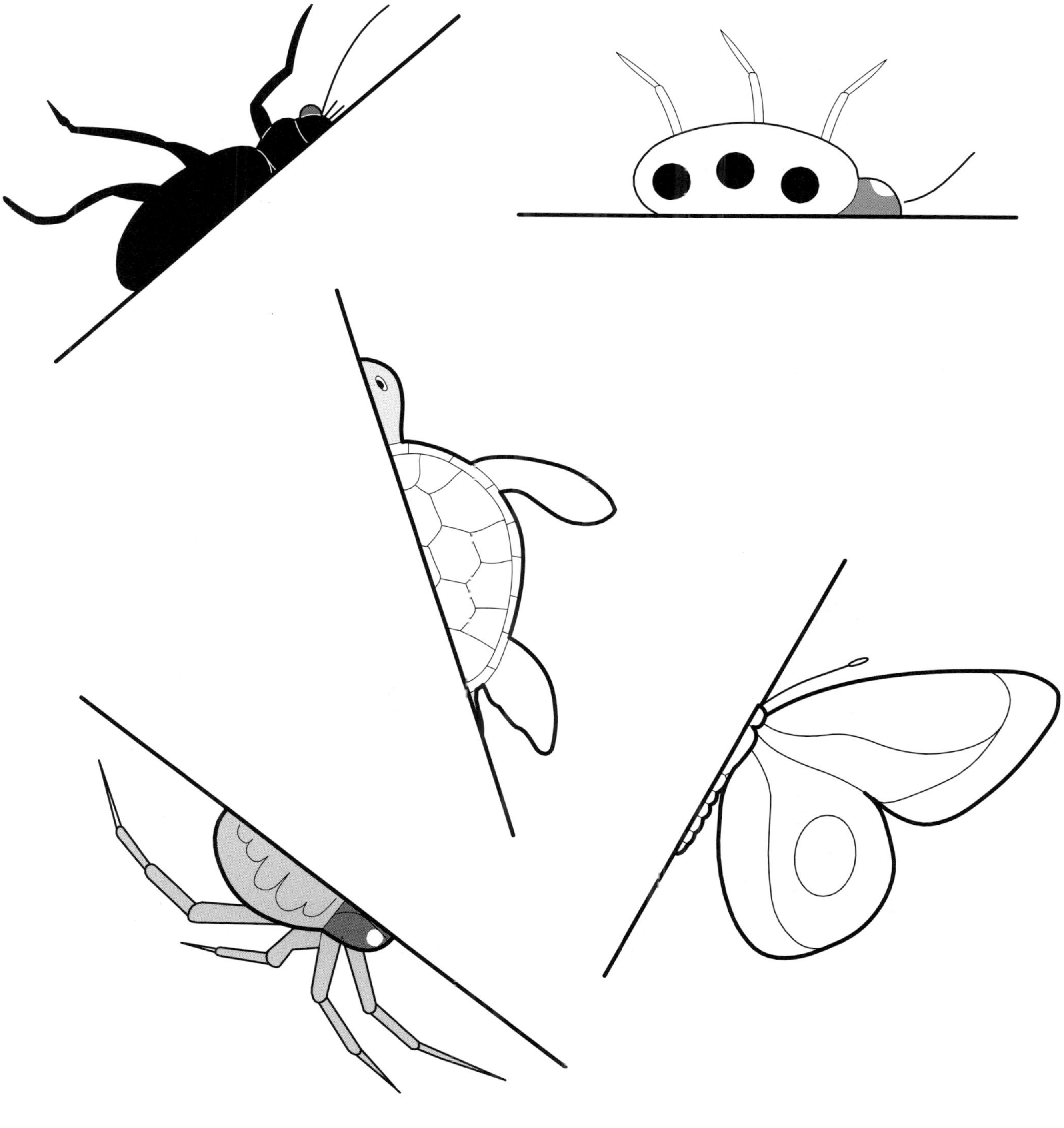

What happens if you colour some parts?

Tick-tock time

Write all the numbers on each clock.

Draw the hands to show different o'clock times.

Slippery snakes

Draw some more snakes which cover ten or more squares.

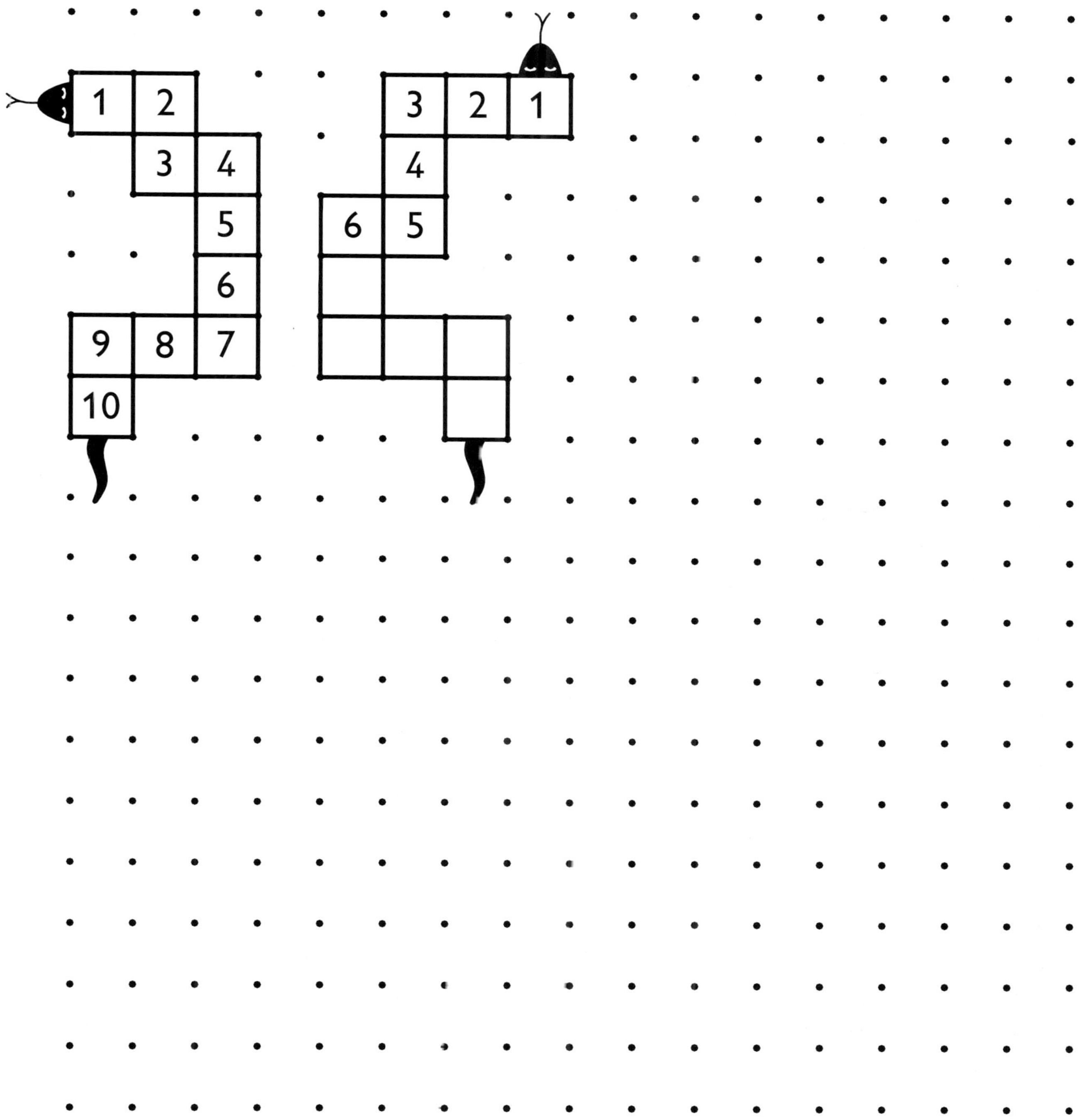

1 2 3 4 5 6 7 8 9 10 11 12 13 14 15 16 17 18 19 20

Notes

Notes